Populism and Performance in the Bolivarian Revolution of Venezuela

performance works

SERIES EDITORS
Patrick Anderson and Nicholas Ridout

This series publishes books in theater and performance studies, focused in particular on the material conditions in which performance acts are staged, and to which performance itself might contribute. We define "performance" in the broadest sense, including traditional theatrical productions and performance art, but also cultural ritual, political demonstration, social practice, and other forms of interpersonal, social, and political interaction that may fruitfully be understood in terms of performance.

Populism and Performance in the Bolivarian Revolution of Venezuela

✦

Angela Marino

NORTHWESTERN UNIVERSITY PRESS
EVANSTON, ILLINOIS

Northwestern University Press
www.nupress.northwestern.edu

Printed in the United States of America

10 9 8 7 6 5 4 3 2 1

Library of Congress Cataloging-in-Publication Data

Names: Marino, Angela (Marino Segura), author.
Title: Populism and performance in the Bolivarian revolution of Venezuela / Angela Marino.
Description: Evanston, Illinois : Northwestern University Press, 2018. | Series: Performance works
Identifiers: LCCN 2017049338 | ISBN 9780810136731 (pbk. : alk. paper) | ISBN 9780810136748 (cloth : alk. paper) | ISBN 9780810136755 (ebook)
Subjects: LCSH: Performing arts—Political aspects—Venezuela—History—20th century. | Performing arts—Political aspects—Venezuela—History—21st century. | Politics and culture—Venezuela. | Political customs and rites—Venezuela. | Venezuela—History—Revolution, 1958. | Venezuela—History—1999– | Populism—Venezuela. | Devil dance—Venezuela.
Classification: LCC PN1590.P64 M36 2018 | DDC 791.0987—dc23
LC record available at https://lccn.loc.gov/2017049338

CONTENTS

ILLUSTRATIONS

ACKNOWLEDGMENTS

The process of putting together a book, I'd like to think, shares something of fiesta politics with its multiple arms of production; less in the streets perhaps, but not without its own saints, beloved devils, and the generous spirit of many who carried this project from its first inklings to the final printing.

Foremost among them are family, friends, and mentors who have passed on during the writing of this book, but whose memory is as vivid as ever: Paul Marino, Francisco "Paco" Alfaro, Randy Martin, Carlos Herrera, Isidro "Cecilio" Antonio Silva, David Craven, Fernando Coronil, and Ernesto Laclau—may their ideas continue to inspire. Román Chalbaud generously shared his indelible appreciation of life with all its miracles. Without him, this book would never have happened. Likewise, conversations with Orlando Rodríguez, Saida García, Saul Rivas Rivas, Jorman Valera and Carmen Zulay Echenagucia, José "Cheché" Echenagucia, Jonathan Scheuer and family, Luisa Benítez and family, Clemis García and family, Roberto Lovato and family, Nora Silva and family, Julio "Ñepe" Concepción, and Luisa García and her family gave shape to the main ideas presented here.

From the book's earlier stages at New York University, I was fortunate to work with professors Diana Taylor, Mary Louise Pratt, Jill Lane, Ana Dopico, and Alejandro Velasco. In addition, Kamau Brathwaite, BKG, Deborah Kapchan, Greg Grandin, Awam Ampka, Richard Schechner, Tavia Nyong'o, and Maya Ramos-Smith were amazing people to be surrounded by. I am so grateful to them for their integrity as scholars. Marcial Godoy Anativia (and other hemifolks of the Hemispheric Institute of Performance and Politics) was one of my favorite people to talk with in these early ruminations and I can't thank him enough for leading me toward the working group Fiesta, Power and Play, which became another important space to think through ideas of this book thanks to Paolo Vignolo, Zeca Ligiéro, Milla Riggio, Rachel Bowditch and others. Among them, I wish to acknowledge the collaborators on the book *Festive Devils in the Americas*, including Silvia Rivera Cusicanqui, Anita Gonzalez, Enrique Lamadrid, Miguel Rubio, David Guss, and Benito Irady, to mention only a few. The American Society of Theater Research's Helen Kinoy dissertation award was a godsend to allow me to continue research (especially on chapter 2), as was the UC Chancellor's Postdoctoral Fellowship, which provided significant support in advancing this project toward its present form thanks to Shannon Jackson and the UC Presidential Postdoctoral Program faculty and staff.

Once at UC Berkeley, my colleagues in the Department of Theater, Dance, and Performance Studies supported this project intellectually, logistically, and in their friendship. I count myself very fortunate to work with such smart and kind people. To mention a few who especially contributed: Juan Manuel Aldape Muñoz, Naomi Bragin, Brandi Catanese, Catherine Cole, Manuel Cuellar, Greig Crysler, Abigail DeKosnik, Marcelo Garzo Montalvo, Mark Griffith, Megan Hoetger, Shannon Jackson, SanSan Kwan, Francine Masiello, Christian Nagler, Laura Pérez, Tonika Sealy-Thompson, Shannon Steen, Amara Tabor Smith, Estelle Tarica, and Lisa Wymore.

The UC Berkeley Institute of International Studies made it possible to receive in-depth commentary from Sujatha Fernandes, David Guss, Benjamin Arditi, Laura Pérez, Charles Briggs, and Clara Mantini- Briggs, who lifted up the whole project to help me see it anew in the revisions process. Zoila Mendoza and Imani Johnson offered reflections on chapter 1 thanks to a research grant from the Hellman Family Foundation. The UC Berkeley Center for Race and Gender, the Townsend Center Performance in the Americas Working Group, the Arts Research Center, and the UC Mellon Global Urban Humanities Initiative provided important spaces to develop ideas.

Many more people contributed to the writing process through research exchange in conferences, publications, and other international networks. A previous version of chapter 3 was published in Spanish for a volume edited by Marc Zimmerman and Luis Ochoa Bilbao titled *Giros culturales en la Marea Rosa de América Latina* (2014), and was later reprinted by the *Alter/Nativas Latin American Cultural Studies Journal* with support from the Department of Spanish and Portuguese, Ohio State University, and a presentation by Abril Trigo. A panel organized by Naomi Schiller and Robert Samet for the Venezuelan Studies section at the Latin American Studies Association (LASA) helped me work through ideas for chapter 4 with comments by Julie Skurski, Luis Duno Gottberg, and, later, Marcia Ochoa. I thank them for their expertise and generosity. Likewise, at LASA the following year, I had a chance to share the revised thesis with Diana Taylor, Charlotte Canning, Leticia Robles, and Sebastián Calderón Bentín, whose response to its more fully fledged arguments gave me the stamina for the last mile.

Some of the most important interlocutors were strangers, but many more became friends, especially Beto Benites, Delbis Cardona, Nadeschda Makaganow, Yanetsi Palencia and family, Franklin Perozo, Zoe Dutka and Benjamin Mast, Dora Farías and Gerardo Luongo, Roberto Lovato and family, Anahir Concepción and family, Luis, Abrahim, Denys, Sra. Carmen Luisa, Rosa and Luis Fermin Uribe, El Tano, and Niky García among them. Marisa Handler, Kate Babbitt, and Morelia Privas expertly helped me make sense of things at different stages in editing and translations. The staff and organizers of such groups as the Misión Cultura, Misión Simón Rodríguez, Frente Miranda, the Cacao Cooperative in Ocumare, the History Museum of Maracay, the Polar Foundation Archives, Fundación Bigott, Biblioteca Nacional, the Museo de Simón Bolívar, Fundacomunal, and CONAC made the experience of research both personable and productive.

When Patrick Anderson and Nicholas Ridout put out the call for this series, I knew that it was a conversation that I wanted to be a part of, and I am immensely grateful to them for including me. The team at Northwestern University Press has been fantastic; thanks to Mike Levine for getting me started, the blind reviewers for their detailed and extremely thoughtful comments, and Gianna Francesca Mosser, Maggie Grossmann, Nathan MacBrien, and JD Wilson for carrying it through to the end with acumen and care.

Finally, I dedicate this book to my mother, Beatriz Marino, who read countless drafts and deftly threw out every sentence over eight lines long. I'm sure a few escaped, but no doubt the book is vastly improved. Maria Morales and Beto Rivadeneyra (with Carlos and Sebas) each helped read and comment at key moments. My greatest thanks goes to Gio, who seemed always to be two steps ahead playing with the answers while I was still coming up with the questions. With them, and the many people who made this book, the road is worth walking.

Populism and Performance in the Bolivarian Revolution of Venezuela

Introduction

✦

Populism and Performance

This book is about the relationship between populism and performance in one of the most influential social movements to emerge in the American hemisphere since the Cuban Revolution. It is called the Bolivarian Revolution, and it was named in honor of the independence leader Simon Bolívar, who is credited with winning the independence of six South American nations, and with a vision of Latin American unification against imperial aggression.[1] Part of that story is about populist leadership, but this book especially focuses on the people behind this social movement who perform a voice of their own. In particular, I examine performance in what I call populist repertoires,[2] or embodied acts such as fiesta dance, theater, music, and everyday performed behaviors that transmit unifying strategies of collective identification.

A hurricane. This was how critics and supporters alike described Hugo Chávez Frias throughout six consecutive electoral campaigns and victories. Whether broadcasting a weekly television show, launching campaigns as a troubadour and folk hero, or performing full-tilt vocalizations of the nation's most popular music, Chávez was framed by the media on both the Right and the Left as a one-man show. What was scarcely mentioned were the constituents of the socialist-leaning movement who rallied around the slogan "Con Chávez, manda *el pueblo*!" ("With Chávez, *the people* lead!"). Indeed, he was a thunderous force, one the press called a demagogue and a dictator, but by spotlighting the statesman as headlining the event, "the people" were readily placed outside the frame.[3]

Since March 2014, with the collapse of Venezuela's economy, violent protests, and challenges to its once-celebrated democracy, there has been a virtually split frame between those defending the crowning achievements of the Bolivarian Revolution and those trying to shut down what has been characterized as an increasingly authoritarian government. While these are issues of paramount concern, this book is not (directly anyway) an assessment of the government, its failures, or its achievements. It does, however, prompt important questions: how does a focus on performance inform debates on democracy and revolution, and what happens to our understanding of populism when it is seen through the lens of performance studies? I suggest that a closer examination of performance in the Bolivarian Revolution reveals the interdependence of populism and performance, and offers new ways to think about the potentials (and pitfalls) of a populism of the Left.

When we look at performance next to populism, their shared root is collective action, a labor within an economy of morals and affect, conditioned, created, and mediated by performance. Performance can *be* populist, and at the same time, performance is a product *of* populism. Both populism and performance are entirely reliant on the bodies that produce them, and the environments where they take place. Whether on stage, in the streets, or at the kitchen table, performance informs the limits of building political unity, just as populism pushes its edge. Performance shapes participation, public space, and collective identities. At the same time, I believe, populism can invigorate the study of performance and the art establishment as it transforms ordinary objects and interactions into aesthetically powerful acts of the political realm.

I examine this intersection of populism and performance across a spectrum of media, from the multitudinous religious processions of devil dances, to the theater and film of the post-dictatorship era in the 1950s, and back to present-day political campaigns and the semiotics of the state. As I will argue, populism is inseparable from the embodied, relational, and material aesthetics of performance, which therefore must be accounted for in the analysis of social movements. This does not mean that performance is a methodological cure or is necessarily predictive. But I do think that we need to analyze populism in situ with a fuller spectrum of performed expression. As political scientist Shirin Rai and performance studies scholar Janelle Reinelt (2015) observe, we need to move beyond nominal theatrical metaphors to understand the shared structures and principles that govern politics and performance. I aim for that in this book by focusing on various populist events and repertoires leading up to and including the first ten years of the revolution (1999–2010).

This book is not a comprehensive account of the debates on populism or performance, nor does it attempt to universalize a theory of populism. But there are some problems that can be circumvented by such a study. Beyond polling and voting records, the political culture of populism tends to evade quantifiable records. Entering the scope of what art critic Nicolas Bourriaud sees as relational aesthetics, populism, like relational art, "take[s] as its theoretical horizon the realm of human interactions and its social context rather than the assertion of an independent and private symbolic space" (2002, 14). Without adequate attention to how performance shapes unified and collective action—through, for instance, an epistemology of the body—the mediation of populism by performance is taken for granted or left missing from the analysis altogether. Where performance meets populism, then, cultural and relational meanings go undetected, are dangerously misunderstood, and handily discredited.

Taking a short look back to the months before Hugo Chávez was elected to the presidency on December 6, 1998, sheds more light on this intersection of performance and populist formation. First, it is important to note that while millions of low-income rural and urban residents joined prominent members of the political establishment in support of Chávez, others were taken quite aback by what one reporter called the "sea of red" (referring to the color red identified with the Chávez movement). Residents in posh neighborhoods on the east side of Caracas, who were a minority of the population, largely dismissed the pro-Chávez social movement as an aberration and, later, as anathema.

Recognizing their miscalculations only weeks before the elections, the two major parties running against Chávez then formed a coalition in support of the opposition candidate Salas Römer. In a last-ditch effort to turn the polls around, Römer suddenly appeared on the front pages of the major newspapers standing in front of a dilapidated housing project wearing a fresh-pressed flannel shirt with a red bandanna. The image replaced weeks of "official" displays of suits and ties, making Römer's impromptu costume change almost laughable. It was also dramatically revealing, not because it convinced anyone that Römer was a champion of the poor, but rather because it offered a glimpse of the desperation behind the scenes. It exposed the fissures in the spectacle of the state. The old-guard political parties were vulnerable. The well-ordered stasis of the political establishment had cracked. Its failure was precisely the unreliability of Römer's relationships to the places, people, and politics of the barrios of Caracas. Its theatricality failed in the way an actor's put-on accent can ruin the credibility of the role. Moreover, it revealed the fact that Römer was forced to change the language, the script, and the location of his performance in response to the seismic shift in political cultures that the country was facing at the end of the twentieth century.

In the days leading up to the elections, red berets began to appear on the small buses that carried people across the city. People were ebullient, singing songs as they mingled in train stations and on street corners. Other people scurried home and shut their doors, as if a storm was coming. *El Universal*, one of the major newspapers in the country, printed a series of headlines suggesting that the United States would withdraw its investments, the economy would crash, and the nation's security would be at risk if Chávez won the election. News anchors cast doubts on whether the long-shot candidate would amount to a real contender. But by then it was already clear that the campaign was happening in the streets, in urban barrios and small towns across the country. When the elections took place, the power of this movement became apparent to all: Chávez won by 56.2 percent of the national vote.

During this transitional moment (one that would later be historicized as the beginning of a revolution), I tried to see as much theater as I could. While hints of current events had begun to spill over into the scripts and improvised acts of popular street performance, the response in the theaters was ambiguous, abstract, and hesitant. Most mainstream venues were unprepared to address or even adequately respond to the political moment. There were some exceptions. In a popular theater in the upscale neighborhood of the Mercedes, a slapstick comedy pulled rapid-fire jokes on all the major candidates, with the audience wincing in discomfort at the too-closeness of it all. A *costumbrista* performance near a centrally located working-class neighborhood, on the other hand, had a mixed crowd of people in stitches by turning a satirical upper hand on the aspirations of the middle class. Further west, in the fine-arts theater complex of Teatro Teresa Carreño, a brilliant performance of Alejo Carpentier's *Concierto Barroco*, directed by Vicente Albarracín, embraced a more inventive vision of a multiracial América among the progressive-minded artsy middle class with a finale that included actual tastings of black beans and rice mixed together, known colloquially as *moros y cristianos* (Moors and Christians). While there was no direct reference to Chávez in the play, the literal consumption of *mestizaje* (miscegenation) seemed to welcome the future of a brown nation, especially coming on the heels of a film in the year before that had scandalized audiences with its depiction of interracial marriage in a family of "high society."

Meanwhile, an adaptation of *Don Quixote* just next door in the Ateneo placed Cervantes's knight and his squire in contemporary Caracas. Actors described it as nonpartisan, but the production took aim at oil rigs, street crime, and political hypocrisy. Staged amid the reigning violence and insecurity in Caracas, this play struck me as a fitting testimonial to the daunting and seemingly insurmountable crisis of the rentier oil economy. Another adaptation, this time of Athol Fugard's *The Island*, poignantly staged two prisoners in their struggle for redemption, recalling Chávez's own coup attempt, imprisonment, and resistance against the state a decade prior to his running for office. Few of these plays overtly presented the social drama at the polls; instead they contributed to the uncertainty with long pauses and empty questions filled with: "We shall see" and "Who knows?" To some degree, theater-makers were not just unprepared for the action of the streets, they were also over-prepared, logistically strapped to schedules in advance. Most institutional art of this first year of the revolution (excepting some street-theater artists) revealed a distance from the millions in the country who were demanding social change. Where in the arts establishment were the radical aesthetics of the early 1970s theater ensembles talking back to the nation (like Rajatabala), or the popular puppeteers and mime actors, or the plays of César Rengifo and Rodolfo Santana? Where was the performance of revolution in the Caracas of 1998? Which stories were missing or only partially visible on the national stage at this crucial time of change?

Of course, the elections in that period of the late 1990s brought out the most interactive and engaging dramas of everyday life. In the back of a Spanish *tavern*, I witnessed a woman from a prominent family break down in tears while remembering that as a child she was disciplined by being told that if she did not behave, people from the barrio would climb the walls of her house to violate her and murder her family. A short time later a woman who cleaned the CELCIT library in San Bernardino told me that she dreamed of one day tearing down the walls that surrounded the barrio where she and her two children lived so they would not be so stigmatized.[4] The coincidence of hearing these two women refer to a common object (a wall) made me wonder if these walls were the same, each side built with different fears and ideas of why they were there and who was on the inside or out. These were real stories that moved people to think and act politically, walk differently in the streets, and otherwise embody a perspective about the nation and one's role in it on an everyday basis. Social divisions became more visible as those who supported Chávez gained power to speak in the public sphere. For some, this was accompanied by elation and incredible hope and energy for change. For others, it spelled terrifying paralysis, and even doom.

Prior to Chávez's election, societal divisions were already palpable for the majority of the population. These divisions mapped on to public space in the city by localized perceptions. People in the central middle-class neighborhoods identified newcomers on the outskirts of Caracas as the source of the city's crime. By contrast, activists from Catia claimed that the real crooks lived on the wealthy east side in neighborhoods such as Altamira and Las Mercedes. Meanwhile, those near the country club hid behind gates, making plans to escape to Miami. The U.S. embassy, a cornerstone of elite society, sat wedged on a hill beside California-ranch houses and flowering hibiscus gardens. These homes lined a winding and well-paved road high above the city, composing a world with its own special horizon, far from the daily migrations up and down the steep barrio stairs, the armies of small buses spewing exhaust, and the old lady huddled in a doorway on the Sabana Grande like Lázaro, with a dozen dogs heaving at her side. What was this rarefied Caracas, to whom did it belong, and who was left out of each view?

While confusion reigned at the embassy, the rise of the newly inaugurated president came as no surprise to people in towns such as Cumaná in the east and Valencia, Puerto Cabello, and Coro to the west. When I asked about Chávez in several small towns of central Venezuela, the answer was unambiguous and near unanimous: *everyone* seemed to support him. On a bus that broke down on the highway to Cumaná just a few months after the elections, dozens of people shared their circumstances and reasons for supporting Chávez in what amounted to a nearly hour-long group conversation while we waited for repairs. At local cafés and markets in the central coastal and interior towns, taxi drivers, cement layers, hotel maids, students, artisans, and street vendors all told me the same thing: Chávez understands, he is one of us. Just as in the buildup to the election, these encounters shared a common thread with the new nationalisms emerging in Venezuela. But for most of the supporters I spoke with, it wasn't that Chávez himself was the story; it was that Chávez fit into an as-yet untold story about a history and a people.

Part of that story appeared in the cultural performances of devil dances in rural Venezuela, but it took me several years to appreciate them as a model for, among other things, healing the effects of demonization in Corpus Christi rites (which I discuss further in chapter 1). The devil dances of Corpus Christi are popular religious manifestations in which devotees dress as fierce—and also playful—devils with brightly colored capes and horned masks. In eleven different small towns, mainly in central and coastal Venezuela, the devils skip, turn, kneel, and pray in choreographed formations of circles and criss-cross lines through neighborhood streets in a daylong and sometimes weekend-long ritual to celebrate the Holy Sacrament of Corpus Christi. Several promoters have described these dances as "folkloric traditions" of mainly Afro-descendant communities. I spoke with many of the dancers and other participants over the course of eleven years between 1999 and 2010—notably the decade *before* the designation of the devil dances as "Intangible Heritage and Cultural Patrimony" by the United Nations Educational, Scientific, and Cultural Organization (UNESCO), which happened in the latter half of 2010. At that time, and up to the year of this publication, almost all of the participants that I spoke with preferred not to use the term "folklore." Instead, they described the devil dance as a devotional fiesta or a religious manifestation. For producers, or *cultors* (culture-makers), the devil dances are an entirely contemporaneous expression of faith in the Holy Sacrament and of ancestral memory that belongs to no one entity but to "the people."

As important as the devil dances are to many communities in Venezuela, this book is not an ontological study of the devil dances. My focus is on the political formations that are exercised by participants within and surrounding these performances, which, I argue, serve as an organizational method of building popular power. To me, similar questions that were being debated in political scholarship were also mediated by the dance: how claims of "the people" are asserted and negotiated, what lies within or outside of the communal order, and who claims decision-making power for the social or public good. Moreover, the dances brought an incendiary character to this mediation: namely, the devil.

In 2006, Chávez gave a speech to the United Nations that invoked the devil in reference to George W. Bush (which I discuss further in chapter 3). This speech—which raised all kinds of issues around political cultures and legitimate dissent—squarely placed the two fields of performance and politics beside the cultural imagination of the devil. It was a strikingly visible example of how the devil carried a political charge. Scandal quickly ensued—one that roiled the media over proper speech conduct and issues of "appropriateness" while missing entirely any of the backstory. What was not well known, at least for U.S. audiences, was that Chávez's UN speech carried over from the Venezuelan referendum elections of 2004, which had already thrust this devil figure from national mythology into the political arena.

At least in Venezuela, the devil in politics was certainly not a new story, and as I continued my research, it became clearer how very *old* the story actually was. As I argue in a previous study on festive devils, following Jorge Cañizares-Esguerra (2006), acts of demonization were not only central to a strategy of "conquest," they were the very basis of an imperialism that *depended* on devil beliefs for land occupation and juridical claims of all kinds (see also Newcomb 2008). While the events of the first decade of Chávez's presidency unfolded, I found myself returning to the question of what the devil dances tell us about the national drama, and the common ground between that drama and the dance. It is a story of colonial history, of modernity and cultural paradigms in collision. Both the devil dances and Chávez's revolutionary state were fighting to tell a story of defiance in which they confronted the ballasts of power that sought to demonize them. This was more than a story of friend and foe. It was about legitimacy and the right to govern—a struggle that went back centuries, yet carried a bold resonance in the geopolitics of the new millennium. Chavista slogans about participation and popular power appeared in daily life, and routine actions on the street were organized around a new sense of (trans-) national belonging. To critics viewing the unfolding events with increasing apprehension, there was a handy label for all of this: populism.

Populism

Since 2016, with right-wing movements capturing attention in the United States and Europe, populism has become a topic of fervent debates in global media. The idea that populism is linked to authoritarianism, xenophobia, and demagoguery predominates this discourse. In this book I contend that there is much more complexity than these characterizations suggest. Populism can take many forms, and it can be allied with a range of political movements and ideologies. While populism can obfuscate and neutralize political debate, it can also catalyze debate and reorganize power. Indeed, I explore here some alternative political possibilities, even the seemingly oxymoronic possibility of a critical populism. What if our understanding of populism could be more inclusive? What if, furthermore, populism could be a force for recentering humanism and a critical activism of the Left?

At its most basic form, populism refers to the politics of ordinary people.[5] Yet there is great variation in who makes up "the people," and how that claim is mobilized in the political arena. Whether "the people" are antiestablishment heroes fed up with the elite, or the uneducated cast under the spell of facile slogans, the people of populism tend to be an afterthought. For some, ordinary people doing politics indicates a deepening of democratic participation among those left out of backroom decision-making (Laclau and Mouffe 1985; Kazin 1998; Laclau 2005). For others, populism can threaten democracy and is viewed as a "disfiguration" or social perversion of liberal ideals (Taggart 2000; Weyland 2013; Urbinati 2014). Margaret Canovan sees this latter tension as an inherent friction between two faces of democracy, the pragmatic and the redemptive—what it takes to make a democracy function and what it takes to redeem it when it fails—where "populism is a shadow cast by democracy itself" (1999, 3). Benjamin Arditi, likewise, sees populism as potentially redemptive but with a dangerous underside that appears and unfolds on the edges of liberalism, what Arditi calls an "internal periphery of democracy" (2007, 53). As "a dimension of political culture" (Worsley 1969, 245), populism may be all of these things: like performance, it is not bound to any ideology of the Right or the Left; it can be ominous or extraordinary (De la Torre 2016), haunting (Arditi 2007), or a manifestation of everyday behaviors, beliefs, and expressions of political life.

I define populism as a unifying strategy of collective identification carried out through the everyday and the spectacular embodied act. This act includes speech, gestures, behaviors, and other embodied expressions, as well as a worldview carried by that embodiment, a worldview that is mediated and actualized by performance. Populism can be enacted or rehearsed in recurrent ritual performance, in the public spaces of the plaza, in the campaign rally, and on the streets. Populism is also highly visible on stages and in media of various kinds such as theater, dance, and film, to name a few. Like Ernesto Laclau, I see a process in which a collective body constitutes itself performatively as a naming act as much as an act *in the name of* a particular group or people. If, as Laclau says, populism "proceeds out of social demands" (2005, 117), then it is agential or, as political scientist Laura Grattan says, "aspirational" (2016, 10) to popular power in ways that I believe people engage with through highly symbolic acts and on a regular basis in their daily walks. My thinking, however, is closer to Judith Butler's approach to performative assemblies as gestural and embodied (2015). Performance as an expressive medium, in both senses of a framed, or staged, "showing" and its performative "effects," I believe, are inseparably linked to populism.

My central argument is that if populism is a dimension of the political, and performance expresses and is also constitutive of politics, then we need to account for how people know and reproduce populism through performance. I think we can delve more deeply into the dynamics of populism by taking into account the ways that performance transmits its own logic and shapes its political outcomes. Thus, while this book focuses on performance, it also lends heavily to studies of populism, primarily through these recurring arguments that (a) populism is a performed practice; (b) populism is also mediated by performance in the social and material environment; and (c) populism carries its own history of reproduction through performance and embodiments, which implies an epistemological (and therefore methodological) shift of analysis. A performance studies approach would help foreground the embodied, spatial, and temporal dimensions of populism both as constituting and representational acts.

In the rest of this section, I address two main approaches to populism that offer some basic framing for intersections with performance. The first approach is a formal aspect of populism as a function of group identification and representation, based on the work of the Argentine philosopher Ernesto Laclau. From his original work on fascism and populism to his magnum opus *On Populist Reason* (2005), Laclau emphasizes populism as a practice, or articulation, in which various individuals negotiate a plurality of social demands (requests or claims), parsing out differences to form what he calls equivalences. To Laclau, these are rational moves that build in tension from the particularity of social demands to the construction of a unified popular identity. Laclau's work perhaps most thoroughly examines the mechanics of populism, tracing social demands to political cohesion in what he sees as a *process or political logic*.

The second approach is known as "ideational populism" since it understands populism as a particular *set of ideas*, or concepts, mainly dualism, or a so-called Manichaean discourse (Hawkins 2010; De la Torre 2010; Rovira Kaltswasser 2014).[6] I became interested in the ideational approach to populism because the concept of dualism that these scholars focused on to define populism was especially relevant to my research in the performances of saints and devils. Ideational scholars chart populist movements on the basis of polarizing rhetoric that reflects a worldview of a purely good will of the people versus an "evil" conspiring elite (Hawkins and Kocijan 2013, 2). Even as I find this approach intriguing, I see the added dimensions of performance strengthening the former (populism as political logics) to critique the methods and conclusions of the latter (ideational populism).

Both the political logics and ideational approaches to populism dedicate considerable attention to how populism unites an "us" against an "other," but interestingly, the actual bodies of people are generally left out of the picture. This could merit a closer look at anatomy to understand how our bodies come to identify and react with particular sensibilities of being/acting together (see Hatemi and McDermott 2016). It could also mean what bodies do to transmit and mediate different forms of populism. The difference is that ideational scholars see populism through recognizable ideas or a worldview with only an abstract sense of the bodies that presumably think and act on these ideas. Populism for Laclau is the making of collective identity; a "performative" process in which "the people" is always an unfixed, contested, and strategic claim (2005, 97). Interestingly, Laclau sees affect as the operative unifying force in this process (what he calls a radical investment) that makes popular subjectivity qualitatively different from a mere collection of demands. Yet, Laclau stops short of explaining the role of affect. His analysis (while replete in other areas) remains fairly limited to enunciation, or naming, as a discursively constituting act rather than an embodied one. More needs to be said about how embodiment and the performance act itself shape these processes of populism.

More recently, Benjamin Moffitt raises this issue to account for embodied aesthetics, actors, audiences, stages, scripts, and mise-en-scènes in what he sees as an argument for populism as "political style" (2016, 38). Moffitt's book *The Global Rise of Populism* (2016) is deeply concerned with performance and points in the right direction by examining gesture, critiquing theories of populism as discourse, and aptly raising important questions of media representation. In particular, I find Moffitt's approach especially helpful in laying the groundwork for advancing a performance turn in populism studies; his book provides a broader assessment of the antecedents in populism theory to argue for a shift to what he calls the "time and space-bounded contours of contemporary politics, which are intensely mediatized and 'stylized'" (2016, 41). It is an analysis that opens the way for new questions, such as how performance works *as* mediation and the relationship between performance and the material environment.

As a performance studies scholar, I agree with Moffitt that these aspects of performance have been overlooked in the study of populism as a whole and that there is more to say about the performative act in Laclau's work. I also see that there is more to develop around the transmission of populism and how we interpret its expressions. We need a more expansive approach to practices of collective identification and embodied language as ways of knowing in the political realm. In the politics that unfolded in Venezuela, it was not uncommon to see people publicly asserting collective claims over political spaces, symbols, and beliefs through the use of performance. There were also moments in which these processes were taking place in ways that were deeply affected not only by questions of style or performativity, but also by the ways in which supporters engaged in performance itself both onstage and in the streets. I see these performances as *populist repertoires* in everyday and ceremonial staged performance. In this book, I focus on performances generally among supporters of the Bolivarian Revolution, but like other performed acts, populist repertoires are not inherently attached to a particular political agenda; despite liberatory ideals, they can also lead to and support fascism, tyranny, and even terror. Populism in many parts of the world enables the exploitation of peoples' desires, fears, or cultural affinities. Once officiating, the idea is that populist leaders install nationalisms in ways that displace, historically freeze, or otherwise attempt to capture the cultural capital of "the people" (Hobsbawm 1983; Williams 2002). In this regard, Jan-Werner Mueller (2014) said that "populists see the people as essentially passive," as an entity to be effectively marshaled into flag-waving elections, but otherwise, to leave the governing to the state (13). Here we see populist repertoires spectacularizing what Néstor García Canclini calls "archaic cultural capital," to pin the impulses of the popular to the state's agenda

(1989). In this sense, to strategically unify through performance seems bound to authoritarian rule.

To me, a purely top-down populism is somewhat antithetical. I'm not sure how useful it is to deploy a word rooted in the *populus* to describe what is ultimately cronyism, jingoism, or xenophobia. Populism without participation, likewise, seems like an oxymoron, even if it refers to an appeal to the people, or sensibilities of the popular projected from on high. Nevertheless, I see populist repertoires on a spectrum from highly participatory and distributive to what can operate through spectacle in the sense of orchestrating the relations of spectatorship though more monist agendas of the culture industry and the state.

While suspicions of the state justifiably run high (particularly of the coercive power of state militarism), I think we need to steer clear of supposing that populism is primarily the doing of leaders and nations. First, because this underestimates the potential alliances of populist mobilizations in the streets, living rooms, and neighborhood groups that can join the state in inflicting harm. But, especially in the context of revolution, populism seen as only top-down from above is not enough to explain the estuary-like complexity of social movements in times of radical change. I discuss this later in the introduction, but for now I point out that the disputes over whether populism is primarily top-down or from some "originary and creative force" of the popular (García Canclini 1989), are, in my view, missing the informal and quasi-institutional forms of political engagement that run parallel to and across municipal or state governance (Joseph and Nugent 1994; Chatterjee 2004). Populism can also dangerously serve as a one-handed dismissal to discredit social movements as ill-equipped for self-rule or as backward to otherwise "modern" progress. The result, as sociologist Sara C. Motta well argues in the case of Venezuela, is to exclude or devalue more innovative democratic experimentations and the political agency of the popular classes (Motta 2011, 43). I thus came to study populism in a critical mode to identify more clearly what was being assigned to the label: perhaps, like the devil figure itself, there is much more bound up within the term.

In Latin America, populism tends to be linked to *caudillismo*, or rural fiefdoms, and to voices of *la clase popular* (the popular class), a term that generally refers to low-income sectors of both rural- and urban-barrio residents, who are more broadly referred to as *el pueblo* (the people). A *caudillo* refers to a boss or leader of smaller groups of families and ranch hands, but the term was later adapted to statesmen who built their power around rural wealth and social systems. The best-known *caudillo* statesman may perhaps be the nineteenth-century Argentinian president Juan Manuel de Rosas, who organized rural ranch hands and the poor in his brand of clientelist politics. The Venezuelan cattle rancher Juan Vicente Gómez (president from 1908 to 1935) is also considered a *caudillo* populist, yet he is best known for selling off the country's oil reserves to foreign interests and for a repressive cadre of secret police that abused the rights of the working class and those who sought political reform. Urban elites tend to view *caudillo* populists as clientelistic bosses with a propensity for tyrannical rule.

Whereas "populism" in the United States is generally tied to rural residents and agrarian reform (see Kazin 1998; Postel 2007; Goodwyn 1978), the term "populism" in Latin America is more strongly linked to *la clase popular* and *el pueblo*, terms that refer to both urban and rural low-income sectors. Leaders such as Juan Perón in Argentina became examples of "classic" Latin American populism, individuals who came to power through alliances with industrial labor unions and class interests. Of course, Perón was made immensely popular in part by his wife Eva Perón, who appealed to union workers via speeches and radio, in what Tom McEnaney calls an "intersectional poetics of radio and literature" (2017, 9). Because of the Peróns and other political leaders such as Getúlio Vargas in Brazil, populism in Latin America became closely associated with the urban poor and the working class. Other terms, such as "popular power," came out of the organizational work of the popular class, again referring to the majority of the population of barrio residents, the working poor, the informal sector, and variably members of the middle classes identifying with regional aesthetics and sensibilities. Particularly in societies with a fairly limited middle class, populism tends to gravitate toward a greater distribution of the state's resources to the majority poor and disenfranchised.

What can be marked cultural differences in populism tell us that the performance space of populism is not empty.[7] The performance studies scholar and poet Ngũgĩ wa' Thiong'o said this of the theater as performance space, calling it an orb of great power, "a magnetic field of tensions and conflicts," tethered to its social relations and histories (1997, 12). The spaces in which populist repertoires circulate likewise are attached to culturally specific histories. We cannot presume that those voices land in the same way in a neutral sphere of debate (Fraser 1990, 60). As political theorist Chantal Mouffe wrote, "any form of social objectivity is ultimately political and . . . must bear the traces of the acts of exclusion that govern its constitution" (Mouffe 2013, 4). A "plural democracy," for Mouffe, therefore does not mean avoiding conflict; rather, it must expose and facilitate an "agonistic dimension" of open debate in which contending voices can be articulated and heard (ibid.). In this sense, analyzing performance in situ helps to unravel a deeper struggle within populist debates over the space of political difference beyond the bourgeois public sphere.

What may appear to be empty in populism, however, are the symbols. By empty, I am not saying they are meaningless, but what matters (for Laclau anyway) is not so much the symbolic contents as the relations that unify through them. In what Laclau calls an equivalential chain, the unification of heterogeneous demands around an empty signifier is one way to construct popular identity, all the while remaining interconnected to the fields of relations and multiple centers of power among its producers. Key to these logics is the inherent tension between the issues and practices people share that holds the chain together and the symbolic inscription that extends it as a totality.

Without pluralism, Laclau warns that fascism can also articulate populist imaginations of the people as one, especially if the working class and the Left abandon the arenas of open debate and elections (Laclau 1977, 111, 124). In order for populism to remain plural (and democratic), there must also be a space for the reconstitution of the equivalential (or differential) logics without coercion, a space in which the signifier can shift and be continuously reshaped by agonistic pluralism. To move forward, we need a close analysis of the conditions of populism through sustained political ethnography, to better understand what forces shape these spaces, and crucially, to promote pluralism and greater equity in democracy.

The ideational scholars also claim to be concerned with pluralism, but they dismiss Laclau's political logics based on what they see as fixed containers of rhetorical opposites. Kirk Hawkins (2010), a political scientist at Brigham Young University, sees Venezuela in the Chávez era as an example of ideational populism, characterized by a Manichaean worldview of "good" versus "evil." Hawkins argues that populist movements such as Chavismo do not solve the problems of their predecessors for two major reasons: first, because they work outside of and at odds with liberal institutions; and second, because they reproduce continued inequalities through a Manichaean discourse that prevents social cohesion between all sectors of society. The "dark side" of populism, as Rovira Kaltwasser adds, is when "allegedly there is no disagreement between the people, but rather a quasi-religious authority that embodies the general will" (2014, 501). Moreover, in this view, to draw on morality or historical injustices detracts from debate where the implication is that populists merely stage "plebiscitary acclamation," without the agency or expertise to actually govern.

While these conclusions can be questioned on a number of counts, the issue I want to expand on here has to do with methods. Hawkins and his team sought to systematically account for Manichaeism, and therefore populism, by collecting the transcripts of suspected populists' speeches and counting the references to good and evil within them. In his research, Hawkins hired coders who were instructed to tick up the numerical score for references to "morality," references to that which is "cosmic" or "across time," and suggestions of a "reified notion of history" (Hawkins and Kocijan 2013). Based on selected speeches, he classified those with reference to the "epic," "messianic," and "cosmic" as populist, contrary to other speeches that were more "policy-specific," "circumstantial," and "limited to material reality" (ibid., 11–12). Not surprisingly, Hawkins and his coders would find a linguistic taxonomy chock-full of Manichaean language in the transcripts of Chávez's speeches, leading Hawkins to the conclusion that Chávez was at the high end of the measuring stick in terms of populism.

I am certainly sympathetic to the potential abuse of power that populism can entail, and even more so in the Trump era of U.S. politics and the ongoing violence on the streets of Venezuela. But upon taking a closer look at how performance plays a role in political cultures, I question Hawkins's conclusion that the populism of the Bolivarian Revolution was merely Manichaean (a concept that is also misunderstood), and in the case of Chavismo, I'm much less inclined to believe that the country faced a deficit of democracy because of it.[8] I think one problem is that Hawkins focuses on only selective examples of de-contextualized transcripts, which omits the broader cultural, spatial, corporeal, and material experience from which these speeches emerged. The result is an analysis that falls short of being able to identify more participatory and inclusive forms of democracy, forms that often exceeded the rhetoric of Chávez himself.

An observation that became increasingly clear after putting performance and populism next to each other is how scholarship, with few exceptions, neglected the performed dimensions of populism.[9] Populism that is analyzed on the basis of logos-centered frameworks strips performance of its political agency as a mode of transmission in its own right. This crucial aspect of public participation and "voice" is, in many cases, missing altogether from the methodology. If in the analysis of populism we shift our focus further toward a performance framework, I think we will have different results, and in particular new insights into the evaluative claims of democracy. Populist repertoires thrive outside print-based discourse, thus expanding an understanding of what counts as political and ultimately highlighting the diverse means by which people enact their own political agency. Most frameworks for understanding populism dismiss the many forms of political engagement that go undetected in textual data. Populism that is methodologically analyzed by only text-based criteria—such as keywords from speech transcripts—leaves out embodiment. The results are consistent with print-based theories of nationalism, effectively distorting our understandings of public engagement and political agency.

If it is correct that performance is an expressive medium of populism, the analysis of populism ought to consider transmission, audiences, reception, and production in ways that engage the broader field of research in performance studies. Randy Martin, author of *Critical Moves: Dance Studies in Theory and Politics* (1998), understood performance as "mediation," or an extension of a political language between social actors and their historical conditions. Take again, for example, the concept of Manichaeans. Does this not depend on how good and evil are transmitted and perceived? In Cata, Cruz María Díaz and Pedro Santana recalled that in years past, dancers would completely cover their faces with the devil masks, and people would run in fear when the dancers came around (Ortíz et al. 1982, 62). But over time, many dancers began perching their masks on top of their heads or letting them hang off of their faces. As the masks became more playfully worn, now instead of people running *away* from the devils, they run *after* them (ibid.). This is one example in which participants shape the performance from the inside to effectively dispose of the fearful effects of Manichaeism. To center the devil figure within the playful and familiar realm of the community effectively diffuses the binary of good versus evil.

The official descriptions may claim the devil dances are a battle of "good versus evil," while the practice of the dance includes so much more. These are multiple-layered performances that respond to a historical condition—one in which the devil dances function more as an antidote to the ideological premise of Manichaeism imposed on peoples and places.[10] Shirin Rai and Janelle Reinelt are inclined to embrace these ambiguities, to see them as starting points. Drawing from Kenneth Burke, they quote: "Instead of considering it our task to 'dispose of' any ambiguity by merely disclosing the fact that it is an ambiguity, we rather consider it our task to study and clarify the *resources* of ambiguity" (1945, xix, emphasis in the original).[11] As resources, ambiguities in performance take new purpose as possibilities for political transformation (Rai and Reinelt 2015, 4). To perform the devil dances is to practice these resources to unsettle the imposed logics of good versus evil.

Moreover, as chapter 1 of this book will elaborate, the very processes of populism are happening within the performance: building interior and antagonistic frontiers, redefining collective will and action, and ultimately opening a space for broad-based networks of people to debate, imagine, contest, and create. In populism, establishing a collective will means that different people form unifying bonds around symbols, figures, or acts in order to build stronger social movements. These bonds, or collective identifications, as Laclau argues, are the very nature of political activity. For him, "populism means putting into question the institutional order by constructing an underdog as an historical agent—that is, an agent which is an *other* in relation to the way things stand" (2005, 47). Laclau sees this as a totalizing relationship—in a certain way supplying the basis of the dualism argument. But there is more flexibility (and complexity) in these relations that play out in the lived experience. Artists working in collaborative and collective art practice, as Grant Kester argues, are exploring ideas such as "the one and the many," a concept that refers to simultaneous identifications of particularity and the totalizing whole, to find ways that the particularism of parts coexists with the whole (2011). Like Laclau, Kester's work shows that unified groups do not necessarily erase the logic of heterogeneous opinion-makers and actors. Therefore, we need to look more closely at these relations to understand populism, and one way to do that is through performance.

The last underlying argument of this book is that many performance-based cultural practices have their own historical lineages that are left out of the genealogy of liberal democracy, which means a true range of political practice has already been excluded.[12] The performances of the devil dances, which were in large part African- and indigenous-based cultural practices as much as European ones, were ignored and discredited as political acts, leaving them outside of law and order on the basis of Eurocentric worldviews. Take, for example, the Tiwanaku artists of the eighth century (located in the Andean regions of Latin America), who developed concepts of good and evil with movement as the mediating force between them. This political philosophy was practiced in performance by generations of people, and when acknowledged, we see that it is precisely about complex processes of signification, interior and exterior identifications, and other social orders.

There is an epistemic dimension to both political and performance practice. Mixing up good and evil is a collective strategy to neutralize dualisms, even while the overarching narrative of the performance may be about the figure of the devil and an explicit story of the "cosmic struggle of good and evil." Performance as a mode of transmission is capable of mediating such ambiguities and boundaries that arise through the production and practice of the dance. Without taking these performance practices seriously, ideational scholars dealing with issues of dualism and Manichaeism erase these complex histories not as "thin ideology," but as straitjackets for political difference. The result is to repeat the ethnocentric biases of their predecessors, where epistemological difference gets muddled in with populism as an easy container to deny the broader pluralisms that they perform.

In sum, my analysis suggests that performance perspectives are necessary to the vibrant conversation on populism. I contend that instead of being primarily text-based and discursive, populism among supporters of the Bolivarian Revolution is performance-based, reproduced and rehearsed within and as performance practice. Populism in this case is quite different from Charles Postel's characterization of United States populism of the early twentieth century as a "reading party," a populism communicated primarily through texts and pamphlets (2007, 4). If this early populism in the United States was a reading party, Venezuela's populism a century later was a "performance party."

Performance

Performance, perhaps in its most basic definition, is an act or presentation, a "doing" and "showing doing" (Schechner 2013, 22).[13] As Elin Diamond wrote, it is "always a doing and a thing done" (1996, 1). It is an embodied act "in the flesh" and an act that is witnessed by others, with implications that carry over to a myriad of debates around ephemerality and staying power, representation and transformation, materiality and the social, to mention just a few.

My approach to performance includes this centrality of the body, combining it with social practice and production. I draw from a range of scholars in theater, ritual, dance, and religion in thinking about how the body transmits sensory knowledge and an epistemic dimension. The performance studies scholar Diana Taylor has been clear about this relationship, calling performance "a practice and an epistemology," a way of knowing and a means of transmitting cultural identity and worldview (2016, 39). Moreover, as a social practice, performance "is inseparable from the bodily co-presence of various groups of people who come together as actors and spectators" (Fischer-Lichte 2014, 18). I think this is especially (although not exclusively) relevant to festival performance in the streets, with many different people participating in a perennial act and means of making collective political space. Gisela Cánepa calls this a cultural repertoire, tying the public constitution of identity in these performances to diverse forms of political action and agency (2009, 32). Indeed, populist repertoires work within our social, historical, and material environment to constitute political effects that are called populism, but at the same time they challenge the very limits of populism as performances that engage politics in very much their own terms.

Most of the performances analyzed in this book raise issues about collective belonging and the revolutionary state. In the first half of the book, I look at popular street and staged performances: fiestas, dance, theater, and film that engaged various actors and participants in small towns and the city. The second half of the book turns more toward representation and the relationship between leaders and constituents of the revolution, and finally, I am interested in how icons and symbols of a state also perform across these interstices of the people and the state. Some of these performances, particularly the devil dances discussed in chapter 1, have been around for decades and generations: during dictatorship, during a supposed opening in democracy, and, going further back, during slavery and colonial rule. They are also fully contemporary and an excellent example of the diverse forms of public deliberation that people return to year after year.

Staged performance in the Chávez era has also largely been about revival and recuperation. Reenactments featuring nineteenth-century historical figures have become commonplace, carrying with them the "passionate patriotism" and "love of country" that surged in national discourse through staged plays and film in the mid-twentieth century (Sommer 1991, 33, 264). Starting in 1999, new theaters were built, and warehouses and abandoned buildings that were once boarded up were renovated as theaters. There are now a dozen such recuperated theaters and cultural centers in the urban barrios of Caracas.

In 2014, I had the chance to see a group of young artists as they rehearsed a performance that paid homage to Chávez's life. Calling themselves a collective, the large cast of dancers, actors, and street performers choreographed several sequences in a warehouse-sized room backstage of the Teresa Carreño national theater with giant props, picture frames, and baroque costumes lining the walls. I sat among a small group of people observing the rehearsals as formally trained ballet dancers alongside circus street artists practiced their routines: stunning leaps and turns, monologues, and full-cast dance sequences. This somewhat unconventional and talented group of artists now had keys to one of the most important stages in the country. All this brought a contagious freshness to a well-known story. Several of the performers described the piece as their personal tribute to Chávez's memory one year after his death. At one point, the young actor who played Chávez was lifted up and through a moving sculpture of bodies, propelled by feet and hands across the stage. At another point, he steps off the stage and conducts from below. María Claudia Rossell, producer and dancer in the collective, said that the intent of the piece was "to show the impact of Chávez's life, which transitioned the country from ruin to recuperation."[14]

In the present day young activists and artists, like the Generation of 1928 that sought to revive the unfinished dreams of Bolívar, also seem to be building new futures through these heroic figures. After leaving the rehearsal, we walked down a winding path newly installed through the fine arts district, where outdoor tables at popular cafés were filled with people, and murals seemed to recall the *brigadas* (brigades) of socialist Chile. This too is a revival where the radicalism of a generation before contributes to a revolutionary aesthetic in which artists who produce these events today are opening new spaces through an homage to the past and a passionate patriotism of their own.

In order to more fully delve into how these performances overlap with populism, however, we must more deeply recognize the ways meaning is made within the body. Populism is an embodied act. The body is at the core of both performance and populism, and yet it is too often secondary in the study of political action. We know that action is beholden to the range of sensorial experience from which we derive and transmit knowledge. As the performance studies scholar Julia Walker reminds us, meaning is "registered within the body's viscera, as emotional or experiential 'knowledge' " (2003, 160). Performance and populism include logocentric epistemes, but when we examine what we know and how we know, these transmissions also generate their own meanings through the body. "Language is not simply an ideational medium," Walker writes, "but 'speaks' to the heart and the gut as well as the head" (2003, 167). The "heart" and the "gut" in this visceral register are often the end point of populism debates; the critique is that emotion is irrational and only sober deliberation can build democratic futures. This critique of populism misunderstands the political role of the senses. Populism is not bad just because it is about emotion and passions. An analysis of affect through performance helps us understand that critical potential.

Embodiment in performance works differently than a logocentric episteme (as fundamentally about words and language). The bodily carries knowledge and a worldview that is a system of perception and transmission operating through the senses. "The performing body is also the sensing body" (Mitchell and Bull 2015). As anthropologist David Howes (2015) points out, "the senses have a vital role to play in framing—or mediating—the relationship between mind and environment, self and society, idea and object" (see Bull et al. 2006, 5). The "heart" and the "gut" are thus inseparable from perceptive abilities. Moreover, as anthropologist Zoila Mendoza (2015) points out, studies of Andean performance suggest that the senses can work differently, for example in unities of hearing, sight, and kinesthesia, in ways that challenge the hierarchy of differentiation of the senses that is often assumed to be universal by Eurocentric philosophies. Perception and transmission are not only culturally specific through the senses; they also point to political attachments and ideals. Our bodies transmit and capture a wide range of this sensory knowledge at a visceral level among others and through our material environment.

Performance, in my view, merges the sensorium with social practice and the environment in the mechanics of *doing*: in backstage production, the rehearsals, the planning, and the networks that make up the performed act. Performance makes social and material evidence of populism visible on stages and in the built environment. Then there are the ongoing relationships, energies, and people that have a stake in continuing a performance over generations. Drawing from the performance-studies scholar Leo Cabranes-Grant's *From Scenarios to Networks* (also in this book series) that in turn builds on Bruno Latour's actor-network theory, to me these networked relationships operate as systems or webs. "Webs of relations," as Cabranes-Grant puts it, is a useful way of thinking about how people, objects, and environments reproduce particular meanings through ritual practice both historically and presently. The interconnectedness of people, stories, and place in coastal Venezuela brings to mind fishing nets and string hammocks (*chinchorros*), which are common in work and everyday life. I appreciate these as metaphors of a broader field of social movements and relationships that performance is bound within. Shannon Jackson (2011) argues that infrastructural support systems (which are often invisible in everyday life) are newly engaged and vital to the aesthetics of contemporary visual and performed arts. This book is an attempt to link these "social works" to political works.

I prefer to use the term "cultural producers" (in Spanish, *cultor*) for those who participate in various kinds of art production, whether they are the people who build the sets, make the costumes, or contribute in other ways to the everyday and more formal aspects of artistic creation. I also use "systems" to refer to the dynamics that move through networks or, as Álvarez, Dagnino, and Escobar call them, "social movement webs," which operate even at the fringes of production in ways that contribute to the meaning-making, aesthetic, material, and social aspects of performance events.[15] To me, these systems of production, however temporary or enduring, are crucial to defining populist repertoires, yet I have to admit that as terms they still seem to me too clunky. Especially since fiestas, carnivals, processions, and other participatory ritual performances turn those systems inside out, onto the streets and in open public spaces, I find that the term "fiesta politics" is another way of getting to the practices of these systems.

The systems of production in carnivals, fiestas, and other forms of cultural performance are not just supports for the event—they *are* the event. The connections between production and performance are simultaneously intellectual, ancestral, and material. Giovanni Arrighi (1994) calls attention to the "organization of processes of production and exchange." From this perspective, cultural production meets the popular discursive space of markets, streets, and plazas, where material exchanges and labor are also mediated through performance (Bakhtin 1968; Martín-Barbero 2008). Thus, while to some degree cultural performance events are, as David Guss suggests, "framed by a beginning and end time," they are also "porous," "discursive," and, importantly, "polyphonic" (2001, 8). In fiesta performance, where its system of production is laid bare in the streets and plazas, the event is both polyphonic expression and a story with a beginning and an end. The performance is inseparably combined with the ongoing ordinary relationships (i.e., among neighbors) that continue well after the event is over and well before the event begins.

Fiestas and other ritual performances foreground these systems of production in ways often associated with disorder, the chaotic, or the upside down. But I see such cultural performances not as discontinuous with political order but rather as expressions of an alternative political order, one very much its own.[16] "Performance," as Jackson writes, is "an art of interpublic coordination" (2011, 13). Linking the ephemeral and the material, these performances are defined by the publicness of their production as much as by the street spectacle and theatricality of costumes, masks, and whirling dances in the central plaza. Processions, carnivals, and popular fiestas, in a sense, walk straight through the back door of the theater, hauling everything out with them—the shop, the costume wardrobe, and the reception lobby—onto the streets. Each function of production—often with its own aesthetic and production systems—may contribute to a joint event, and yet originates from different corners of the neighborhood.[17] Between political performance and popular fiestas, there are some obvious differences of scale and in the complexity of navigating in and out of open town spaces, but the organization of these "processes of production and exchange" requires a great deal of systemic management. Rather than merely the disorderly, the ludic, or the *festejo* (party), these processes of production and exchange hold their own rules, cultural specificities, and logics.

Community-based performance approximates the kind of multiple-armed production of fiesta and carnival. By multiple-armed, I mean that there are many source points of agency that hold up a social body and shared meanings of the performance event. While sometimes staged indoors, fiestas as community-based events are generally organized very differently from mainstream institutional theater. According to Jan Cohen-Cruz, in the latter, "those able to leverage the most money are on top, be they producers or stars. The playwright is generally second, demonstrating western civilization's bias for written expression over the oral and physical. Next comes the director, then the rest of the 'creative team,' designers, composers, and choreographers. Then the actors, mere interpreters, followed by the even more lowly technicians, mere 'skilled workers.' Last and least, if discussed at all, is the audience" (2005, 6).

In processions, fiestas, and other cultural performances, however, "actors" are only one part of the performance process, and each part is generally interdependent with another. Costume makers and mask makers, cooks and guardians of the saints—all are integral to the performance process in ways that expand leadership and authority. The "technicians" are often the ones who say what the show should actually be, and the "director" can be a group of people guiding the action on one end of the street with little to say about what happens on the other end. In ritual and popular fiestas, where hundreds and sometimes thousands of people take part in walking with the saints or devils in a procession, the "audiences"—or, as Augusto Boal says of forum and legislative theater, "spect-actors" (spectators that become actors within the play)—are also capable of intervening and participating; instead of just observing the event, and in many cases they *are* the event.

Ritual and community-based performances maintain their own systems of agreement and regulation. We must not presume that all ritual is "antistructural," an act opposed to or outside the rule of law, one that operates under the principles of disorder and/or anti-order, not just as chaos, but also as the separation of ritual from law.[18] It makes sense that ritual performance can be resistant against the law. It also makes sense to think of the law as if it were ritual.[19] I am saying that we might also see ritual as if it were law. There is a mutually reinforcing, even circular relationship between the law as predictably ritualistic and the understanding of ritual, even apart from the legal system, as following certain prescribed norms and routines. Fiestas and carnivals are ordered with rules both codified and also dynamic so that people, space, and resources can be organized year round (and year after year). In short, these performances carry their own politics. Just think of the massive scale of organization that goes into carnival preparations in Brazil, for example, where the samba schools, *blocos* (carnival "blocks" are organized groups that dance and play music together), or other kinds of street mobilizations are institutions of major power. So when I think of performance in terms of ritual, I'm referencing these formal and semi-formal organizational systems of the practice to argue that they overlap and, in many ways, are contiguous with political society.

We also might be tempted to see a social drama unfold in the political realm on the basis of these performances. Turner applied ritualization as social drama to four phases of social activity over a span of time—a breach of norms, crisis, redressive action, and reintegration—mirroring the rise and fall of Aristotelian dramatic structure. In some cases I think that is accurate.

But I am also drawn to a more episodic approach, or what Eric Selbin calls the "microstories" of revolution (2010). In particular, as the political culture of the Bolivarian Revolution unfolded, I became interested in Selbin's observations that revolution is often not an act of singular heroes and tragic form, but rather a web of particular stories that make up the macrostory, which is what builds up to a cohesive narrative of revolution (2010, 44). Again we see webs, and this time in terms of content where parts of the story, bits and matched patterns are tied together through networks. These are microstories that spread, or build traction through lived experience.

The spread of these meaning-making webs makes up the more unifying scenarios of social movements. Here my use of the term "scenario" follows the performance-studies theorist Diana Taylor, who calls it a "formulaic structure that refer[s] to specific repertoires of cultural imaginings" (2003, 31). Moreover, of interest to me is what those scenarios then make possible to reproduce in the local. In other words, as Taylor argues, without the repetitive enactments, the scenario would likely not adhere to widespread social movements, but also, to a certain degree, vice versa. We might consider these microstories as composing, as Susan Buck-Morss suggests, a particular kind of universal history, "an infinity of connecting links . . . lateral, additive and syncretic" (2009, 151). In the politics of historical reproduction, an episodic approach challenges a totalizing version of a single unifying story. To draw open the tension between the two, however, provides a rich context in which to analyze up close what happens when a unifying story does take hold across a popular movement. In the process, we shift the emphasis to perhaps more pragmatic issues of who, how, and when those stories are reproduced and retold, and the production of history, with its recursive phases and absences in relation to power (Trouillot 1995). Selbin argues that the revolutionary process is precisely about this transfer, which takes place in a language of storytelling, back and forth from the microstories to the grand narratives of revolution and so on. To me, the scenario and Selbin's macrostories are strategically upheld and reciprocal to the choices people make on an everyday basis to uphold their political reality.

The active reproduction of history in the revolutionary state arrived at the very heart of debates that are also taking place within both populism and performance studies—debates about official and unofficial narratives, inside or outside of the social body, representation and embodiment, performativity and the performed. One such debate revolves around the term "performative," which Laclau deploys in his theory of populism. The term "performative" as first developed by J. L. Austin is about the power of words to produce an actionable result. For example, the utterance "I do," given proper procedure, performs a marriage (Austin 1975, 5). For Austin, this event depends on its explicit status, legally conferred or authorized to warrant action from words (ibid., 28). The marriage is only actionable if a priest or judge pronounces it so. Yet, for Laclau, "performative" refers to the reiterative, discursive practice that constitutes subjectivity, a model he derives from the groundbreaking work of Judith Butler. This means that ordinary people express particular demands and agreements in the equivalential chain as they are "hailed," or through a reiterative citationality (and practice of refusal) that constitutes identity. For Laclau, populism is thus agential by its mechanism, a process that rejects the need for a proper officiator. Authorization is transferred from officiating individuals (priest, judge, etc.) to a broader system of moral authority through the equivalential chain, a process in effect constantly ratified by facing one another in assembly.

Recognizing this difficulty of officiating performatives, Taylor proposes another term next to performatives that she calls animatives; rather than performatives as "referees on the field," animatives explain the "ruckus that breaks out in the stadium" (2007, 1417). Akin to Antonio Negri's constituent power that resists domestication, Taylor describes animatives within the realm of what Jack Halberstam calls "the wild" (Taylor 2016, 131). Like Halberstam, Taylor reaches outside Eurocentric philosophy, suggesting *olín*, which means "movement" in Nahúatl. She writes, "animatives are part movement, as in animation; part identity, being or soul as in anima or life. The term captures the fundamental movement that is the life of (that breathes life into) embodied practice" (Taylor 2007, 1417). *Olín* as repetitive, ordered, and cosmic (breath) seems to present a continuity in relation to the political affect of the scream. As animatives capable of riot or the gritty determination to survive, and performatives at the moment of agency, both emerge as important components of the performance and/as politics enjambment, centering the body with its different senses, desires, and demands within continuous (or repetitive) forces that move through it.

The way I see it, populism is closer to the political potential of animatives, the action in the stands that is organized amid the seeming ruckus. To link animatives to populism means to insist on movement and "soul" in ways that "challenge or exceed discursive formulation" (Taylor 2007, 1417). Like Elizabeth Maddock Dillon's "performative commons" of the Anglophone transatlantic, these unofficial and yet performance-charged events enable political cultures to flourish. Animative practices bring attention to the unofficiated demands among the multitudes in the theater, on public squares, and in other performance spaces. Like populism, Selbin's microstories and Taylor's animatives tell us that performance has a broader and much more intensified relevance to political cultures that have historically and presently been discredited, cast aside, or appropriated. To "take performance seriously," as Rai and Reinelt call for, then, is also about recognizing an ongoing struggle for cultural legitimation.

A performance studies approach also sharpens what we know about agency, participation, and the enacting of inclusion and exclusion to provide a crucial counterbalance to (or at least critical questioning of) foundational biases within the institutions of the Western sciences. To omit this dimension of performed political practice, I believe, is to exert yet another act of bias to distort democracy. The possibilities of democracy actually depend on widening this analytical lens while maintaining a critical activism and a constant questioning of what constitutes the common good.

As has been well-documented, the appropriation and exploitation of "the people" and romanticized projections of the "common good" can reinforce dominant ideologies. And this is where the critics are understandably suspicious of populist movements. Stanley Brandes, in his study of social control in rural Mexico, describes fiestas as events in which participants develop a tacit dependency on dominant party interests (1988, 4–5). Often in the guise of "community," campaigns that champion solidarity are the first to exploit the struggle of the oppressed. In Peru, Alberto Fujimori's populism sought votes by handing out televisions and kitchen appliances, claiming to represent the working class; instead he plunged the country into a "Fujishock" of austerity reforms, extrajudicial killings, forced sterilization of thousands of indigenous women, and the list goes on (López 2014). The suspicion of the collective runs deep, especially when the good of some uncritically claims to stand in for the good of all. Populism in this sense can lead to false representation, abetting phony schemes to appropriate signs and symbols for the enrichment of the promoters at the expense of producers.

In this book, I will explore what it means when ordinary people act as protagonists of the political future of the revolution. Outside a lens of liberalism, in which singular voices each take their fifteen minutes of fame, what are the possibilities of envisioning collective action, and what are the implications of the people as "actors" or "audiences" of revolution? What does it mean for artists and activists to engage with a broader-based social movement of Bolivarianism, particularly in a political process that works simultaneously within and beyond nationalism and when those previously holding power have for a long time been the minority? Revolutionary performances of the Chávez era have generally been produced by collectives, and yet, interestingly, several have chosen to spotlight the lives of historical figures; a pantheon of heroes cycles through murals and stenciled street art, on stages, and in films, from amateur and low-profile to the highest-budgeted films in the history of the country. Are these heroic performances of the state that excavate the past for its own consolidation, or do these performances and producers fulfill a radically different future?

In the last decade of socialism in Venezuela, previously excluded actors and ensembles have found a place to thrive. Betwixt and between both official and unofficial discourses of Chavismo, they have expanded spaces such as theaters, community centers, and plazas for the fight against racism, sexism, and other forms of violence. They have strategically (and tactically) used available funding and spaces for public arts projects and open arts education in the central and peripheral neighborhoods of the city, making "outreach" a moot point because these projects originate within. Rather than an imported false divide between the arts and social welfare, endogenous organizations restore the role of performance as attached and integral to issues of labor and the economy, health care, and environmental rights, to name a few.[20]

The result in the arts is a stronger emphasis on outdoor, public theater and festivals that are connected to working-class and poor people. Some of this work perpetuates the trend of larger-than-life heroes as subjects even as it simultaneously exercises tremendous creativity to transform these figures on murals, or in performances like the work at the Teresa Carreño Theater. For the street artists and independent professionals who now have keys to the national theater, the recuperation of space reflects a shift in priorities; these "shrines of power," to borrow a phrase from Ngũgĩ wa Thiong'o, become newly enshrined with greater access and the reproduction of popular cultural knowledge.

But what about the compulsory function of the state to unify and to represent? Is it not always a game of power between who is on the inside of the state, and who gets shoved to the margins? While new opportunities have appeared, in a practical sense it was also clear that artists and activists were constantly in a process of negotiation with the Chávez administration over its implementation of structural reform.[21] Sujatha Fernandes (2010) describes the ways in which cultural arts producers negotiated the terms of a changing system as "one of strategic ambiguity." Her work with artists and activists in the urban barrios of Caracas suggests "the porous nature of society's interface with the state" (254). When Chávez took office, the government relied substantially on the formal mechanisms of a liberal state, distributing millions of small booklets of the laws and constitutions that govern it. It also conducted regular elections to verify these mechanisms (see Pastor and Dalmau 2001). At the same time, questions over the new role of more than 30,000 state-funded organizations (known primarily in 2013 as the *comunas* and *consejos comunales*) have challenged liberal conceptions of the necessary separation between state and society (López Maya 2004; Buxton 2005; Hawkins 2003). According to Fernandes, activists and cultural producers of these organizations "question the abstract and formal principles of impartiality, rule of law and procedural democracy invoked by Western observers and technocrats as a means of masking forms of privilege and domination. . . . This logic of accountability differs from that of a middle-class civil society, with its postulations of a sharp boundary between state and society" (2010, 253–54). Fernandes makes clear that these forms of political agency are not just exercised from above. They also follow their own political logics from below.

Bottom-up state formation, a concept examined by Gilbert Michael Joseph and Daniel Nugent, suggests a more nuanced understanding of the multiple ways in which official projects of the state are coproduced and shaped by ordinary people of the popular sector (1994, 12). Partha Chatterjee calls this "political society," distinguishing political society from an understanding of "civil society," which he saw as comprised of a privileged sector of "culturally equipped citizens" aligned with elites and the status quo (2004, 38, 40–41). This understanding of civil society harkens back to the neoliberal state prior to Chávez in which most institutions (including and sometimes especially cultural institutions of the arts) were governed by boards of directors that were heavily, if not entirely, invested in the maintenance of the political establishment.

Both Fernandes and Chatterjee document a domain of political difference that is made possible by a "widening of the arena of political mobilizations" and by "building on communication structures that would not be ordinarily recognized as political" (Chatterjee 2004, 47). What kinds of communication structures might be taking place in these repertoires that contribute to a widened frame of the political? It is no coincidence that both authors, and Cánepa mentioned earlier, consider the importance of cultural assemblies and religious festivals in their analyses. Fernandes explores them within an urban context, claiming that "the celebration of popular festivals in the barrios of Caracas are an important form of cultural expression through which communities appropriate public space, emphasize their commonality, and revive their social and historical origins as the basis for urban popular movements" (2006, 51). It is this recognition of fiestas and cultural performance as *bases* for popular movements that is the specific work of this book.

I see fiesta and large-scale religious manifestations and cultural performance as forums for performance-based politics, sometimes defining themselves specifically against political institutions as an alternative or contending political order. Central to my argument is that fiesta and other kinds of popular performance are more than popular culture; they are also practices of popular politics. One approach is to look at the systems of production. Fiesta, for example, includes production that extends beyond the norms of staged theater. Within an enclosed space, whether scripted or not, with a stage on high or down low, there are different systems of control over access and the environment. At the same time, radically different forms of organization take place among fiesta's participants, both actors and audiences. The networks that organize these performances carry with them these diverse histories, cultural specificities, and logics. The devil dances—performances that move through the streets in a public procession—that I will describe in the first chapter are a striking example of a socially and politically broad-based and populist performance.

Ocumare

This book opens and closes in a small near-coastal town called Ocumare, about 150 miles northwest of Caracas in the state of Aragua. Ocumare is a name that likely derives from the word *cumari*, which refers to a plant used for making hammocks and baskets in the indigenous languages of the

Caribe-Cumanagoto and Tacarigua peoples. It also recalls the Candomblé deity Oxumare, the serpent rainbow who is always in motion. This land was first inhabited in three waves of indigenous migration: first by Arawak peoples of the Amazonia about 4,000 years ago, then by a broader base of Arawak or Lokono peoples, from present-day Colombia and Mexico, and last by Kali'na (Carib) and Taíno peoples who migrated from the greater Caribbean just before the European invasion.

Throughout the seventeenth and eighteenth centuries, the coast of present-day Aragua was the arrival point for tens of thousands of Africans who had been forcibly removed from fourteen recorded African ethnic groups, mainly from Central and West Africa, including Congo, Fon, Mandinka (Mande), Mabembe, Bantu, Akan, and Efik-Efok. Fewer in number were Portuguese, Dutch, and Spanish Europeans, and *criollos* (a term that refers to American-born European descendants).[22] At present the majority of the people living in Ocumare are of mixed race (mestizo) indigenous and Afro-descendant ethnicity, with many families that can trace their lineage in the area back for centuries.

Nearby Puerto Cabello was one of the first landing points in South America for the Spanish fleet carrying the Venetian merchant Amerigo Vespucci. This was one of at least three journeys taken by Vespucci between 1498 and 1503—journeys that would lead an amateur German cartographer to place the name "América" on his 1507 map of the continent.[23] Over the next century, Puerto Cabello became the principal shipping port in South America for the Spanish Crown. Just east of Puerto Cabello is a much smaller port known as La Boca, which is about three miles from Ocumare. Francisco de Miranda docked on the shores of La Boca just outside of Ocumare in 1806, on an expedition financed by Haití. Simon Bolívar landed ten years later on his own mission, again financed by Haití. Ocumare was also known as the Venezuelan dictator Juan Vicente Gómez's personal hacienda during the 1930s, the town itself thus becoming metonymical of his backyard domestic holdings.

For the Dutch, English, Portuguese, and Spanish, Ocumare was considered strategically important as the heart of production of one of Venezuela's main exports at the time, chocolate. The cacao industry in northern Venezuela most likely began as early as the mid-sixteenth century, and by 1579, following a crash in production in Mexico, it was recorded as a lucrative export for Venezuela (Vivas 1993, 378).[24] The demand for product drove the surge in slavery in the region, which was known to have continued in Ocumare up through 1880—three decades after slavery was officially abolished.[25] In 1875 the production of cacao comprised 87 percent of Ocumare's economy (Mörner 1993, 49). The distinctive fruity flavor of Ocumare's and nearby Chuao's chocolate was highly sought after and considered exemplary of South America's finest products. Yet, by the mid-twentieth century, with the exploitation of oil, the chocolate industry became practically defunct. A cacao cooperative more recently organized by small cultivators in the region has revived the chocolate production of Ocumare and surrounding communities, receiving support as a cooperative business from government micro-investments. With limited hand-selected production and a process that ferments and then dries the beans in the sun, raw cacao and chocolate products from Ocumare (and Chuao) appeal to artisanal markets around the world.

Most people in Ocumare live marginally off of local tourism at the nearby beaches of Playón and Cata. Some people fish, some farm, and some work for the municipal government that funds day care and schools, a large hospital and clinic, two recreation facilities, and local food markets. Walking through the plaza in Ocumare, one sees a plain handwritten poster announcing a community meeting or fiesta tacked to the wall across the street from the pharmacy. Several men mingle on the corner in front of the church. An open garage door of a community center that holds public workshops reveals a collection of drums and books. Kids line up to use the computers in the library across the street. A film is being shown at the technical school across from the stadium, and a group of men play dominos under a giant tree. At a different corner, several friends and family sit around a circle of drums long into the evening to celebrate the birthday of the same señora who, a few nights later, sits among a dozen or so ladies under a single street lamp in a rosary circle, solemnly reciting prayers and sliding beads along a string. Cars drive by on the main road, sometimes like lightning, other times slowly and with the latest *reggaetón* or a classic salsa streaming out. City dwellers from Caracas and Maracay drive by; sometimes they stop for a bottle of water or an empanada at the *panadería* on the north corner of the plaza owned by a Portuguese family, but mostly they cruise right past on their way to the beach towns of Playón or Cata. On the plaza, on the side of the street, in front of houses, or in any number of pay-per-seat taxis or motorcycles zipping along the Aragua coast, conversations take place about the marketplace or the roads, about the latest government projects, and about family. These many levels of sociability and exchange hold particular patterns and rules. Perhaps more so than any single entity, group, or individual, the devil dances and other fiestas of the town create a space that reflects who a people are and what they value in a way that is complexly layered, carrying its history as it is constantly being remade.

Chapters

A few words here on the structure of this book and how its argument proceeds. The first half of the book is dedicated to how populism manifests within street and staged performances. The second half of the book then takes a reverse approach to look at how performance turns up in what is more commonly identifiable as populist politics. Here the concern is to show how campaign politics (discussed in chapter 3) and symbols as seemingly consolidated as the national crest of arms (discussed in chapter 4) are dynamically remade through performance. The case points discussed in this book thus map a spectrum from what is conventionally considered performance—dance, theater, and film—to what are more typically understood as political acts, such as election campaigns and symbols of the state. In the arc of the chapters, I am also stretching to find the limits within the overlap of performance *as* politics, where it seems that even a performance that is expressly apolitical can systematically exercise a politics of its own. Likewise, in what might appear to be a highly constituted symbol of the state—such as a flag—there may in fact be evidence of a dynamic embodied interaction with audiences, actors, story, and staging.

Chapter 1 centers on a long-practiced annual performance in a small town on the coast of Aragua called the *diablos danzantes*, or devil dances. In this chapter, I argue that people rehearse populist logics, as Laclau theorized, in the production of the performance. These notably "popular" performances—popular in that they are large-scale, produced by hundreds of people, and held in open, public spaces—become forums of political engagement. The devil dances are also a quintessential example of an event authored by no singular entity but rather "by the people." Within the event, individual and collective agreements, as well as the constant tensions that threaten to break them, are made. A process of informal deliberation over who claims the inside versus the outside of the communal order takes on embodied and symbolic form in the public arena of the streets. The devil dances provide a site for considering the ways in which populism works as a system of political conduct created by ordinary people and by participants in large-scale performance-based cultural events—as Boal says, a forum for the political.

In our discussion of the dance as a public forum of the political, there are two significant implications. First, for those who participate, "the people," as authors of a collective event, are a moving target that is constantly negotiated and rearticulated through the performance and its production. I call this "fiesta politics," where people come together to contribute different resources to a unifying event, problem, or concept. In such an approach, we must consider the distribution of power and agency among a wide number of participants, not only those "onstage," but also costume makers, altar makers, local guardians, and historians, since the performance itself is composed of this broad base of production that sustains it over generations of its reenactment.

Second, if populist logics, including fiesta politics, are transmitted through embodiment, then that embodiment implies a range of sensory experiences that exceed a text-based transmission. The multimodality of embodiment includes sound, smell, tactile, spatial, and other forms of sensorial transmission. Rather than taking place "out of time" or "upside-down" or otherwise in opposition to the rule of law and order, populist logics are enacted *through* embodied performance. Populist repertoires are not just the result or product of politics; it is the medium itself that does the work of populism. Scripts, or logocentric systems of knowledge, operate in their own interpretive schema, one that receives information in texts like this book with print in black squiggly lines, or online, or on paper. The text on this page is not, however, video, and it is even less of a vehicle for the sensorial, material, and social complexity of the devil dances.

This first chapter attempts to situate saints and devils in the center of this sensorium and includes a discussion of the multiple ways that polytheism and devil beliefs circulate more broadly in society. How do people understand the devil? Do they understand it as the ultimate "evil" of a Manichaean logic, or as this ultimate evil mixed in with various other qualifying meanings of the devil, of evil, and of the contexts in which those meanings adhere? How do multiple saints, as figures of devotion, stand in for one, or the one Holy Sacrament stand in for all? I suggest that these performances show that both are possible, which is a very different, decentralized model for how people work through and beyond Manichaean logics, a model that informs both politics and populism, from fiestas and religious manifestations to the highest offices of state.

In the second chapter, I trace what happens when populist logics transfer to different kinds of embodied practice and cultural production, namely theater and film performances. I focus on urban political formation in the era leading up to Chávez's electoral victory, from 1958 to 1998, examining in particular the work of the playwright, director, and filmmaker Román Chalbaud. I argue that cultural production of this era contributed to the making of the popular class, "the people" of the urban working class and the poor, in part through the space of the barrio. Chalbaud's earlier theatrical work helped to break the wall of invisibility in staging the barrio. The latter case of a film, just preceding Chávez's elections, reimagines those spaces of the barrio to reflect an insurgent utopianism of the popular class. In both, the evidence of populism was as much in the bodies of these characters as in the material evidence of the buildings, pathways, and spaces that they inhabited. The cultural and material construction of spaces in effect opens from *inside* the barrio, creating a "we" of political subjectivity from within. In this case, fiesta politics carries over to theater and film to shift the iconic centrality of the barrio into a mainstream populist imagination of *barrio adentro* (inside the barrio).

Although the performances discussed in chapters 1 and 2 were developed quite differently—one as a grassroots cultural performance over centuries of practice in a rural area, and the other by a small group of urban artists and intellectuals who challenged state power in art and media—both are examples of how performance generates popular culture, and perhaps more importantly a *culture of populism*. The distance between performer and audience in the performance discussed in the second chapter produces different inclusions and absences, effects and environments. Within the "fourth wall," that imaginary separation between action onstage and off, we are taught to suspend our disbelief of its illusion. And yet we also know that performance carries cultural memory and its own genealogy. Migrants from around the country brought fiesta politics with them to the urban barrios. These populist logics learned from organizing fiesta performance contributed to the political culture of change in Caracas and across the nation. I see this political formation as one shaped by longtime particular histories and performance practices—practices that were carried into a new wave of media and the political opportunity of Chávez's election—rather than as a spontaneous upsurge of populism taking effect only in the Chávez era.

Chapter 3 examines one such election campaign when performance became an important mediation of the newly forged relationships between people and state in the Chávez era. The focus here turns to how the state mobilized story-making in the 2004 recall election, where the pro-Chávez campaign activated the legend of "Florentino and the Devil"—a story in which a humble campesino (peasant) outwits the devil in a duel of musical riddles. As the state distributed more power directly into the hands of citizen-action groups, these groups wielded that power to their advantage. And as David Cahill has pointed out, the question is often "Who is appropriating whom?" (1996). Chávez supporters appropriated the mechanisms of the state for their own demands; the state strengthened itself by drawing on the popular culture of its supporters. In other words, as Michael Taussig said, "it is a circle" (1980). In this case, the circle depends on the extent to which its constituents are able to wield the reins of state for their own interests, inasmuch as the state appropriates the energy of its base to strengthen the new hegemony. Of course, others see this exchange as less evenhanded, claiming that Chávez and his supporters reconfigured the state, shaping and defining its new functions in order to maintain its hold on power.

These deeper political tensions play out in this pinnacle moment of the Chávez era when performance and populism were inseparably and, to a certain extent, problematically intertwined in the 2004 recall election. I inquire into how the political culture of the campaign was enacted through performance. The focus here turns to how the state mobilizes story-making; I discuss the Chávez campaign's activation of the legend of "Florentino and the Devil"—a story in which a humble farm laborer outwits the devil in a duel of musical riddles. I argue that both the state and its supporters broadened their platform through this national legend by effectively shifting the debate on the terms of the participatory democracy that they proposed.

In chapter 4, I explore further the limits and possibilities of the popular state. I begin with an analysis of the reaction to an executive decision to change the direction of Bolívar's horse on the national coat of arms. The decision, for its critics, exemplified the spontaneous "anything goes" attitude that Hawkins attributes to populist leaders' excessive disregard of due process. Although the decision was technically handled by a separate bicentennial executive committee, reversing the direction of Bolívar's horse was, in a sense, a creative act, a performance of state, and I argue, a response to much broader demands for national redemption. In this case, joining populism and performance complicates the singularity of state power, pointing to populism's interminable attempt to unify through representation. Chapter 4 pairs this representation of Bolívar with a local history project in Ocumare de la Costa that was conducted by educators, cultural organizers, and oral historians, who situate Bolívar and Chávez amid the revolutionary struggle of Afro-descendants in the region.

While it is Bolívar's horse that is on the official flag of the state of Venezuela, the festive devil is everywhere else. The devil is a ubiquitous symbol of Venezuelan popular culture, one that appeared throughout colonial history and still appears in common speech, songs, and stories. First introduced to Venezuela in, some say, the late sixteenth century in Coro (a coastal port city west of Ocumare), the annual performances of the *diablos danzantes* (dancing devils) were practiced on the Aragua coast from the early part of the seventeenth century onward. In a sense, the devil figure guides the reader through this book: from Ocumare, to the capital city of Caracas, and back again; from its manifestation in present-day dance, to its colonial-era history, and back again to its appearance in contemporary media of the Bolivarian Republic of Venezuela. It is a figure whose meanings have shifted radically over centuries of abjection, revelry, resistance, and recreation. I am referring to the *festive* devil figure, which in Venezuela is derived from polytheistic African and indigenous belief systems perhaps more than from an embodiment of the antichrist in the Judeo-Christian tradition. Festive devils typically wear horned masks, ribbons, and colorful capes; they dance in what is widely promoted as a cosmic struggle between good and evil. The devil's role in these dances is clearly also that of protector and mediator. Thus it seems appropriate that the devil is, in a sense, a mediator for this text—hopefully with some playfulness and the critical distance of the trickster—as much as a guide for organizing the material of this book.

Throughout the book, performance allows us a glimpse of how this devil is recalled in specific moments of history. In some ways, the devil may be viewed as a counterpoint to the "official state," at times strategically distant and at other times merging together as one and the same. Never static, it spins through history. As David Guss writes, "These dizzying reversals confirm once again that which defines the popular is its relation to the dominant order and not some inherent quality or content" (2001, 16). This festive devil traces the path of the popular in populism's dangerous double edge, negotiating what is inside and outside the political order, constantly redefining the boundaries of the social good and questioning who has the right to decide.

Chapter 1

✦

Corpus Christi Devils and the Performance of Populism

Isidro "Cecilio" Antonio Silva set his calculator at zero and slowly started subtracting. "Sixteen-seventeen," he finally pronounced, displaying the digital numbers on the tiny window. This was Cecilio's estimated date, counted back by generations, for the first performance of the devil dances in Venezuela. We were sitting outside his house on the main road to town, a thinly paved, quiet road under draping *samán* trees with only an occasional collective taxi passing or a neighbor walking by on foot. The nearest market, about a half mile down the road, was a small brick bodega painted all white with a quote by Chávez in large red lettering across the wall: "To work with the people, the principle of everything revolutionary."

It was spring 2008, almost time for the annual Corpus Christi celebration, and the devil dances were about to happen again. Cecilio and his teenage niece Nora Aliver Silva were among the musicians who would lead the Corpus Christi procession from house to house to the front of the church at the center of town. Earlier that day, Nora and I had walked through the ruins of the Spanish *obras de piedad* (works of piety), also known as *obra pía*, an old mission and labor outpost across the street from Cecilio's house. This was the site of one of the earliest and largest seventeenth-century plantations that produced cacao. Lucrative chocolate seeds were harvested as pods off the trees; these were fermented, dried, and then shipped all over the world in an industry of chocolate production that triangulated Venezuela and other parts of the Caribbean, West Africa, and Europe in a matrix of transatlantic colonial economies (López-Cano et al. 1998). Only part of the structure of the *obra pía* still remained: a staircase and a landing with broken stones that protruded out of an open patio. The flat, claylike area, hardened like a giant *comal*, or cooking pan, reminded me of the drying yard in the cacao cooperative in Ocumare where piles of the chocolate beans soak up the sun, musty and syrupy-smelling like stewed berries and moss.

In the seventeenth century, the *obra pía* was one of the first outposts of the Catholic Church, and it lay at the center of slavery, forced labor, and religious conversion. Considered a "charity" project, the *obra pía* was the nexus of this system, and it was eventually surrounded by free black, Afro-indigenous, and mixed-race (*mulato*) families of Cata who traded cacao with Dutch merchants in the nearby island of Curaçao. Later it served as an orphanage during the long struggle for emancipation throughout the nineteenth century. In the beginning of the twentieth century, the property was purchased by Juan Vicente Gómez, a dictator known for brutal repression of his opponents and for selling the country's oil reserves to foreign interests. Gómez profited substantially from his landholdings until his death in 1938.

As we were leaving the site, Nora pushed aside the weeds to uncover a stone plaque on one side of the steps. The plaque marked the reconstruction of the edifice centuries after it had been first built; the numbers were barely visible. But what Cecilio had so carefully figured on his calculator made sense as the story unraveled and moved over three centuries from the construction of the mission and the first performances of the devil dances to the Gómez era. "*Ves*? [You see?]," he asked, holding out the calculator for both his niece and me to look at. That "*ves?*" implied many things: Do you see how old this dance is? Do you see how closely intertwined these histories of the dance are with the plantation-slave economy and the church that founded the "works of piety"? And then, did you see what came along with a glimmer in Cecilio's eyes: how those numbers were calculated without the internet and with no encyclopedia? Cecilio's gesture, relating his experience, and our attention to that experience authorized yet another layer to this history. It was not just about the building, the dance, or the dates.

Cecilio Antonio disappeared into his house and returned a few minutes later with a large book of essays and oversized photographs, one of fewer than a dozen published sources on the devil dances in the 1980s; this one had been produced by the National Institute of Folklore. As he thumbed through the pages, he explained that researchers had come to him twenty-five years earlier asking him about the history of the dance. For Cecilio, the book was a treasure, something he contributed to, but what he most enjoys, he said, is talking about it. This is a living history, he said, reminding me of those same words "*historia viva*" painted on a mural in the arts district of Caracas.

In most written material, the devil-dance performances of Corpus Christi are described as a cosmic struggle between good and evil, a contest born of the Christian faith and sanctioned as a fiesta in 1264 by Pope Urban IV.[1] Corpus Christi was considered the grandest of the fiestas in the Americas, held nine weeks after Easter. It was established and promoted during a time when the structural weakening caused by territorial expansion and the Reformation challenged the influence of the pope. The waning of church power concerned its leadership, and Corpus Christi was its answer for a popular revival. The fiesta was to be a joyful occasion; as one papal decree said, "no expense is to be spared" with theater, acrobatics, and elaborately decorated arches and altars in the open streets.[2] From as early as the sixteenth century, the church scripted these "new world" performances to promulgate a message of purification and Christian supremacy in which the dancing devils, as symbols of paganism, were purged amid abundant revelry.[3] As the Corpus Christi fiestas spread throughout the Spanish colonies, they became one of the church's most widely attended events by promoting its popularity through the incorporation of "native dances" as representative of this pagan "evil" that must be purified from the social body.

The "scripting" of these dances has largely remained the same over the hundreds of years of their enactments. The devil dancers begin by gathering in the house of one of the senior leaders of the dance to prepare themselves for the day. They wear colorfully painted horned masks and carry *maracas* and leather whips or sticks with strings. Just as the Mass is coming to an end, they leave the house and dance through the streets in a procession to the church. The devils then approach the church and, crouching low and constantly switching places, they furtively stand by the door. After Mass, the priest confronts the devils. He holds the monstrance of the Holy Sacrament high above his head, performatively banishing them from the parish. Seeing the sacrament, the devils bow down and retreat back into the street. The priest then pushes on with the sacrament in front of him to symbolically drive the devils out of town, with the parishioners following close behind. As the devils retreat, overpowered by the effect of the monstrance, they "surrender to" each of the altars that are set up at various intersections along the adjoining streets of the central plaza. The priest then blesses the altars, fortifying the faith of the altar-makers, to eventually purify the streets of his parish.

Mission friars and other church authorities were responsible for following the regimen of the Corpus Christi ritual to purge the devils or non-believers and at the same time to facilitate the dispersion of the fiesta as a means to recruit new members to the church services. The idea of purification in the Corpus Christi festivals goes back to medieval pageantry and the auto-da-fé rituals of the Inquisition. In these rituals, church officials sought to discipline transgressors through public shaming and forced acts of repentance. Those accused were led through the streets to trials with devil insignias and crosses sewn onto their hats and clothing. If the accused refused to repent, they were tortured, imprisoned, or, in some cases, immolated.[4] The documents of the Inquisition made clear that individuals subjected to torture were not the church's main concern; this punishment was for the sake of the "public good," "to induce terror in others so they would not commit the same evils" (Eymerich 1578, book 3, 137, col. 1).[5] In these terms, it appears Corpus Christi began more as an anti-populist festivity designed to repress popular opinion that was moving away from the church.

By no coincidence, the original "devils" in both the performed rites of the auto-da-fé and the devil dances of Corpus Christi in Europe were Muslims, Jews, and those accused of witchcraft (often women). As the Spanish colonial enterprise expanded, Corpus Christi celebrations symbolically incorporated those who refused to convert to Catholicism or who were deemed to be heretics, mainly Afro-descendant and indigenous peoples in the Americas accused of practicing "sorcery" or "witchcraft" through "pacts with the devil" (White 2005).

In these frameworks, good and evil were clear domains: the "good" was the Holy Sacrament and followers of Christ, and the "bad" were the "devils" that symbolized, initially anyway, those subjects who defied the church. The didacticism of these performances on the part of the European colonizers was explicit: so-called paganism was evil, and so to purge the devils, the procession dramatically performed the exorcism of "evil" (the devils) from the social body of "good" (the church). For most people, however, the occasion also meant a day off of work, and, whether enslaved or "free," people could mix, play music, and dance in the fiesta. Corpus Christi was thus an important promotional tool for the church, claiming to joyously celebrate the multiple races and cultures of the world, while also wielding a weapon designed by the church to eradicate beliefs and practices that did not conform to Christianity. The Corpus Christi fiestas thus became the public relations arm of the church's punitive system in which the body of Christ was the symbolic battlefield.

While early enactments of the devil dances involved a wide range of festive practices that incorporated "native rituals," it is important to keep in mind that Corpus Christi was mainly developed—at least by the church—as a tool of religious conversion initially intended to reproduce the colonial logic of the church and the institution of slavery.[6] Devil dancers were mostly, if not all, indigenous and black Afro-descendants, and they were recruited by *cofradías*, or fraternal orders, that were regimented by the church. While the *cofradías* offered some privileges to dancers and other participants, they also worked within severe measures of control (see Acosta Saignes 1962; Guerra Cedeño 1984). Historically, black *cofradías* negotiated the rules of the devil-dance performances, playing a key role in their conformity to church rules and their preservation of cultural traditions (see Ortiz 1921; Salazar 1984; Foster 1953). Akin to the Cuban *cabildos*, or guilds, the *cofradías* today—which often operate independently of the church and more closely with the municipality—are one of the central organizational mechanisms through which many families have maintained or claimed ownership of the dance over generations of its enactment.

As Cecilio showed us the book, he pointed out the people in the pictures and explained the diagrams of complex choreographies, musical scores, and instruments. He paused over several pages, noting the details of colorful wire-mesh masks as if he were looking at a high-school yearbook. "That was me," he said, pointing out a man in his forties with a *cuatro*, a small four-string guitar, in his hand. He was standing on the edge of where the devils were dancing, alongside a few other hip-looking men in wide-legged jeans. "Back then we were only a handful of dancers, and now, can you imagine? How many now, Nora?" They looked at each other pensively and started listing names, concluding somewhere in the range of twenty-five dancers in Cata. "And how many now in Ocumare? There's got to be a lot." Cecilio said his brother-in-law would know, telling me where he lived and which neighbors to ask in order to find him.

During these conversations with the people in the small towns on the coast of Aragua, the actual origin story of the devil dances was often brought up with curiosity and great interest, but it was also a device for something much larger and more important. Each person had a bit of information that led to another person and another. The stories lead to a network of people, to the roles of the members of that network, and to more living ties and relationships. In short, it is a system of producers, each of whom has his or her own part to play in this cultural performance that almost everyone agrees belongs to *el pueblo*.[7]

Along the way, I encountered not a cynical dismissal of "the people" as a chimera or invention of co-optation, but insistent claims that "the people" were indeed the authors of this dance. Most producers I spoke with suggested the devil dances are about faith, and communal bonds, and a way of doing things by a network of many rather than by a homogenous, or singular, subject. Behind the term *el pueblo* there is a complex web of relationships. It is about practice and the face-to-face exchange that is not without its internal tensions and conflicts. Ultimately, the ways in which people tell the story seem to outlast any foregone conclusions. As Diana Taylor said, "it's all about cultural adjustment and adaptation" (2006, 76). In other words, beyond Corpus Christi, there is a constantly remade practice of knowledge reproduction, unfolding and flexible, that keeps the devil dances going long after the old mission had crumbled back into the ground.

Over the rest of the afternoon, Cecilio explained how the dances are presided over by musicians playing the *cuatro*; their role is that of guide and protector. It's the musician's responsibility to ensure that each dancer reaches home safely on the night of Corpus Christi and throughout the rest of the weekend when the dances take place. While the church celebrates Corpus Christi as one of its most ebullient fiestas, for those that perform, it is also an extremely sober event, one that brings the potential of actual dangers. On the night of Corpus, as several leaders of the dance contend, real devils have been known to appear, and the *cuatro* player's duty is to protect the dancers by playing a rhythm that repeats over and over, never ceasing. This unbroken rhythm shields dancers, who are particularly vulnerable during the time of Corpus Christi. This is Cecilio and Nora's role: armed with the *cuatro*, they are guardians and protectors. Cecilio is also a historian and mentor, telling the history not just to me but also to his niece—a future historian, *cuatro* player, and mentor for the next generation.

Nora played a few chords and told me she would be accompanying the dancers the following year; it would be her first time as a musician in the

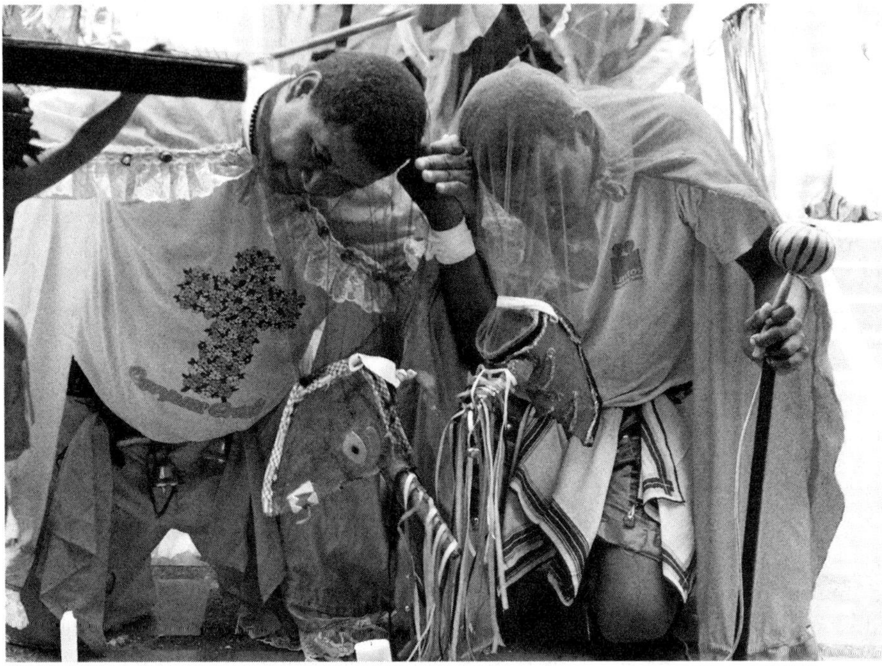

Figure 1. Devil dancers in Cata "surrender" at the front entrance of the church in devotional prayer. Shirts read "Corpus Christi" and "Juntos/Poder Popular" (Together/Popular Power)." Author photo, 2008.

dances of Cata. Later, she pointed out the processional route, stopping to tell of her own memories of the church, the bell tower, and school projects. She wanted to be a community historian, and attending a newly established university in the nearby city of Maracay was now a possibility, and so she was debating whether to go. That afternoon, we sat in the cool shade inside the seventeenth-century church of Cata while saints on both sides of the high adobe walls peered out of their *nichos*, or nested alcoves I tried to imagine what it would be like in just a few days with all those saints on the inside and the devils dancing at the door.

In contrast to the medieval rituals of the Inquisition, however, the devil dances of today mix devils and saints all the time. Rather than marching in penitent shame, the devils are honored, and they perform by blessing the altars that neighbors set up along the processional path and in their homes. Children grow accustomed to seeing their fathers, uncles, and other family members (mostly men) in fantastic horned masks and capes. In Cata in 2008, the priest was not present at the dance; instead, a family of three generations (a grandfather, a teenager, and a small child) held a modest cross on the inside of the church while neighbors, friends, and family stood both inside and outside of the church. A small basket filled with church contributions (*limosnas*) of bills and coins was placed at the foot of the cross as the devils dropped to their knees in pairs, praying with total surrender and a raw devotion that washed away any conception of evil.

For years a debate has taken place between the archdiocese and the *cofradías* over whether the devils should enter the church. After centuries in which the devils were banished to the streets, more recently the priest in the parish insists the devils should come inside the church to be "cleansed," since outside on the streets they are, in the priest's words, still "demonic."[8] Some people agree that the devils should be allowed to enter the church, but in order to signify that they are no longer banished. The majority of devil dancers and other participants in Cata and Ocumare, however, disagree. For them, the devils should *not* enter the church. Rather, the priest should leave the church to join the devils outside on the streets and fulfill his obligatory duty to bless the altars in the public procession. I discuss this in more detail later in the chapter, but for now, I merely want to point out the spatial dimensions of these debates.

For the people who produce the dance, the streets are where the devils take on the role of public service. In most of the towns on the Aragua coast, after the devils dance through the procession, they come back to the plaza and the streets to visit houses. Even in cases where the devils exorcise themselves from the plaza, they don't actually leave. They go around the back of the church and reenter the main streets, this time to bless the entrance to the cemetery and the individual houses of the elderly, especially those who are ill or housebound. Rather than discreet spaces of the sacred (church) and the profane (streets and cemetery), the devils are constantly moving in between.

Thus, while the devil dances uphold a story of good versus evil, in actual practice the devils' role crosses over into "good," dissolving the dualism that is at the foundation of the Corpus Christi rites. Of course, this was not always said in the literature. In most mentions of the devil dances they are almost always described as representing a "cosmic struggle between good and evil." The church attempts to maintain the primary order of holiness (inside), but it concedes that the devils have transformed from once being representative of the demonic outside, to now desired subjects for purification. The more I witnessed the dances, the more ambiguous good and evil seemed; especially for the devils, the emphasis was more on regeneration than on any fixed notion of dualism. As Taylor and Townsend write in the case of a Corpus Christi performance in Mexico, the result is anything but final (2008, 51).[9] These dances indeed seem to constantly revise and reorder the Manichaean binary of good versus evil, just as it reorders the temporal logic of finality.

In populism, performance is an important medium for recognizing these divisions of power, and for finding ways to produce an alternative. The many people who contributed to this dance made it possible to reproduce a political-theistic logic altogether different from the one the church originally conceived. While the friars indeed sought (and still seek) to instill the concept of absolute evil, the popular politics within this dance rework the devil figure as a strategic function of power. Performances like the devil dances (notably symbiotic with Venezuelan popular culture) turned the Manichaean discourse of diabolism into a more manageable, even playful, contestation. By family members taking on the role of the devil figure in homemade costumes, centering the very object of so-called evil as a devotional art practice, the performance transforms the devil figure into a familiar, and even lovable, dynamic agent of power. Thus, where the performance in theory upholds the good-versus-evil narrative, in practice the devil dances move beyond dualism into a new story with a much broader array of meanings. What I emphasize in this chapter is that this happens by virtue of the social systems of popular production, what I call a fiesta politics, where embodiment, spatiality, and the senses are at the center of this paradigm of reversal.

In one way, the devil-dance performance has the power to undo the racist didacticism of the church because the dance takes place in the streets. If the inside of the church is the place of order, the institutional order that founded the concept of good versus evil, then these dances undoubtedly turn that dynamic around. The streets are where many are present and participate as a broad-based network of producers, thus transforming the performance into a people's forum that ultimately offers an alternative epistemology of the political. While Venezuelan theater scholars such as Susana Castillo (1980) were insightfully writing about the uprooted condition (*desarraigo*) of Venezuelan society prior to Chávez, and while in the United States cultural producers are still searching for ways to generate sustainable social systems that can effectively transform pervasive demonization in our own communities, this centuries-old practice is an important example to study.

Festivals, carnivals, and fiestas such as Corpus Christi are participatory performances. Take community-based theater, add the dazzle effect of spectacle, and then multiply it across twelve generations in the same town. The "wow" of the devils swooping their colorful capes is a fantastic visual and sensory experience that goes hand in hand with the dance's participatory nature. Musicians, altar-makers, caregivers, and guardians of the saints move through the streets, sometimes with candles and other times praying or witnessing along the processional path. The spectacular attraction of these performances—at this point, anyway—is not about selling tickets or hotel rooms. In Ocumare, the dance is not a commodification of experience, since there are relatively few tourists outside the local economy. Instead, the performance is closer to what Victor Turner understands as *communitas*, a transcendent moment of communal integration. However, the performance is not removed from the networks and experiences of everyday life. From the viewpoint of participatory politics, popular religious manifestations such as the devil dances are as much a spectacular devotional experience as they are a regulatory practice of communal norms.

Corpus Christi was enacted through a top-down mandate by the church, which devised a highly structured command and hierarchy within the dance, yet today the concentration of power is dispersed among the dance's participants. Every year, dozens of families participate, with hundreds and sometimes thousands more coming together to watch. The devil dances on the coast of Aragua are not produced by any centralized institution; they are distributed systems, not owned by any one person or entity.[10] In many communities in which fiestas are part of the organizing systems of a town, this dispersal of production is not unusual. Different people control access to different elements or parts of the performance: food, costumes, altars, choreographies, and so on. As Sabino Augusto Dorantes Cantor, one of the organizers of the fiestas in Tepoztlán, Mexico, said, "Institutions come and go, people remain" (see Taylor 2006, 83). If these systems of production were mapped as an organizational chart, the devil dances would look like constellations or clusters of relationships that are flexible and moving, yet interrelated and contingent. Particular claims or duties are legitimated within the social, neighborly, and kinship networks outside; such networks allow for a broader range of participation. I see this as a popular politics expanding an alternative order of political logic and practice among these networks.

As networks, again, I'm referring to people as part of a system of relationships, rules, and agreements that composes and negotiates politics; this is, in practice, a politics of the many. I don't think it's necessarily a mystery (or magic) that the devil dances produced a transformation from an ideological dualism to a performance of pluralism, or from an imposed religious authoritarianism to a populist mode of transmission. The work of organizing people and public opinion toward a broadening of popular performance—physically, conceptually, ideologically—comes out of the production process itself.

So far, I've introduced some of the ways in which politics, as fiesta politics, more generally appear and operate in and around the devil dances. The rest of this chapter is dedicated to more specific ways in which performances of the devil dances reproduce populist logics: first, I focus on the formation of a space of collectivism, or the social body as "we." Second, I turn to a case in which participants used the performance itself to reconcile two situations of conflict, one between the church and the people, and the other among different producers of the event. I consider the claiming of "the people" as an inherently contested act rooted in problems of representation. Conceptually, a claim such as "the people" is easily shot down: it is a nonentity, a monolith, and an unrealistic portrayal of a unified bloc. But here I try to take such claims as a starting point to understand contending power and negotiation; rather than as an end to the discussion, it is a place to start.

Scholars are right to condemn state machinations to usurp control over popular events such as the devil dances. However, protectionist attitudes over appropriation by the state can also do the very thing that they purport to criticize: strip the agency, credit, and rights for making these performances from people without institutional backing. The departures, interruptions, and compromises are part of a deep level of contestation. Some claim control to push others out when the legitimacy of the event comes into question. Claims of authorship can hang in the balance for dozens and even hundreds of years. Just as David Guss's (2001) important work on fiestas and the state reveals, cultural performances like Corpus Christi continuously negotiate power in what can amount to a "semiotic battlefield" (10).

My approach is to consider the multiple ways in which people identify on the inside or outside of the "we" within those battles, with the understanding that "the people" (and the devil) are always strategic (and heterogeneous) claims. In these examples, social systems enact political agency through performance, showing them to be sites in which Laclau's antagonistic frontier is expressed through such a practice. I'll explain this further in the three sections ahead ("Arrivals," "Rehearsal," and "Procession"), in which stories about arrival, a rehearsal days before the event, and the procession of the devil dancers to bless nine altars in the town of Ocumare point to integral components of the performance in which participants negotiate the limits and inclusions of the social order.

Arrivals

In 2007, my then three-year-old son Gio and I were traveling from Maracay to Ocumare by bus when we met Eduardo. The bus swerved back and forth over the switchback turns of the coastal mountains of Henri Pittier National Park, and Eduardo, with kids of his own, kindly helped me keep Gio from sliding down the aisles. The pull of the engines bore us around each corner, with a rolling *cumbia* rhythm keeping everyone, especially the driver, in a focused dance between the mind and the road. Giant banana leaves whipped past us as the sun flashed across our faces like a strobe light. Over the course of the trip, it turned out that Eduardo was on his way to Ocumare to dance the *diablos* for Corpus Christi. When Corpus Thursday approaches, no matter where he is, Eduardo comes back to dance with a group in Maracay or Ocumare wearing the cross of his grandfather.

Eduardo was born into a family of dancers from the town of Turiamo, where the devil dances had been practiced for generations as they have been in Cata and Ocumare. However, in Turiamo the tradition was abruptly uprooted when the dictator Marcos Pérez Jiménez (1952–58) announced plans to build a naval base in the town. Thousands of residents were forced to relocate, including his family. As a result, Eduardo was born and raised mostly in the nearby city of Maracay with his extended family. Even decades later, he told me, without the dance, he and his family feel as if they are in exile. Eduardo described the sense of loss associated with being uprooted not only from his family's hometown but also from the practices of the dance, which provided a sense of community and belonging. This story was not just about Eduardo's experience; it was the story, he said, of many of his friends, family, and neighbors who had been forced to migrate to new communities.

As we made our way to the ocean side of the mountain, I asked Eduardo what he thought of the devil. What is the devil? What form does it take? He told me that ever since he had been a child, he had imagined the devil as a dog, a vicious dog that would grow out of shadows. He then began to tell a story about *sueltos* (loose ones), the devils who run along the side of the road.[11] He said that old-timers talked about *sueltos* as figures that sometimes appeared with a chain and huge ball attached to one foot. Eduardo recalled that a *suelto* once appeared during a devil dance wearing a full mask and costume and the ball around his ankle. A few other listeners in the bus had tuned in to our conversation over the waves of music and blaring horns. The masked figure would join the dance and then was gone as quickly as it had appeared. Here, as the bus made its way around the mountain a week before the event began, symbols were transmitted and took hold among those of us listening: the cross, the dog, the ball and chain, the *suelto*.

Although many of the symbols in stories such as these, including the figure of the devil, are accompanied by laughter, intrigue, and play, they also circle around personal loss and the trauma of exclusion, political persecution, and displacement. A year later, an elderly security guard in a museum in Maracay told me about prisoners with giant balls chained to their feet, most of them political adversaries of the Gómez dictatorship, who had built the road to Ocumare, the very road Eduardo, Gio, and I had traveled. The guard remembered seeing them digging along what was then an old mule path. With a grand gesture of stooping low and heaving up an imaginary train of fabric, he told me how his mother would tie up her long skirt, and with a knife tucked inside her boot, she would haul her children over the mountain to sell sacks of flour to the villages on the coast.

In this Caribbean region, as in many other parts of the Americas, demonization extends far beyond the prisoners of the Gómez era. Systematic racialized oppression in Venezuela is trenchant and at the foundations of civil society. The region's history as a plantation-slave economy seeps into all aspects of social and political life, including and sometimes especially within the church. As historian Arturo Rodríguez-Bobb noted, "the ecclesiastical logic of colonial society culminates in what amounts to the annihilation of the black man" (2004, 93). This annihilation began in the sixteenth century and increased in severity in the late eighteenth century after Haiti's successful revolution of 1791. In an exhaustive study of the devil in Venezuela, historian Rafael K. Strauss links this racialization to the devil figure, concluding that "in the consciousness of white European colonialists, the black man was the devil" (2004, 107). This legacy of demonization, abjection, and violence that founded Corpus Christi was embedded within the dance, and carried over to those that performed it. Ever since, cultural producers have contended with, and effectively transformed this premise over many generations. It is an institutional racism that haunts these performances and, indeed, the politics of the nation. Yet today, in Ocumare, the dance is all about cultural pride, family, and renewal, and for some like Eduardo, Corpus Christi is deeply devotional and syncretic, where the performance is as much about Afro-descendant cultural recognition as it is about the Catholic Church. This is not to say that these concepts are seamlessly blended, but certainly for many, the ideas of Afrocentricism and Catholicism are tightly woven in contemporary religious practices.

What makes these linkages important for the present work on populism is that this transformation from dehumanization to a process of humanization through the performance of the devil dances could be considered as much political as it is cultural or spiritual. Performance is the medium of this transformation, which is capable of recoding the meanings of good and evil that it was founded on. This resignification, I believe, is a spiritual, cultural, and political work that takes place through the performance practice, and, like populism, it is a work that has been discredited, ignored, and even persecuted by various forces in society.

But signification is not limited to the spectacular event on the day of Corpus Christi festivities. It is a process that overlaps the edges of the event both spatially and temporally. It is on the way, days before the event begins, and long after the event is over. It takes place on the streets, in houses, and on the bus, beyond the central plaza. The next section continues this discussion of signification, but this time to emphasize that fiesta performance, like populism, is not all necessarily unruly or mere chaos. Within the overlap between the performance and the social systems of everyday life is the regulatory function of the devil dances. The social networks that the dances are situated within help generate both the capacity for transformation and new limits to the social body and the public good.

Rehearsals / Rules and the Limits of the Social Body

Two nights before the first devil appeared in front of the church, Gio and I watched the rehearsals near the house of one of the guardians of the dance, Señora Luisa Benítez. At dusk nearly 50 young men between the ages of 13 and 30 lined up on either side of the street, wearing loose T-shirts and shorts. They arranged themselves in pairs as they practiced the steps, crossing one leg over the other, switching places in a scissor jump and slide, and ever so slowly edging the line toward the altar at the end of the street. As each pair reached the end, they leaned, bending their knees, and switched places and shook the maracas in this crouched position before the altar while offering prayers to the *Santísimo* (Holy). They then turned in and, with a sidestepping skip, made their way back to the end of the line. Once there, each dancer lay on the ground, watching attentively, on guard to protect the others. Several women were standing nearby, conversing and keeping the dancers in line. Cheché, as *capataz*, the leader of the devils, was in the middle, calling out directions. People brought lawn chairs into their yards or sat on curbs or rooftops to watch. The boys stopped to joke around, drinking from water bottles and laughing with friends.

Out of the corner of my eye I noticed Gio at the far end of the street totally fixated on the older boys making their crisscross steps. A few minutes later, Gio started to play with two other little boys his age (between three and five), still watching intently from the sidelines as the dancers practiced. They skipped back and forth from one foot to the other, shaking pretend maracas in their little fists. It was so cute. I pulled out my phone to take a picture, remembering people freely snapping pictures on the day of Corpus Christi and Cheché's acceptance of it. But the rehearsal was the real deal. Cheché gestured to hold off and I quickly put my phone away. I realized that these boys (and I) were learning about what to do or not do with respect to the dance. Several women sat nearby, and, as the boys were playing, we started chatting and they told me about how they were making an altar at the corner of their street.

More people came out of the house, until several women were conversing, and from them we learned more about the rules of the altars.[12] They showed Gio and me one of the most basic rules of the ritual of Corpus Christi: not to turn your back to the altar. Even if the *santo*, or saint, has not yet been placed on it and it is just a few pieces of bamboo held together with baling wire and string, the altar is still a site of meaning and respect, and certain actions such as turning one's back in relation to it are considered sacrilege. The rehearsal, or "training," if you will, comes long before the crowds and brightly colored displays that appear on the morning of Corpus Christi. During these rehearsals, important lessons take place on the sidelines about how to move one's body, and behaviors are reinforced through familial and informal relations, the social networks that tie the event to a broader sphere of influence.

Rules are at the center of this performance, and by means of the open-forum rehearsals on the public streets, the women on the corner, and the very prominent guardians, such as Señora Luisa Benítez and others, a wide range of people are able to participate in the negotiation of these rules. Perhaps these micro-interactions with a broad range of individuals have had a greater influence than any "official," singular authority in the dance.[13] These rules and the oversight of them within the social networks of the community are crucial to the overall production of the dance and even to the performance itself. There are rules and yet there is no manual; they are devised out of an entirely embodied populist logic that maintains a certain degree of flexibility, even in the highly structured context of the performance. It is true that those who dance the devils do so through devotion, as a way of giving thanks, and out of *promesas* or pledges that they made to the Holy Sacrament, but dancers and organizers are also very aware that they play a part in working out a much more complex historical condition. A look at how dancers negotiate the structural hierarchies of the dance makes this clearer.

The leadership includes the *capataz* as the top devil (the overseer) and the *perreros* (literally "dog runners"), who are middlemen or foremen. The newer devil dancers, who constitute the majority, are known in some dances as *milicias* (soldiers) or *esclavos* (slaves). About midway through the rehearsal, the *capataz* goes through the line to count the dancers. The act recalls how enslaved workers were counted in the early morning and evening rituals of daily life in plantation society. Foremen were expected to enforce punitive laws. In the dance, *perreros* carry whips to swipe at ankles if a person is out of line, whether that person is a dancer or a spectator. In the forced-labor conditions of plantation society, the count and lineup at 5:00 a.m. and the count late in the evening at the end of a workday were means of preventing people from escaping, another embodied form of discipline and social control. If someone was not present at dawn when the church bells rang, the consequence meant severe bodily harm and even death, not just for the person missing but also for his or her family and friends.

The counting ritual in the dance today, however, is not for those who are missing. Instead, it is a precaution against an unwanted appearance of the real devil (Echenagucia 2007, interview). One might consider this a form of parody or mimesis of the plantation practice. But in the dance, the practice of the count adheres to a different premise altogether. The dancers and practitioners—all devils, at least among the leadership—now *own* the count. It is no longer an act to determine who is missing and therefore subject to punishment; this new authorship transforms the social body to see the roll-call count as an act of protection for those on the inside. The meaning of the count thus shifts from a declaration of exclusion to one of inclusion. To accommodate this shift, the practice expands the threshold at the edge of both exclusion and inclusion; the social network (those watching during the rehearsals and on the day of the event, with the audience as witnesses and co-participants in the performance) becomes a frontier and display of how limits are decided.

Clearly, power and authority are being performed and are always subject to the potential of abuse or coercion. Yet the counting ritual associated with the devil dance makes an important readjustment in power dynamics. First, the ritual is a statement that those who control the count are *inside* the intergenerational system of production of the dance, a system that is tied to the community and is subject to accountability by virtue of those ties. Second, through its performance and display in the public arena of the streets, the count exposes who controls its rationale. No longer are the "devils" counted in order to determine who is *out*; now the lineup and count are resignified as a practice to determine who is *in*, an inside made possible with the ever more mysterious potential that a *real* devil might appear. Indeed, a real devil on the outside still exists, but it is a vanishing figure, turned toward legend.

The transformation of interior and exterior identifications of the social body is practiced and rehearsed in a way that prepares producers and participants for more than the day of Corpus Christi. The inside of this dance is constantly negotiated and works to absorb and transform the exclusions from the past within a new moment that is tied to communal responsibilities, witness, and faith. One might say that performing the devils reveals and potentially heals the damage caused by the exoskeleton remains of the plantation system from which the dance was born. The roles in the dance that are filled by the *capataz*, the *perreros*, and the musicians transform leadership from a policing down to a form of guardianship from within—by the devils, the guardians of the dance, and the broader networks that participate and witness.

Sometime during the rehearsal, I noticed that Señora Benítez was making sure that several of the *perrero* leaders of the dance were set to meet the next day in order to cut bamboo poles to build the altars. They assured her that they would bring others with them and be ready to work with machetes and buckets of concrete to anchor the altar frames. Whereas Cheché was the official *capataz mayor* (main overseer) of the dance, Luisa Benítez and several other women guardians of Ocumare were clearly the overseers of production.[14]

Procession / One for All, or All for One?

Clemis García, guardian of the saint San Juan Bautista (St. John the Baptist), stood inside the House of San Juan and smoothed a blazing red fabric across the altar table. She pinched the seam with one hand while she carefully pinned with the other. As she prepared the altar for San Juan, whose customary color is red, she described the extent of the network that builds and supports the procession. As far back as Clemis could remember, individual families or a small group of neighbors have been responsible for each aspect of the production in Ocumare, in particular the building and decoration of nine different altars along the processional path.

Altars have been a part of ritual performance in the Americas since long before the Catholic Church began to present them in Corpus Christi processions. One could imagine them as what performance studies scholar and poet Ngũgĩ wa'Thiong'o calls "shrines of power" (1997, 13). Like a courtroom, the theater, or a newspaper, the altars become sites where the frictions of power and representation are most visible. Individuals and small groups build altars and bless them during Corpus Christi events, carefully choosing multiple objects to offer to the Holy Sacrament. Each altar maker decides how the altar celebrates Corpus Christi, what to place on the altar in that

Figure 2. Clemis García (*center*, holding San Juan), guardian of San Juan Bautista of Ocumare de la Costa, and others from the neighborhood decorate the altar of San Juan Bautista, also known as the patron saint of Afro-Venezuelans. Author photo, 2010.

celebration, and why it is important. Just as the costumes in Ocumare are different, all the people and neighborhood groups practice relative autonomy to build their own altars as they see fit, but they are all working toward the goal of uniting the social body. Thus, the Holy Sacrament carries a double meaning: it is the embodiment of Christ and it is also a symbol of communal union.

In Ocumare, there are nine altars dispersed throughout the town on a processional route that circles the church in a two- to three-block radius in every direction. Altars are set up at the same intersections every year, usually a couple of blocks apart and closest to the families who decorate and present them. In addition to the altar of San Juan, which is the first, there is the altar of Jesús Cristo by the Muñoz family, the Corazón de Jesús by María Jesús Bolívar and her grandchildren, the Virgen de Caramoto by the Arebalo Bolívar family, the Virgen del Carmen by the Manrique Vásquez family, La Caridad del Cobre by Yajaira Concepción, the Imaculada Concepción by Luisa García and Yamelis Lira, the altar of San Pedro by Reina Delgado and her children, and the final altar, known as the *altar mayor* of La Cruz, is by Luisa Benítez, all presented in honor of the Holy Sacrament. Decoration includes draping the altar with cloth and adorning it with various religious figures, flowers, tiny palm leaves, rosary beads, small statues, and flowers. Some families prefer to leave the altars very simple, with only an offering of an image of the Holy Sacrament, Christ, or one saint.

Residents on the southeast side of town gathered in the late afternoon to decorate an altar that had been set up on their street corner. It was the day before the Corpus Christi processions, and they had their hands full getting the altar ready with drapery and other adornments. Two women held a large transparent cloth over bamboo poles that had been set up the day before on the corner of their street. Several neighbors gathered to decide what to place on the table under the canopy. Luisa García retrieved some objects from her house that were "always placed on the altar" and explained what each one meant. "Some are very Venezuelan," she said, referring to the small figure of Dr. José Gregorio Hernández, the patron saint of medicine, the disabled, and the infirm, dressed in a top hat. "These are saints that we always cherish as Venezuelans." Then she showed me the small palm leaves that were placed in a tiny glass of water. "These are all our blessings," she said. With extra emphasis, she added, "Each and every thing we place here has meaning" (García 2007, interview). The altars hold an array of valued, faith-producing, and culturally specific symbols.

Cultural producers of the devil dances emphasize the pluralism of this tradition (interviews: García 2007; Valera 2008; Echenagucia 2008). Like the altars, each costume and mask is unique in Ocumare. Dancers make their own masks, buy them from local artists, or craft them with friends or neighbors. Most dancers have family members help them design their brightly colored capes, which are decorated with tiny bells, ribbons, and other adornments. Sometimes they sew their own. Moreover, costumes and masks are constantly being reproduced; most dancers wear different masks and costumes each year. In 2010, I met several young people making masks in the street in the week before the event; the streets had turned into a papier-mâché and paint workshop for small children in the neighborhood. During the annual procession, devils may be the ones running through the streets with the sound of jingling footsteps and maracas and crisscrossing lines of dancers, but before and behind them there are an even greater number of family members, participants, and producers of all kinds.

While contributions to the performance are unique and pluralistic, they are also guided by regularity and rules inscribed by cultural traditions. For decades, dancers have made their way from the church to each of the altars, which are always in the same places, organized by longtime residents. That is why—even after a centuries-long history of struggle for rights and for recognition of this important cultural tradition—no one was prepared for the priest to publicly reject the altars in Ocumare yet again in the twenty-first century (well, kind of unprepared—let me explain).

Figure 3. Devil dancers take to the streets on their way to the church plaza in the morning before the procession in Ocumare de la Costa. Author photo, 2010.

In the early morning on the day of the Corpus Christi ritual in 2010, the devils took over the streets of Ocumare like they do every year. First they came out to dance in front of the church, then on to the procession to submit themselves to each of the altars. Later in the afternoon, the devils dance once again in front of the church and then they go visit people in their homes before retiring for the evening. That year approximately 115 dancers participated, a huge number compared to years past. In two lines they skipped, prayed, and knelt together to the strumming of the *cuatro*, wearing all the customary adornments: capes and crosses, brightly colored masks with snarling teeth and horns, bells, and ribbons. Around 300 onlookers lined the streets and clustered on corners to accompany the devils through the residential side roads of the town toward the church. This time, however, things were different.

All the tradition of this centuries-old religious manifestation came to an abrupt halt when the priest—who had recently been assigned to the Ocumare parish by the archdiocese—turned his back and refused to bless the altar of San Juan. At the first stop of the processional dance, directly in front of the cacao cooperative, just as the *diablos* approached the altar that Clemis and other neighbors and family had so carefully prepared, where San Juan

Bautista stood with blazing affection in his red dress, the priest stopped and turned away. The crowd was visibly disturbed. Some began to murmur in outrage. Turning one's back on the altar is sacrilege, so when the priest literally waved his hand, turning to walk away, his disapproval was palpable and profoundly injurious. A few people peeled away from the crowd and followed the priest. The majority, however, remained standing in clusters and along the street in silence. Several very long moments passed. People looked at each other, at the priest, and then back at each other. Some held hands. Several people cried and were visibly upset. Everyone in the crowd watched with rapt attention to see what would happen next. Then a remarkable transition took place.

Among hundreds of people in the middle of the procession, a popular decision to elect another priest to lead the ceremonies was made. Fermín Uribe Naranjo, a young black *padre popular* from Ocumare, stepped forward from his position holding the canopy behind the priest, and was ratified by public assembly to offer the prayers at the altar of San Juan. It was a collective action authorized by the altar makers, the *cuatro* players, the devil dancers, and other participants who stood in observance, and the sequence was conducted with no words; it was entirely through gesture and embodiment. The way it happened was this: the dancers rose and made way for Fermín to move forward. Clemis nodded and stood firmly by the altar she had so carefully prepared. Several people murmured encouragements, asserting their agreement with the new appointment, while the crowd waited in close anticipation of the blessings and to observe their own faith to the altar. Fermín, who wore a red T-shirt that day, then slowly picked up a simple cross that was made out of wooden sticks that had been tied together, and the *cuatro* players strummed on. The cue by the musicians, again the protectors of the dancers, and the movements of the dancers themselves signaled that the act had been decided. Later, several dancers told me that they had no idea in advance what was going to happen and that they were simply going with what they felt to be the right thing to do, following one another and their sense of what was happening in the crowd, carefully basing their actions on what was transpiring around them.

Although people were deeply disturbed by the actions of the priest, the crowd approved of Fermín as an alternative. The decision to have Fermín bless the altars was made without documents and speeches, yet it was clear that he was a popular choice. This was the man who had already given blessings at many of the non-official fiestas and at numerous occasions for funerals, baptisms, and house visits for the infirm when the priest was unavailable, so Fermín was familiar to many of those present. Several people cleared a space for the new entourage. The monstrance was carried by a former *capataz*, who referred to himself as "*el guardián de los negros de Ocumare*" ("the guardian of the black people of Ocumare"). As soon as the procession was moving again, people swarmed in together and started talking about what was going on and what had happened, hashing it out step by step, asking questions, and supplying their own input and analysis to whomever would listen. A young local filmmaker recorded the event as Fermín made his way to the second altar at the entrance to the river path at the southwest intersection of the road.

What happened in the procession of 2010 was, like many more occasions before and afterward, nothing less than an extraordinary act to uphold the ownership of the event by *el pueblo*. In a way, this was what Jason Frank calls a "constituent moment," in which "the underauthorized . . . seize the mantle of authorization, changing the inherited rules of authorization in the process" (2010, 8). Constituent moments provide a way of thinking about the heightened moral state of agreement that justifies the breaking of institutional rules for the sake of an extrajudicial transformation of the system

It was also, in a sense, an election of leadership conferred on Fermín by people who approved of his role in offering the blessings. Fermín was perhaps already familiar, and was known as someone who would offer the prayers for funerals, fiesta days, and other events when he was called for service. Nevertheless, the extraordinary moment when the priest left the procession and Fermín took up his role was unforgettable to many present that day. As Frank so rightly points out, these moments have a mythology and appeal that keep us enthralled by "the drama of the exception" (2010, 32). Yet what is left are the episodic and repeated "moments of constitutional crisis . . . in the fabric of everyday political speech and action. It posits a history not of epochal constitutional shifts but of micro-political enactments across several rhetorical and political contexts" (33). The events of the Corpus Christi performances are complex yet very practical. They rarely begin with spontaneous impulses; they operate within a repeated framework based on precedents. Yet extraordinary acts may emerge, such as the public acceptance of Fermín as the leader of the prayers. It is this relationship between the micro-political and populism that turns up in these moments as closely intertwined.

If this was a constituent moment, or an act of higher law, it was created by bodies in performance.[15] In this case, the devil dancers took on the major role of legitimating and leading the new procession through sequences of embodied choreography. The devils knew their steps, and the musicians, picking up after the moment of confusion, carried on without missing a beat. Yet, authorizing gestures, such as Clemis's firm stance next to the altar, showed that ownership belonged broadly (beyond the *cofradía*) to *el pueblo*. Animated by the initiative of the devils, the crowd was especially attentive, trying to make sense of what was taking place. Gradually as the dancers picked up momentum, the few hundred people who lined the streets relaxed and followed the rest of the procession. The show would go on, priest or no priest. Their act to follow Fermín was decisive. The devils, and by then an especially conversant crowd, continued until each of the nine altars had been blessed.

Figures 4 and 5. After the priest of the Ocumare parish refuses to bless the altars, Luis Fermín Uribe Naranjo extends his hand (*top*), and with the support of witnesses, takes over to lead the prayers at each of the nine altars, including the one dedicated to the Immaculate Conception, whose guardians are Luisa García in collaboration with Yamelis Lira and family (*bottom*). Author photos, 2010.

Word of mouth flies quickly in Ocumare, a form of communication colloquially known as "Radio Bemba," or the news that spreads from mouth to mouth, effectively broadcasting important information as quickly and as far-reaching as radio.[16] Within hours, the prevailing explanation was that the priest had said he felt he was unable to comfortably rest the monstrance of the holy sacrament of Corpus Christi on the table because "it was too crowded."

"Nonsense," said Clemis García. "There was plenty of room on the table. The problem is that this priest is new to the area, and he doesn't know that we in Ocumare celebrate the *diablos* with all our saints put together." She continued, "The priest's objection is the same in his sermons, which prove he has no interest in preserving the traditions of the town." For Clemis, the multiple saints and other objects on the altars are an essential part of collective identity. "This is who *we are*," she emphatically told me after the event. "We'll write a letter and take care of this at once, because he [the priest] has to know that here in Ocumare, we invite *all* our saints to the party!" (García 2008, interview).

"This story hasn't changed," said Jorman Valera, one of the dancers and also a historian and militant activist with the Cumbe Afroragüeño, a group dedicated to the vitality of Afro-descendant public life. "We've been in the same struggle for centuries, and what we've built for ourselves is a culture of resistance. This is not a resistance culture, but rather a *culture of resistance*. The dancers eventually kept going. The altar didn't change. We know to keep going because we always keep going. That's just the way it is. Through the rest of the day we danced at each and every altar the same way we always do" (Valera 2010, interview). It is important to emphasize the point that both García and Valera made: what enabled all participants to stand their ground was that they were doing what was *customarily done*.

García's and Valera's ideas made me think twice about the activism that I had been used to, which tended to gravitate toward the terms of rupture and breaking away from a given order. As someone influenced by anarchist thought, I imagined building what could be called a "resistance culture." Yet, for García and Valera, they were building on something quite different, something based on culture first, a culture that stemmed from constancy and adherence to historical precedence. Rather than the disruption of a social order, it was about cohesion. From this precedence, one would derive an even more powerful stance of resistance that could stand guard against those who attempted to intervene. To "resist," in other words, meant to defend and hold ground, to enact repeated behaviors and prevent intrusions on the order a community has created; even, to a certain extent, to adhere to the scripted norm. Participants thus reinforce a system of their own rules and legitimation, revealing the ritual as a powerful system of popular sovereignty.

Too often, "populism" is confused with meanings acquired within highly commoditized cultures as fleeting and even shallow. That which is popular may indicate an ascending trend rather than a sustained system of distributed power. The first three letters of the term seem to invoke this notion of a momentary eruption, or exploding trend of the times, as if the popular were interruptions of more enduring, time-honored "high" or "elite" culture. Jorman's idea of a popular resistance operates outside of these dyads of high versus low, eruptive rather than constant. Instead, fiesta politics tends to suture these divides, or expose them. But what is important for our purposes here is that the devil dances present more than a moment; they are both an enduring and flexible politics of ritualized assembly in the performed act of claiming "the people." What I found especially notable is that these political logics were taking place in an almost entirely embodied way, regulated in the presence of others within the performance itself, bound to the paradox of performance's own lasting impressions, repetition, and impermanence.

If we consider the procession as a kind of public forum or convention, it's a moving one, both flexible and enduring.[17] The word "convention" here is interesting to me because it refers to an occasion, a meeting in a particular moment and time, and also repetition and tradition. That which is conventional holds a familiar practice to return to after a traumatic break like the priest's refusal. Resistance is not a fleeting act; rather, it is made possible by enduring relationships and attachments. In the particular moment, defying the priest was not spontaneous, but rather the consequence of physical, spatial, and spiritual conditions that had been reinforced through repetition and practice. Participants held more firmly to their routine: the altar makers prepared for the blessings, the musicians played, the crowd watched and followed, and so forth. In ways reminiscent of Augusto Boal's (1979) understanding of theater as a forum, the devil dances also created this space for communal problem-solving *through* the performance.

At the center of the agreements there were also internal conflicts, of course, not to mention the struggles over competing paradigms of belief that date back to the extirpation of "false idols" during the Inquisition. Land occupation, cultural rights, language, and basic understandings of law and society are wrapped up in this conflict. The priest's disrespect of the altars was not an isolated event in the history of the devil dances; in this sense the event was also a popular assembly, with the means to legislate over an enduring struggle for cultural rights that weighs in on the side of *el pueblo*.

However, ritual, as we know, is not necessarily created a priori by unified forces. Ritual, like Laclau's self-constituting "people," is a product and process of multiple tensions that play out in various conceptual, material, and embodied attachments, in this case to the church, or to any other institution, individual, or belief. The brilliant ritual theorist Catherine Bell called this the strategic function of ritualization to manipulate its context and re-create itself through the process (1992, 100). As Jean and John Comaroff write, "It is in this sense that ritual is always a vehicle of history-in-the-making: at times it conduces to sustain and legitimize the world in place; at times it has the effect of changing more or less pervasive features of that world; at times it does both simultaneously" (1993, xxix). Ritual is as much a vehicle for transformation, contingent on dynamic circumstances, as it is a repetitive process of practicing tradition, or in this case, practicing methods of assembly.

Corpus Christi in Ocumare is a religious fiesta regulated by a *cofradía* (church guild) that is now independent of the church and by the municipal government, whose hand in the religious affair dates back to the sixteenth century. The municipal government and the *cofradía* have typically shared the responsibility of supporting the event by paying for food, street cleaning, and some decorations, such as flowers. However, that day, as in many years past, it became clear that this event belonged to a broader base of popular production. While popular production arguably builds it, the fact that the event has also been shaped by top-down administration should not be dismissed. Producers of the dance have a variety of relationships with political and religious leaders in the church and municipal government.

These systems of production work both in and out of institutions and need to be examined closely in order to understand the heterogenous relationships that undergird this important transition from the social logics of difference to the political logics of populism in the devil dances. Historically, Corpus Christi is a fiesta that was principally organized by the municipality, not the church. The Ocumare mayor's office has at times exercised its power to make changes in the dance. It is not unusual to see a police officer at some point during the procession in Ocumare, where the crowds have grown to thousands of people. A resident on the far western edge of the village claimed that in the 1980s the processional route included more than a mile of the riverbank that led to the ocean. Apparently, the municipality altered the procession path in order to facilitate foot traffic in places where it was harder to access the pathways that were closer to the river. The routes changed over time to accommodate more dancers, and create more "efficient" access between the altars.

The extent to which the municipality sponsors the event has been somewhat contentious. Many residents feel the government should be more involved. "*Aguardiente* [a popular liquor] just isn't enough," said one participant in 2007, referring to the mayor's traditional practice of distributing alcohol on fiesta days (which is customary regardless of the party in office). Participants that year felt that the government should have done more, since it was widely known that many of the altar makers in particular often traveled at their own expense to Maracay, a larger city two hours away on the other side of the coastal range, to buy flowers.

The mayor's office (at that time run by the Acción Democrática Party, not Chavistas) claimed that it did its share to ensure that the town is beautified. The municipality often makes improvements and upgrades around the plaza in time for the major fiestas. For example, just before Corpus Christi in 2007, the lampposts around the plaza were freshly painted and the municipal government hired people to clean the streets and trim weeds. The municipality and the church both played functional but ultimately minor roles in the event, leaving most of the negotiation to the *cofradía* and others.

On the morning before Corpus Christi in 2008, Señora Luisa Benítez and others were preparing food and transforming their living spaces into hubs of activity where kids practiced dance steps and relatives perched on lawn chairs on the streets to watch the happenings. Señora Benítez had been cooking for hours and had just received a delivery of hundreds of carnations. She showed her grand-niece how to arrange the flowers that were piled in a box by the door. "This is the Santísimo Sacramento," she said reverently, gesturing toward a tiny translucent orb nestled in a large, white, ornate framework that took up the wall of the first room of her house. "This is big," she said, referring to its power. "It's a profound expression of who we are, it is the center, the *ojo*, the eye of creation and where we gather our strength as a community. For us, it represents everything, *everything*." I didn't ask more about what was so big at that moment, because the answer seemed to be obviously both the Holy Sacrament and religious devotion. There was also the other obvious reality of a giant pile of flowers just inside her doorway, and the magnificent altar frame being decorated in her living room. She had two giant pots on the stove, cooking smells filled the house, and several visitors and relatives were at the door. I knew my cue to make room for this production, offer to help, or stand out of the way. It was not only the activity, though, that surrounded Luisa. She made sure that before I left that afternoon I would have no doubt that this was a religious manifestation that came from the spiritual bonds of the Santísimo Sacramento, or Holy Sacrament. For Señora Benítez, this bond was about the One Santísimo and the spiritual unity that He embraces. It was about faith, and gathering family, friends, neighbors, and activity that would celebrate this powerful and singular manifestation.

During the events of 2010, Luisa Benítez agreed with the priest that the Santísimo should be the only thing on the altar. For her, it was not necessary to put multiple saints and other meaningful objects on the altar; in fact, she saw them as distractions. She agreed with the priest that each saint has its day and that Corpus Christi essentially encompasses a wholeness of faith, a concept best expressed with the unifying symbol of the Eucharist. However, Luisa Benítez also agreed that generally the practice is that each altar maker builds their altar the way they choose. When I asked her if those rights continue even when the priest disapproves, her answer seemed more ambivalent. I realized in talking with her, however, that my own understanding of "rights" was unclear. For Luisa, this was not a question of individual rights; what was more important was the continued flow of practice among the broader community. Maintaining the practice took precedence over the idea of some universal law that everyone should abide by.

In many ways, both Luisa Benítez and Clemis García receive power through their positions as guardians in the dance. Carmen Alemán (1997) calls this a "moral prestige" that enables producers to establish strong positions of influence. This is especially the case among the women altar makers, whose positions are not necessarily defined hierarchically (in contrast to the dancers, who are appointed in a clearly defined pyramid structure of the *capataz* at the top, then *perreros*, and finally the *diablos*). Luisa and Clemis both enjoy this power, one that is made visible by the number of people who gather in a circle of chairs in front of Luisa's house during the Corpus Christi weekends and by the fact that Clemis, as the guardian of San Juan Bautista, has the keys to the building on the plaza that is home to the saint. The ability of both Luisa and Clemis to uphold the belief that everyone has a right to make the altars in the likeness of his or her own devotion is an extension of and even an incentive to this power.

The fact that Clemis García and Luisa Benítez might disagree about what is best included on the altars and continue their practices in different ways shows that there is room within the wholeness of the event—within the authoring of *el pueblo*—to defend different positions regarding the altars, even when the frontier of the event is challenged by the institutional order of the church and they unify against it.

The wider network of participation in the performance allows the Santísimo Sacramento to function as a powerful signifier for different participants without diminishing their devotion and belief in the Holy Sacrament. The success of the populist moment, however, requires some agreements over what the Holy Sacrament stands for. When the priest walked away from the altar, he disrupted his own participation, threatening to either derail the event or provoke his own exclusion. The producers of the dance maintained the dance without him. They found another priest to fulfill that role and thereby reinstantiated the authority of the people. If one person does not agree to hold their place in the equivalential chain by, for example, being unwilling to participate in what they may view as an intolerable profanation of the Holy Sacrament, the chain may break. Of course, this relies on the degree to which participants allow, however loosely, each other's differences to supply meaning to the whole.

In the populist logic of the devil dances, differences exist and are allowed, but aside from the priest's sermons that pretend to authorize right or wrong, the altars are typically not policed by any central regulation. There is no one regulating body, even though participants uphold authorship to a totalizing claim of *el pueblo*. Instead, it is about subregulating microsystems. In some ways, a certain amount of power and motivation is bestowed on the altars and those who make them by virtue of the people who see them.[18] In other words, the motivation for having one's altar blessed in the public procession is the desire to give and to be accepted into the social body as much as to honor the saints. It is, in a sense, a gift economy, where the act of the offering is signified within the larger social systems among the people who produce them (Mauss 1954, 1). Yet, if this is what Marcel Mauss calls a "total social phenomena," it is the micro social economy that keeps the event happening.

Several things are important to emphasize at this point. First, it is significant that the social rules of the altars are not entirely constituted forms of control. They are examples of distributed power. The social rules are formed and supported by multiple sites of power, literally many hands that build them. Their claims to authorship are material and embodied, regulated within smaller family and neighbor groups. Year to year there are those who participate. They come out to the street corner and decorate, deciding what cloth to hang, what decorations will be placed, and so forth. In the process, people make agreements and sort out differences by insisting on some demands and sublimating others. This process of sublimation is important, but it is even more important to consider how each person chooses to remain in the process to uphold the event.

Second, while the altar-making that I saw was generally cooperative, makers certainly don't always agree. In order for the chain of equivalence to maintain democratic populism, says Laclau (2005), there must also be an antagonistic frontier where there is difference and debate. And there is the key. Differences emerge first in the formation of the social body of "the people" contending with whatever becomes the exterior, the "vanishing devil" (i.e., the *suelto* which endangers or otherwise threatens that social order), and second, in how individuals or groups debate among each other about what counts as an exterior limit or boundary. Although each popular subject position, in this case, is the articulation of each altar-maker independently, in that articulation a unity is expressed and there is a reinforcement of the broader "popular" front needed to contend with or against the church. The devils' performance contains these multiple, heterogeneous forms of activity while also producing a unified act of the people, one that is being negotiated year after year.

Third, the story of good and evil was not the end result. It was only a means of beginning the transformational tale of how the devils become agents of good as they join the saints as guardians of *el pueblo*. In 2010 it seemed like each person, or small group took a slightly different stance in regard to the presentation of the altars and the role of the priest. For many, it was not enough to simply dismiss the priest (an agent of institutional authority). Several people I spoke with said they felt that the priest had an obligation to fulfill his duties of the blessings in order to play out the story of paganism and Christianity. The majority of participants wanted the priest to abide by the traditions of the people in completing his part of the production in the streets—and not in a facetious way. But again, it was not so much that people thought the devils should be more under the auspices of the church. Many people believed that the procession affirmed the transition from church authority to the authority of the devils, from the priest to the people in the streets. While the performance is outwardly about the struggle between good and evil, ritual acts allowed participants to effectively join the devils and the saints with a sincere request that that relationship be blessed by the church.

Last, the procession is a physical movement of people through the streets, who, with their bodies, agree to uphold the greater union as witnesses to the event. In this way, the procession itself acts as what Paulina Ochoa Espejo calls a "people in process," as an assertion of popular sovereignty. On this path, the altars and the various processes of negotiation undertaken by people moving along it present an embodied model of differential logics, and by their ultimate confrontation with the priest, as we have established, those logics constituted a totalizing identity of "*el pueblo*." But if we accept Laclau's understanding of the "institution of the social," we might also recognize both Laclau and Ochoa Espejo's search for popular sovereignty beyond autonomy, and more as a source of democratic legitimacy. As "people in process" between institutions and the fleeting moments of indeterminacy, there is a search for what is "flexible enough to admit change, yet realist enough to recognize the staying power of institutions and the dangers involved in both change and stability" (Ochoa Espejo 2011, 13). Walking the procession brings these complexities into closer view, moving both alongside and within, and also capable of rejecting what does not belong.

Indeed, it could be that peace between neighbors is ultimately more important than assuming a confrontational stance among participants or asserting what is right or wrong about the altars. Clemis García's statement that "all the saints are invited to the party" and Luisa Benítez's act of making room for what she views as the "one and only Santísimo" are both populist ways of engaging in collective action. Both views coexist and are authorized by a system of familiar, repeated acts. But does this personal interdependence squelch real debate? The dances after the Mass, the retreat of the devils, the procession, and the dancing devils' blessing of the houses of the elderly and the infirm mark so much more than a ritual of magical transformation to resolve problems. To return annually to unresolved questions is ultimately another means that people utilize in order to better deal with the conflict. The populist logics of this performance would tell us that the most difficult issues to arbitrate are at times more effectively addressed through routine and repetition, or return.

In Ocumare, many producers agree to allow plural forms of representation: as discussed, dancers wear different kinds of masks and other regalia, individual participants make altars that express their own beliefs, and so forth. On the other hand, a small group within the church rejects the dance because it feels the dance does not conform to its understanding of the celebration of Corpus Christi. What will become of this dissent?

Years later, I had the opportunity to talk with the priest Jesús Amando Osorio and his assistant Gerardo Arias. Osorio was clear that what bothered him was that very few people attended his Mass and that the events of Corpus Christi had turned into, in his words, "chaos and disorder" (2017, interview). From the priest's perspective, syncretism was a profanity that was ruining the religion. The devils had taken over, he said. It was interesting to consider this view and how Osorio and Arias, with the support of the archdiocese, find themselves on the other side of *el pueblo*. Where might they go to gather support for their position? The obvious move would be to rally support from another outside body. If, as was the case in Ocumare, *el pueblo* rejects the priest, he makes the choice to conform to community practices, build his own events, or reach outside that social body in an attempt to generate a network of his own to overtake the one currently in place. The antagonism continues.

More recently, with the *diablos danzantes* now funded as cultural patrimony, the dynamic once again changes, bringing an even more complex layer bound within privilege to those with access to new resources while others are left behind.[19] A lineage of micropolitics through the production of the performance informs these dynamics of agreement and dissent. To reach further, what are these histories, and how might bringing them up in relation to the devil dances reveal the battle lines that have long existed between institutions (such as the church) and popular power? To answer these questions, we need to get closer to a history of the ritual orders that made it.

Ritual Orders

The most elemental organizing body of the devil dances are *cofradías*, or church-affiliated groups or societies. *Cofradías* are basically guilds that have worked alongside informal networks of leadership and authority in Venezuela since at least the late seventeenth century. There are presently eleven *cofradías* for the dancing devils in Venezuela. According to Benito Irady (2015), president of Venezuela's Centro de la Diversidad Cultural, these are long-established organizations, some of them hundreds of years old and others more recently founded in the nineteenth century.[20] In addition to organizing, disciplining, and recruiting networks of participants for the devil dances of Corpus Christi, these guilds, for a large part of the history of these organizations, administered the local affairs of the church. These duties gave *cofradía* members a relative amount of power and religious authority within the community.

One of the overlooked, and yet incredibly important roles of the *cofradías* was to administer social services such as health care, funerals, burials, and the visiting and care of the elderly. Black and mixed-race *cofradías* of the colonial period handled these social services for the majority mixed, African, and Afro-descendant families living in the area. They were responsible for funeral services and burials, baptisms, record-keeping, and the distribution of pensions among the remaining family of the deceased. Members of a parish paid the *cofradía* an annual fee in addition to a *limosna*, or church collection, in order to ensure a proper burial for themselves and their families (Alfonso 1854, 17n39).[21] Generally the oldest member of a *cofradía* was responsible for distributing the funds of the society, imposing fines on subjects, and managing other disciplinary actions. These forms of leadership established the basis for certain kinds of privilege and proximity to wealth and power in terms of prestige and access to resources.

Many scholars make it clear that *cofradías* should not be confused with ideal or utopian free-black societies. *Cofradías* were highly regimented by the church hierarchy, often contending directly with and contributing to persecution and systems of oppression. While the *cofradía* was an essential vehicle for preserving cultural traditions in the dance, it also acted within a rigid hierarchy of vigilance and control (Acosta Saignes 1967, 72). Dancers would pay penance in the form of one *real* to participate, and often participation was obligatory. According to Acosta Saignes, *cofradías* limited or prohibited practices that fell outside the acceptable limits of church authority. While restricted, *cofradías* also played a significant role in negotiating among various social circles within the confines of plantation society.

In addition to fulfilling duties related to social services, *cofradías* produced fiestas and large-scale religious manifestations, such as the devil dances, within networks of production involving the trade. In managing multiple functions even within the religious fiestas—functions such as building altars and fixing, cleaning, and sweeping the streets—the *cofradías* enabled friars to expand within and beyond the direct control of the church. It is important to recognize that white society was virtually entirely dependent on the labor of mixed-race and black society from as early as the sixteenth century; they were carpenters, wood-carvers, masons, midwives, ironworkers, craftspeople, launderers, locksmiths, and sailors, to mention a few of these trades. Although, as two mid-twentieth-century historians put it, "the ironworker never [had] iron and the carpenter [had] not even wood to burn a cooking fire" (Marsland and Marsland 1954, 85). Given the debilitating effects of poverty, the labor involved in producing fiestas of the magnitude of Corpus Christi must not be overlooked in an economy of production, for it was in this capacity that networks were formed and maintained.

Passing down knowledge through generations is a part of these networks as *compadrazgo*, or kinship networks.[22] According to Irady, "in the Dancing Devils, oral tradition and imitation of the elders are the key vehicles for the transfer of intergenerational knowledge" (2015, xx). These networks or systems of production involved key holders, timekeepers, ushers, traffic controllers, guardians of the saints, tailors and clothiers, artisans, healers, midwives, vendors, and oral historians who worked within neighborhood and familial networks both in and at the margins of church and state authority.[23] *Compadrazgo* is an integral part of the social and material organization of society.

In the spring of 2007, I went to a Caracas bookstore when an academic journal with the title *Cayapa* caught my eye. I had just been thinking about the *cayapa*, which refers to a cooperative or shared labor system, but in published scholarship at that time I had not yet found the depth of descriptions that seemed evident when I talked to people like Cecilio, Nora, and others on the Aragua coast. Midcentury scholars recorded that the *cayapa* was an indigenous term with strong similarities to African-based institutions such as the Dokpwe in Dahomey.[24] The journal that I found in Caracas was focused on social economies to serve, in part, as a vehicle for examining the organization of the emerging cooperatives in Venezuela, which were rapidly increasing in the country during the new Chávez administration. On the inside sleeve, the journal defined its name *Cayapa* as a "group of people that together manifest a work" (Nuñez and Pérez 1994).[25] This brief description was elaborated slightly in the editorial notes, which stated, "The word originates in indigenous traditions of communal labor in large works of infrastructure for particular and collective interests" (Velasquez 1979). The *cayapa* is a form of organization in which members take part in shared work projects, barter exchanges, and reciprocal labor among members of the cooperative.

More recently, a steady flow of circulation, recognition, and activism in Venezuela has brought interest in the *cayapa* to the forefront of national discourse.[26] On the web, several sites feature early calendars, petroglyphs, and other archaeological evidence in ways that aim to bring awareness to these long-established forms of social and political organization and alliances, mainly among indigenous and Afro-descendant groups in the region. For example, one site shows how the Mariche-Cumanagoto, who were marine navigators in the Caribbean and common ancestors of the Maya, Nahua, Warao, and Yanomami peoples, recognized thirty different forms of *cayapa* communal activity around food production, timekeeping, shared work assignments, defense, and the acquisition of resources (Prieto 2010, 11). Historians such as Jesús Chucho García (2004, 2007) and Jorge Veloz (García and Veloz 2003) and other producers of the Afrodescendant Network (*Red Afrodescendientes de Venezuela*) and the Ruta Histórica project in Ocumare (discussed in chapter 4) are expanding research on the *cayapa* through the language and epistemology of African-based knowledge systems. More recently, a blog site called *Cayapa Visual Revolucionaria* features hundreds of short videos or "windows" into the communitarian projects of the revolution by local organizers.[27]

While the journal had begun to use the term at its inauguration in the early 2000s, the *cayapa* was nothing new to members of the devil dances in Ocumare. One day I asked one of the *perreros*, Señor Julio "Ñepe" Concepción, if he could tell me more about the *cayapa*. Just down the street were two of the projects of the Bolivarian government: a health clinic and a local empanada café, the latter a cooperative that people in the community had built. I had heard that those who worked there referred to these projects as a *cayapa*, and so I was curious as to what Julio thought of it. For him, though, the issue of who was promoting it meant little compared to the actual terms of labor and obligation that the *cayapa* would imply once within the project. For instance, the questions of the *cayapa* boiled down to whether one would get paid up front or later, or whether participants would trade for reciprocal labor or a share in the profits, and so forth. Julio thought the projects were doing positive work in the community. He knew people who were employed by these works. As collectives that worked on building their locales, they now operated and owned them. Generally, Julio had positive things to say about the *cayapa*; the clinic clearly served the neighborhood. But again, for him, it was always a matter of negotiation to figure out the terms of the project, whether it was the government-supported empanada café or a boat that needed fixing by a relative or neighbor.

Unlike the *cofradías* that officially worked within the auspices of the church, the *cayapa* mostly represented shared work projects, spread through familial and neighbor networks by word of mouth. It's the work people do to help out an elderly neighbor who lives next door or the ways in which people might share large tasks, especially when they have limited means to pay for it. Early-twentieth-century *cayaperos* were the fire brigade of the community (Liscano 1950, 210).[28] Interestingly, these affiliations are almost always locally named, rarely constituted in one definition, and suggestive of a range of collective action and work exchange known in different regions as *brigadas*, *cambalaches*, and *trueque*, to name a few.

Networks of production make the *cayapa* a political system as much as an economic one. In this rural and coastal town of 9,000 people, now decidedly socialist while still dependent on certain forms of capitalism, many people work in the informal economy. They sell fish to a large distributor in La Boca, work in the informal tourism industry in Playón or Cata, and often supplement their income by growing food on small plots of land. Others have government jobs, have small shops, or work for the nearby hospital or schools. When there is work to be done, the *cayapa* is one way to organize a group of people to clean up a plot of land, build a house, fix a boat, or otherwise carry out a project that would be too much for any one person to do. On the other hand, a much less positive use of the term that also bears a political edge was well in circulation: the slang expression "fall into a *cayapa*," used in popular vernacular in Venezuela, means to get into trouble with a gang of people, to be entangled in the politics of a group, or to be stuck in a problem where the irrational or unfair prerogatives of many overtake the needs or desires of one.

The double meaning of the word *cayapa*—as mutual aid or mob politics—bears particular relevance in the study of populisms. What is "unsaid" or "unwritten" in this linguistic slippage gets to the heart of the dispute. As the relations of a group change, they are not always fair or safe. The issue of the *cayapa* needs more careful attention—not idealism or dismissal—within these kinds of social contracts. Why the slippage? Was it the degeneration of a potentially good idea into the problems that arise from practice? Did the *cayapa* become slang for the "bad experiences" as a result of a failed system, or were there other conditions? I don't think the *cayapa* is a bad idea, but I agree with Julio that it is a system requiring constant discussion and debate over the terms. Whereas written contracts divorce the relationship between client and provider, the *cayapa* requires a particular ecosystem in which the terms are to be continuously reaffirmed and negotiated within a relational exchange. Work being done among ordinary people, whether in labor for a clinic or for a fiesta, is dependent on a social system—and whether the rules are written, there are still rules that follow the "conventions": meeting, assembly, covenant, and law.

Before returning to a discussion of rules and law, however, I want to recall a historical context in which these production systems surrounding the fiestas—in particular the systems that surrounded the *cofradías*, such as the wider networks of fiestas and the *cayapas*—were heavily persecuted and dismissed by the church (and state). I suggest it has something to do with how fiestas presented a kind of counter-campaign that supported but also significantly challenged the logics of colonial power. If the broad-based production of performances like the dancing devils has endured for hundreds of years, it has done so against a systemic effort to disparage not just the belief systems but also the social and political systems that surround them: in effect, fiesta performance, in many cases, counteracts the longest-running demonization campaign in the history of the Americas.[29]

So far I've been discussing *cofradías* and kin networks like *compadrazgo* and the *cayapa* in relation to the dancing devils as systems that combine fiesta performance with what often gets categorized as social welfare. This involves visitation and care of the elderly; presiding over funerals and managing burials; the placing, naming, and construction of altars in the streets; the broader social and familial networks of people who produce within an artisanal economy; food production and distribution; and the maintenance of public plazas and buildings. These are just some of the things we know that go into performances of this magnitude, and the list goes on.

We also know that (mainly but not exclusively) members of elite society—both Catholics and Protestants—continuously described these performances as lawless, disorderly, and highly corrosive to societal ideals. Complaints about the profanity of the dance and accusations of heresy increased during times when the vulnerabilities of plantation society were most exposed. The historian Oviedo y Baños's 1723 account of Venezuela refers to *indios* and *bárbaros* (Indians and barbarians) who worshipped pagan gods that colonialists saw as *demonios* (demons) (35). During the lead-up to the Haitian Revolution (1791–1804), the efforts to control the fiesta were compulsive (see Ramos-Smith 1998). When a Catholic bishop visited the parishes of Barlovento in 1784, he reacted with horror at the fiesta associated with San Juan Bautista, a saint that the devil dancers of Ocumare hold in high regard.

> These people are led by a passion for dancing, not just at parties or celebrations on holidays or when some baptism occurs but also at what they call velorios, both for dead children and on the eves of

> festivals, all of which leads to a sorry disorder, with men and women in a confused mess, especially at night. And they go on this way during these festivals with endless dancing for nearly the whole night, so that they wake up worn out and tired, incapable, and prohibited from satisfying the Precept of Mass, burdening their consciences, and, knowing the risk to which they expose themselves, still do not avoid these ridiculous and earthly diversions. Therefore, in order to end these so-called disorders, we must of course prohibit under penalty of excommunication such velorios, in which wild dances and other suspect gatherings occur; and we must send and order that the priest of that congregation in frequent sermons and exhortations make his parishioners understand the pernicious effects resulting from such dances, of which one Church Father has said, "They are a circle whose center is the Devil and circumference his Ministers." (as quoted in Chacón 1979, 33)[30]

A century later, Afro-Cuban processional performances were commonly referred to as "vulgar," "disgusting," "fearsome," and "noisy" (Ortíz 1960, 13). Venezuelan anthropologist Daisy Barreto points out that throughout the nineteenth and early part of the twentieth centuries, negative terms such as "primitivism" and "barbarism" were commonly associated with indigenous and Afro-descendant cultural life (1995, 10). These descriptions, typically derived from the attitudes of elite society, discredited what were otherwise considered highly "ordered" and "structured" performances (Brown 2003, 49). It may seem that one person's ideal order is another's mess, but there is so much more at stake than simply a world upside down.

Both ritual and populism share this legacy of having been negated and even shamed in secular as much as religious institutions of power. Pierre Ostiguy charts these behaviors on a "high-low axis" in which populism appeals to the low end of his axis as "immediate," "colorful," "earthy," and "grotesque," as opposed to anti-populism on the high end, which is described as "cultured," "refined," and "distanced" (2009, 5). The idea is that the "low" is less mediated, somehow "raw" and less restrained. As Benjamin Arditi said, populism is the awkward guest at a polite dinner, likely to "disrupt table manners and the tacit rules of sociability" (2007, 78). Populism, like ritual, is immersed in racialized class-cultural assumptions relating to issues of appropriate conduct and norms in political activity.

To draw a critique of ritual into the analysis of populism reveals these more deeply embedded biases that transfer notions of "irrationality" from performance to politics, and at the same time, within political analysis about populism. While midcentury scholars generally agreed that ritual is symbolically meaningful and even in some cases highly esteemed (or glorified), its very definition relied on its capacity to detach from, negate, or transcend the social and political systems that produce governance rather than be recognized as coterminous with its production. In particular, ideas of liminality within ritual theory were positioned as counter to law and order, where liminality began to subsume other forms, and even in some cases define ritual. Victor Turner, one of the most prominent scholars of ritual (and considered the foundational theorist of liminality), believed that ritual was indeed a meaning-making act, and capable of a "perduring social system" (1974, 132), and yet he also routinely positioned ritual as "a time and place of withdrawal from normal modes of social action" (167). Whereas rules and regulations are attributed to liberal forms of governance ascribed within a Western Eurocentric model, rules of performed ritual still tend to be theorized as highly symbolic, pertaining to mysticism, religion, and spiritualism. The problem was not so much adopting these approaches for analysis (as these are indeed important areas of study), but as symbolic, as mysticism, as religion, and so forth, ritual analysis tended to strip the social networks out of the practice, effectively depoliticizing its contents and form. The result is that performance was first depoliticized by Eurocentric religious doctrine, and then again depoliticized as a resource of secular liberalism.

In the context of colonial Venezuela, an all-out disdain for the political potentiality of fiestas can be traced to repressive measures of plantation society. The barbaric penal codes established by both *criollos* (those of Spanish descent born in America) and Spanish-born whites suggest that the ability to control what was considered a rogue outpost of the colonies, such as Venezuela, was limited. In 1635 there were twenty-five *encomiendas*, or land grants by the Spanish crown legitimating forced labor, in a region that stretched almost the entire length of the northern coast of the colony (Ferry 1981, 615). Predominantly white institutions, such as the church, and municipal governments desperately tried to maintain control, mainly through violence, in a region in which hundreds and sometimes thousands of enslaved people arrived each year, mostly from Africa but also from other parts of the Caribbean. This went on for over 400 years. As black and mixed-race professionals, merchants, and tradespeople gained power throughout the region, white *criollo* elites increasingly relied on the mestizo class to assert and uphold authority. In places where the ability of whites to control institutions was thin or nonexistent, African-based and indigenous social and political forms of organization had a place to thrive. Aisha Finch's (2015) book on slave rebellions in Cuba emphasizes the role of this black and mixed-race middle class in organized insurrections. When paired with Jill Lane's (2005) now-classic book on blackface performance in Cuba, it becomes clear how these sometimes conflicting social relations entered theaters, fiestas, and everyday life.

Pressure from the church to purge what it viewed as pagan practices thus presented a dilemma for ecclesiastic authorities in the Americas who needed to restore the popularity of the church. On the one hand, the church instructed those who organized Corpus Christi celebrations to spare no expense and incorporate "native rituals" to win the hearts and minds of those it sought to govern; and, on the other hand, church officials found themselves desperately unable to control the members of their parish and the rapidly increasing exodus to *cumbes* throughout the region.

Several communities on the Aragua coast are known for their histories as *cumbes*, which is also a word for both dance-fiestas *and* self-liberated spaces, or as *palenques*, where thousands of people built civic societies apart from colonial enslavement throughout the region. The most famous, and perhaps most long-established one is San Basilio de Palenque (located in northern Colombia). Self-liberated Africans on arrival in the new world founded the village under the leadership of Bioho Benkos (from the region of Bioho in what is now Guinea-Bissau). The villagers of San Basilio fought for the liberation of other Africans and their descendants throughout the region from the late fifteenth century to the present day, preserving kinship networks of the *ma kuagro* that distributed responsibilities and protections for the community through interdependent (and at times competitive) generational squads or groupings.

From the mainly persecutory rants of church officials, like the bishop mentioned previously, and their desperate attempts to reinforce the didactic teachings of Christian (and white) supremacy, we can deduce that devil dances and similar rituals of Afro descendant peoples had in fact created a space where neither the church nor slaveholders could exercise total power. The church desperately tried to suppress such rituals without success. It seems that plantation society "could not avoid . . . forms of slave agency" (Laviña and Zeuske 2008, 330) and the increasing popularity of the devils in the events of Corpus Christi. Although organizational systems surrounding these fiestas, such as the *cofradías* (and arguably the *cayapa*), were subject to increasing pressures to conform, networks of production in the dance likely extended far beyond what the church might have imagined.

In these accounts of plantation society, we might also take a second look at what the bishop meant when he described the fiesta practice as "a circle whose center is the Devil and circumference his Ministers." It is curious that a children's game common in the Caribbean mirrors precisely this relationship, with the contrapositive figure of the "virgin in the middle." In the game, children (as ministers) hold their hands tightly in a circle to "protect" the child in the center (the virgin) from another child tapped as "the devil" whose task is to charge the circle and capture the virgin. Especially when we consider that the devil-dance manifestations have long been described as a battle waged between good and evil, unraveling one layer of the church's prevailing strategy of demonization leaves us with the fiesta as a mirror image of its own power: only this time the devil is a leader surrounded by a circle of ministers. In other words, in the minds of church leaders, the fiesta was an organized adversary of its own likeness that the church deemed evil.

In the Americas, however, not all devils were ever really bad. There was no word or direct translation for "devil" in most indigenous languages. Instead, several words were used, sometimes interchangeably, to refer to various messengers, healing locations (such as hot springs or *temazcalli*), serpents, and flying birds or dragons. Deities and forces connected to the earth, death and transition, or travel were assimilated into diabolism and only scarcely survived the persecution of idolatry as long as they were labeled diabolical. As a result of zealous extirpation, violence, and displaced meanings, the devil figure never lost the traces of heterodox meanings that proliferated through thousands of religious practices in the Americas to authorize travel, heal and transform, reorganize land rights, and reconnect with ancestral beliefs (Rivera Cusicanqui 2014).[31] The devil in fiestas thus became a charged and complex figure enacting the deities of non-Christian beliefs and practices, most of which were polytheistic forces that did not necessarily conform to dualism or what some call Manichaeism.[32]

While Corpus Christi has its particular history from the church perspective, the dances are as much Congo, Luongo, and Bantu as they are European, and are known to many producers today as an Afro-Catholic fiesta (García and Veloz 2003). Caribe, Taino, and Arawak groups also influenced the dance. As *areítos*, or song-dances, the devil dances may have been performed as political assembly as much as acts of devotion (see Scolieri 2010). With these major influences on the fiesta, it is no wonder that entire epistemes (including methods and mnemonic systems) are transmitted through the social and sensorial experience of performance.[33] What is at stake are the broader forms of knowledge, history, and power sustained in these practices, calling for a wholly revised epistemic model from which to understand the repertoire of devils and the cosmic struggle of good versus evil.

This more integrated and expansive approach to ritual practice is also directly about the political in performance genealogies of the Americas. In relation to the dancing devils of the Aragua coast, it is important to note that when I refer to the political or to populist logics, I do not mean that the devil dances or their participants use the dance to engage in partisan electoral politics or in demonizing individuals for political gain. Nor am I claiming that these dances are populist in the sense of affiliation with the state, or any governing official. The devil-dance organizers generally agree to *not* endorse candidates or express opinions about political policies or a particular group of people as outsiders or real devils. Several participants and leaders in the devil dances point out that the practice has survived generation after generation precisely because it does *not* affiliate with campaigns or political parties.

José "Cheché" Echenagucia, the *capataz mayor*, explicitly made this point that the devil dances are not partisan, a fact that is crucial to their survival (2008, interview). The *cofradías*, the dancers, and most producers that I spoke with are clear that whatever their own beliefs might be, the dance stands apart from the shifting fortunes of one party or another. As Cheché put it, what would happen if the dance organizers openly sided with one party and then that party fell into disfavor in the next election? Within the

Figure 6. Illustration by the Venezuelan artist Iván Lira; the message below reads "The Devils Are Ours, Thank God!" Image courtesy of Iván Lira, 2017.

wider network of the dance, however, some people do express their political affinities. For example, the people who stand in their doorways to observe the dance or the crowds who gather to watch may visibly identify their support for the Chavista revolution by wearing red clothing, hats, or buttons. However, others made it clear to me that they do not support the PSUV (pro-Chávez) party. By looking at audiences for the devil dances, it may appear that partisan politics are visible, but each person is free to wear what they want.[34] In Ocumare, I saw that producers with more enduring commitments to the dance tended to welcome the fullest expression of difference within the fiesta. For these reasons, it makes sense that many producers discuss the dance as a cultural event instead of an expression of a particular partisan politic.

Certain kinds of political logic in the dance, however, are in parallel and overlapping relationship to the ways in which populism theory identifies its own issues and concerns. Many of these logics are negotiated at the level of production. In popular performances like the devil dances there is no "backstage," thus these many arms of production (costumes, masks, altars, etc.) are actively engaging multiple publics before, during, and after the event. The system of production in *making* the event offers the most salient "sites" for the logics of populism, but they are distributed systems, again not to be confused with a top-down state: this is a system that extends from the families that reunite each year to see the dances, to the municipal and local authorities that hire the street cleaners, to the oral historians and altar makers who decorate and adorn the saints, to the water bearers who bring pitchers out to dancers in the sweltering heat, to the vendors who sell sweet iced tea on the corner, and to the many observers along the streets and plaza—all of whom contribute in their own ways to what makes up "the people" or "*el pueblo*" in these performances. All of these elements involve negotiation on a political level about issues of representation, labor, and resources, and to a certain degree, a willingness to uphold the terms of collective ownership in the performance practice.

Within these performances, political logics overlap with more familiar understandings of populism such as the slogan in figure 6 exemplifies, in which the powerful transformation of the performance of devils is expressed as a quintessential populism: "The Devils Are Ours, Thank God!" The plural first person identifies a collective "we" precisely at the frontier between God and the devil that these performances enact. The message is a play on the reversal of the devil and God, but more specifically it reverses the role of the devil dancers as outcasts (outside the "we"), emphatically suggesting that the devils belong within the popular. I see this as a populism, as some say, from below, where popular production within the devil dances transformed the dualisms that were (and are continually) intended by the church to be reinforced, however unconvincingly from the beginning this may have been. The result of this continuing struggle has been to not just reverse the sacred and the profane, but to diffuse and work against the Manichaean logics historically and presently imposed upon the people and the practice of this dance.

In the devil dances, people practice both difference and a unified voice through this articulation of the "we," a claim that is flexible and open, reliant on multiple points of agency in the system of production. Structurally, there is no *one* authority in popular performance; instead, that authority is dispersed through the multiple foci of the event and the corresponding arms of production. Producers of the dance agree to claim a collective authorship that is identifiable in common histories and experience. Yet claims are also generated by heterogeneous demands and differing points of view. These various claims are held in tension by a precedence of rules and agreements. Devil-dance communities have created a system that facilitates negotiation about the unstable meanings attached to devils, saints, and the people. This negotiation is also a practice of sublimating difference to reach agreements about what the dance as the social body does and becomes. Given the differences of opinion about what symbols of the dance are or could be, what the dance itself is, and what people constitute the dance, it is understandably a slow process that builds from long-term commitments and repeated encounters.

The devil is obviously one of the symbols that plays out in these performances. Instead of being a fixed symbol of evil, the devil functions as a floating signifier in which ideas of inclusion and exclusion are worked out. The meaning of important symbols such as the Holy Sacrament are mediated by the dance: the Holy Sacrament can unify as all for one, one for all, and one of many, sometimes simultaneously. Saints and devils will all show up to establish the boundaries and overlap and the movement in between. Each of these symbols performs a different function and is the product of negotiations that establish a realm for understanding who is on the inside of the social order and who (or what) is on the outside. And if the image above is any indication of the articulation of a "we" on a local and a national level, then clearly the potential of the performance practice—again, under the pretext of a cosmic struggle of good versus evil—is evidently capable of inclusion and capable of expansion. The devil dances of Corpus Christi in Venezuela show populism at work in this embodied way. And if the devils upstaged the priest, they did it through a political epistemology that is integral to the history of a people.

This chapter started with the question: what are the connections between performance and populism in the religious manifestations of devil dances in Cata and Ocumare? One way to answer this question is to examine the processes of production, even in ordinary interactions outside of the actual event. Boundary lines of inclusion are formed on the way and are always arriving as the social body is negotiated from the inside out. Symbols, such as the devil, are signified in stories that people remember and make their own, a process that takes place in rehearsals, as the altars are being prepared, and as various people claim their space within the procession. These micro-political acts are more than random. They are more than spontaneous, spectacular, or about the rupture of the status quo. I agree with Jorman Valera that a culture of resistance is constructed through continuities in practice. The visibility of these performance-based forms of politics, therefore, is contingent on the conditions of a regularized practice, one made possible through a rehearsal of collective action where people—through an embodied act—create strategies of decision-making, unification, and conflict resolution through performance.

The result is the transformation of the social body, where the church would ultimately yield its power to the several generations of families in Ocumare who maintain the norms of the event. This was made possible because people such as Clemis, Luisa, Cheché, and the many other dancers, mask makers, and costume makers own vital parts of what they need to organize this performance event. Had they relied on the priest for the keys to the church or needed to ask permission to use the altar cloths, this kind of popular assembly might not have been possible. Thus, the populist presence in this performance is powerfully articulated by the multiple points of agency that each producer has at their disposal in the event. Populism in this case is a method of participatory production, a method that strengthens the capacities of collective action, and thus, their own authorship of the dance.

Fiesta performance, like populism, is about claiming a space for ordinary people to inhabit. Claiming a space in the presence of others is one way that individuals form a "we" of a town, or of a people. On the days of fiestas, the town is cleaned up and repairs are made. People position and adorn their altars. Relatives come by and neighbors sit in a circle of chairs. In this way, people in Ocumare and Cata, like in many other communities, take control of the streets, effectively using their own bodies to maintain an order. Thus, the performance becomes a way to create and optimize a *forum*, which in Latin means specifically "an open public place." In another sense, it is a convention, because the power of the dance to claim space builds on precedence and the practice of coming together.

If fiesta performance is a populist repertoire, however, it makes sense that popular production and reasoning would be enacted in the performed event. The procession becomes quite literally a chain of equivalence, where bodies of individuals stand for their demands and interests. One might imagine the altars as nodal points, or sites in which equivalential logics are negotiated. Each demand or interest is different in the forum. It is a heterogeneous mix. In the articulation of shared demands in the altars, tensions arise as to what the many producers of this dance will uphold within the communal "we": one altar or multiple, the priest or the procession, all the saints or one? The performance is what contains this chain of equivalence to hold together the devil dances as a communal act, enforced internally by a sense of devotion and duty through the *promesas*, or promises, that are passed down through generations. Thus, claiming a public space through intergenerational networks informs the political culture of that space, where the populist repertoire articulates a unified stance of that popular subjectivity against a contending other.

This recalls for us the ideational view of populism, such as Kirk Hawkins's argument that populism in the Chávez era prevented social cohesion by what he calls a discourse of Manichaeism, or a "cosmic struggle" between good and evil. Hawkins's "cosmic struggle" makes an uncanny parallel to the same wording used to describe the devil dances; that in my opinion, is not merely a coincidence. As an icon of popular culture in Venezuela, the devil dances indeed perform this cosmic struggle every year in sixteen different communities throughout central Venezuela. Yet, as I've described in this chapter, an analysis of the actual performance of the devil dances yields far different conclusions than Hawkins's populism. The performed outcome, once applied, could be considered altogether different than the reinforcement of Manichaeism and social disintegration, of course depending on whether one stands with the devils or the priest.

For now, let us stay with our example of the devil dances in Ocumare as a way of understanding the function of performance as mediation. Perhaps, as Aristotle would have it, the devil dances are a drama to purge societal anxieties, to rid us of our tragic flaws through catharsis. In another way, as seen through kinship networks, as I've argued in this chapter, this performance is more about socially enacted transformation through production and a politics of inclusion. As Clemis and others bring all their saints "to the party," and as the devils continue to be the beloved family members who protect and pray for the well-being of the community, the notion of devils as the embodiment of evil and the church as a singular good is continuously negated and recombined.

A well-rehearsed culture of resistance, as Jorman Valera would say, is constantly and necessarily working through the performance to undo the dichotomous view of good versus evil that was imposed on the devils in the first place. A collective work reliant on broad-based systems of production ultimately undoes the dyad of good versus evil even while, on its surface, the struggle between the devils and the sacrament carries on. I believe performances like the devil dances can hold this multidimensionality of seeming contradiction by their flexible and reflexive qualities. When speeches and other public events take place, the true meaning of what transpires is often unavailable in the verbatim transcript. It is a script without stage directions, without actors, and much less an audience. Neither is it enough to suggest that the actor at transmission or the audience at reception will follow scripted meanings at face value of what is assigned. To predict the tone from textual messaging is to invite an exceptional confirmation bias to obscure the multiple meanings registered within the performed act. To put it plainly, there is so much more to the performance than can be accounted for in the text. I am not saying that text is not important, and much less am I making any sweeping statements about literature and the art of script-making. But to understand ideas or ideational approaches to populism, I believe the performed act must be included in the analysis, an analysis that recognizes its spatial, temporal, and bodily dimensions. This is especially true in a system like populism—a relatively uncharted practice—where any valid interpretation, in my opinion, requires a deeply situated, interdisciplinary, and historically relational perspective.

In sum, populist repertoires include a great deal of systemic order, and performance as an exercise of group relations helps us understand this systemic dimension. The devil dances are religious manifestations that model their own political culture—one outside of partisan politics, and which are collectively sustaining as a culture of resistance. These logics, from one end of the spectrum of populist repertoires, are about social networks, routines, and negotiating the inclusions and exclusions of collective action. It is a participatory system of communal action that opens a space within which to negotiate the inside and outside of a social body or network. The devil dances in turn reproduce a populist logic that is woven into other repertoires, and carried on in these events for generations to come. Rather than assimilating to western European political frameworks, cultural producers on the Ocumare coast are calling this liberated public space the *cumbe* (see chapter 4), a self-named and self-proclaimed space, and one that was, and is, constructed and held open through culturally specific practices. I extend this idea in the context of the urban barrio and around systems of production that I call "fiesta politics" in the next chapter.

Centuries after the devil dances of Corpus Christi began in Venezuela, the performance still reveals the conflicts, negotiations, and agreements made among its producers. It also reveals the means by which informal order and institutional histories are unevenly told, entangled, and erased from view. Performance is one way to work through these tensions that are layered one on top of another, as people sort them out and continuously reclaim the collective means to agree and disagree.

Chapter 2

Fiesta Politics in the Making of the Urban Barrio

This chapter puts theater and film next to the construction of public space in the urban barrio to suggest that this relationship contributed to the political culture of populism. It focuses on two performance productions that bookend a historical period of representative democracy prior to the Chavista revolution: one in the mid-1950s, at the moment that Marcos Pérez Jiménez's dictatorship began to crumble, and the other in the latter part of the twentieth century, just before Hugo Chávez was elected. What follows is an analysis of these two performances, both written and produced by perhaps Venezuela's most prolific playwright and director, Román Chalbaud: *Caín adolescente*, a play that debuted in 1955 at the Union House Theater in Caracas, and the film *Pandemonium*, released in 1997.[1] Both productions joined people and a place with a particular populist sensibility—a populism literally built from the cultural and material construction of the barrio and those who live there, many of whom identify as the popular class.[2] This urban populism arose from the informal, peripheral settlements of Caracas and other cities, commonly referred to as barrios or *ranchos*, that climb the hills surrounding the burgeoning metropolis.

Caín adolescente (Adolescent Cain) opens on such a "typical Caracas hillside" on the day before Christmas Eve in the mid-1950s. Juana and her son Juan have just arrived in the city after a long journey from the interior of the country.[3] They unpack and settle into a humble home at the edge of a winding stairway. Light slips through cracks in the walls made of cinder block and tin. A doorway leads to the outside where beggars, launderers, and neighbors pass by. The set, designed by the artist Alberto Paz y Mateos, included two wide ramps on either side of a narrow bridge that stretched across the upper width of the stage with a landing, a street below, and a horizon line of other shack dwellings. Electric lines and laundry hang in the distance like crosses while three washerwomen discuss the death of a neighbor. "Yesterday Francisca died," one says. "Today she will be buried," replies the other. "Tomorrow nothing will be left of her but a shadow," says the third (Chalbaud 1991, 21). By the end of the first act, when Juana injures her hand as a house-cleaner and Juan is exploited by his childhood friend Matías as an

Figure 7. A typical barrio street in Caracas; narrow staircases lead to housing farther up the hillside. Author photo, 1999.

unpaid apprentice, we are led to wonder if the newcomers will disappear like Francisca, leaving nothing behind but a shadow.

Juana and Juan face a predicament not unlike others arriving at the margins of Caracas.[4] Full-throttle industrialization of the country's transportation, oil reserves, and agribusiness under Pérez Jiménez caused mass disruption in rural communities. In 1957, for example, Pérez Jiménez ordered the construction of a 1,800-acre naval base in the town of Turiamo, which displaced hundreds of families. Despite the fact that the base was not built, the military kept the land and denied the rights of residents to return. Simultaneously, a promise of middle-class ascendancy lured hundreds of thousands of mostly rural poor and young people to the city to look for work and education. By 1965, nearly 70 percent of the nation's population had relocated to the major cities of Venezuela, with the majority moving to the capital city, Caracas.

The result was a major upheaval in which entire communities were dislocated along with their cultural traditions. The acclaimed scholar and literary critic Ángel Rama describes this midcentury displacement as "a cultural axing of the historical continuity of the country" (1984, 34). Deep networks of cultural production were indeed fractured by the modernizing program of the 1950s in Venezuela. However, rather than being entirely destroyed, in many cases these networks transformed and reconsolidated. Like Eduardo's experience, which was mentioned in the preceding chapter, evicted residents sustained a decades-long struggle to reclaim the rights to their land and maintain their networks and particular forms of cultural practices. Meanwhile, fiesta politics rekindled and found new space as migrants gained footing in the city. The next section looks more closely at how these networks were sustained by a new center of populist formation in what was called barrio law.

Barrio Law

Just a few years after the play *Caín adolescente* debuted, in the late 1950s, a binational team of U.S. and Venezuelan social scientists conducted a study on social and political formations in the barrios of Caracas. Their in-depth interviews and observations were conducted during a time when over 50 percent of the population of Caracas was comprised of recent arrivals to the barrios who, like Juana and Juan in the play, were transitioning from the rural sector to the periphery of the city. The study found that barrio residents formed political alliances and jurisdictions that were (quite literally) foundational to the construction of these informal settlements. It also described the political formation of *juntas*, or governing groups—which were in some cases one and the same as fiesta councils—practicing what the study authors called "barrio law."

Law, according to the authors, consists of the rule-making processes and agreements that contribute to communal functions of social activities (such as fiestas, celebrations, and cultural events) and various aspects of governance (such as the construction of housing, the maintenance of sewage and drainage systems, and trash collection). Particularly in the context where state institutions ignored new settlements, barrio law was the order of the land, and it is important to recognize that these formations—consistent with its history that I describe in chapter 1—combined cultural performance with other forms of material and contractual jurisdiction. In the absence of the state, residents maintained this system of dispute resolution, family law, property claims, and other kinds of legal matters next to, and as a part of, fiesta and other cultural events in the barrio.

For the Pérez Jiménez regime, on the other hand, the growth of the barrios threatened to unravel the seamless outward face being presented to foreign investment. A clean and modern city image was paramount to an enterprising global Caracas, an enterprise that prided itself on a likeness to Miami with the added bonus of a safe haven for foreign-capital oil investments. Yet as the "boom" grew, so did the barrios. By the end of the 1950s, the population of Caracas had doubled. The response of the Pérez Jiménez regime was to eradicate the barrios—to bulldoze houses and relocate people to giant superstructures known as *superbloques* that were inaugurated as the *2 de Diciembre* housing projects in commemoration of the date on which Pérez Jiménez took power (see Velasco 2015a).[5] The *superbloques* were designed to house 85,000 people in 35 buildings, yet some claim that at least 100,000 people lived there (ibid.). Within ten years the infrastructure (elevators, plumbing, roofing) of these buildings had collapsed into disrepair.

Contrary to the Pérez Jiménez regime's view, the study on "barrio law"—which was conducted in still-standing barrios at precisely the same time as the fever-pitched campaign that wished to destroy them—concluded that barrio residents were steadily increasing investment in their own properties and that these trends allowed residents an eventual integration into city life. The study authors observe, "Barrio life is not glamorous; these are relatively poor communities that have major problems. But by any test, barrio residents are not those alienated, normless hordes which populate middle-class myth in Caracas" (Karst et al. 1973, 72). In short, the study refuted (and thus documents the existence of) "a Caracas myth that the barrios were teeming and ready to sack the city at any minute" (ibid.). Indeed, residents were building their own spaces, and, through the development of the barrio, they enacted their own law and order: "As the barrio becomes established, not only do concrete walls replace packing-boxes; other kinds of institution-building go on as well, such as the formation of some kinds of credit arrangements, the regularized resolution of land disputes, and cooperative public-works activities" (ibid.). As relatively uncharted institution-building from the 1950s, it is important to recognize that social and political life was primarily organized through *juntas*.

Junta is a word derived from the verb *juntar*, which means "to join together." It refers to an organized collective, but it is also a term—perhaps like the *cayapa*—that is fraught with other connotations, including a negative association as armed groups aligned with military rule. In the barrio of the 1950s, *juntas* varied widely in their jurisdictions and generally consisted of loose and informal affiliations (Karst et al. 73). These groups were made up of working-class or informally employed people, usually living in the same vicinity, who helped to adjudicate issues in the neighborhood. Instead of following management systems outside the neighborhood, *juntas* handled the duties of shared infrastructure in the barrio in a model of locally based governance.

The physical spaces of the barrio, according to the study, were developments built from the ground up, where people would make improvements on an as-needed basis. Rather than developing from a master plan, these settlements grew as people squatted on land and built their own shelters; houses were built adjacent to or on top of one another. As a workshop or new bedroom was needed, it was added on to existing structures. New facilities and infrastructure were built on this contingent basis to accommodate the influx of residents.

The "boom" was a formidable and complex process of migration and economic growth that also led to greater exploitation of the informally employed and low-income sectors that surrounded the urban center. As new residents arrived, extended-family members and hometown acquaintances often provided assistance in getting settled, building networks of relations from rural to urban districts. Not all of these relations developed alliances. Certainly, tensions among incoming residents and those previously established were, as Velasco states, "riven with ideological differences for over sixty years" (Velasco 2015b). In some cases, established residents, like Juan's childhood friend Matías and Juana's new friend Petra, whom she meets later in the play, leverage themselves against the new arrivals for greater advancement, revealing the inequity of the insider advantage. Nevertheless, what they shared was the state's relative absence in this midcentury period. Instead of the state or municipal officials controlling the barrio, fiesta networks in *juntas*, councils, and small-town associations facilitated the expansion of nearly a million new dwellings over the course of the Pérez Jiménez dictatorship and the decades that immediately followed.

As the study authors write, "The model of development found in the barrios is that of *participatory development*—developmental activity by large numbers of people at the lower levels of the society and economy. This model implies a redefinition of personal and group goals: a sense of destiny control, a concern for achievement, a willingness to take moderate risks, a concern for the common good, a sense of participation" (Karst et al. 1973, 74). When I read this, I could not help thinking about the participatory political culture of the fiesta-making practices described in chapter 1. These terms appear again in the rhetoric and practice of participatory democracy that flourished in the first decade of the twenty-first century as the Bolivarian Revolution.

In the barrio, given the vast differences and potential conflicts among barrio residents, participatory development may have been the only method of governance that *could* work. In terms of the effects, however, the study authors conclude, "The barrio resident who builds and improves his own home, unlike the head of a family who is handed the key to an apartment in a *superbloque*, takes some risk, achieves, gains confidence in his control over the future, becomes interested in community development projects, and gains a stake in a system that he has made to work in his own interest" (Karst et al. 1973, 75). The participatory process may indeed have succeeded in fostering some degree of autonomy and communal self-determination in the face of adversity, particularly when the government had abandoned or ignored barrio developments altogether (see Ledwith and Springett 2010, 15). Participatory practice expands the dialogic process around the negotiation of values within a community. It is a process that creates, as Mo Griffiths calls it, "political public spaces" (2003, 126).[6] These are spaces in which debates and decisions are conducted and organized around different orbits of decentralized production.

Román Chalbaud's staging of theater and film across the second half of the twentieth century depicted these continuities of fiesta politics in the public space of the barrio. Chalbaud's work represents the barrio in ways that join sociality to the materiality of the barrio space. His work is not just about showing poverty; it is the cultivation of an "inside" social space, generating a communal identity: a "we." Yet, when it comes to ideational critiques of populism, these skills and negotiations, the relations, and even the material evidence of barrio constituency are conveniently erased. These elements are lumped together as a simplistic binary of inside or out, one of us or one of them, leaving out the complexity of negotiations and institution-making that go on *within* the barrio.

The ideational critique views populism as an ideology of "good versus evil," a polarization that denies debate, pluralism, and the interests of minorities. The idea is that populist leaders reject the legitimacy of other opinions in a rash and simplistic way, thus denying the divisions of interests within and across the bloc of "us" or "them." To be inside or out, according to this view, is all or nothing. But inside or outside of *what*? Is it a place, or are these boundaries constructed as more broadly social, by cultural or religious ideals? Perhaps there is in fact no *one* interior, but only strategic identifications among multiple publics.

The social theorist Michael Warner (2005) rightly makes "publics" plural, referring to multiple and often contesting ideas of who stands in for one public or another.[7] *Caín adolescente* is very much a play about conflict inside the barrio, but an even more fitting theme that can be seen in this work is Warner's idea of common publics—notions of group identity such as the "we" of "the people" that are undoubtedly a fiction but nevertheless provide a powerful image of a common people and a place. I suggest that Chalbaud's barrio works do both. The barrio is not a singular space. It represents multiple contesting publics, and it also contains a "we" as the interior identification that would develop into slogans in the revolutionary era such as *mi barrio* (my barrio), *barrio adentro* (inside the barrio), and *nucleos*, referring to collective groups of artists and social services in endogenous organizing models. Chalbaud's major works throughout his career revealed this pluralism from a perspective of the *barrio adentro*.

First, in *Caín adolescente*, one of Chalbaud's first plays, the insider "we" is a social and material condition in which none of the characters remains pure. Spaces and action in the play are constantly shifting, in transition, and often fragmented. The stage directions call for the domestic space and the alley walkway to be simultaneously visible where action takes place intermittently, dialectically, between the domestic interior and the public exterior. Juan stands outside the door talking to his mother inside while Matías presses him to get back to the mechanic shop. Encarnación, Juana's future healer and lover, runs past the house in an effort to escape the police, while just inside her doorway Juana burns in pain from her injured hand. People are constantly passing through the alleyway: neighbors, a homeless man, and visitors whose transit and alternating dialogue cross over between domestic and public spaces.

In the crossovers, there are also new spaces that open possibilities for the characters in the play. When Encarnación takes refuge in Juana's house, Juana strings up a bedsheet across the corners of their domestic space, saying, "Now behind this sheet, in this beautiful darkness, there is a new world that belongs to us. This will be our corner." The sheet *creates* a space in the play where Encarnación and Juana find spiritual and amorous transformation, a sacred space. Juana and Encarnación are seen only as shadows behind the screen, hidden from the audience, retaining a privileged place in the play as a sanctuary. It is an interior shelter, a private space within the domestic space that ultimately dethrones the imagined privilege of the singular exterior-society-state.[8] The state is not the only source of governance and rules, thus opening up a possibility for multiple political forms. Most importantly, there is no simple binary between the interior and exterior, despite the common distance felt from the barrio to the downtown center of municipal and state power.

These locations of the "we" are not discrete and exclusive. Social separations are pronounced within both domestic and public spheres in ways that multiply in the play; there are *two* double sets of spaces: two domestic interiors (inside the house and behind the sheets) and two public exteriors (the barrio streets and the urban center). The barrio public is distinct from the interior of the house and the double interior behind the sheet, yet it is also distinct from the urban center: it is a street space, a public space, and also a barrio space. It is the place where the washerwomen discuss the death of the neighbor. It is the space where the masked lovers escape in the carnival. It is also the space of betrayal, where Matías confronts Juan for taking over his life after his accident, now running his shop and engaged to be married to his ex-girlfriend Carmen.

Juana and Encarnación's experience marks the limits of the barrio space where their "new world" behind the sheets in their house meets violently with the police state of the dictatorship. The police intrude and eventually arrest and imprison Encarnación. Juana, who mourns for the loss of Encarnación, spirals into alcohol like Petra. At the end of the play, just as Juana and Matías seek closure and redemption, they are crushed in a procession stampede from the church at Easter Mass.[9] All characters in the play confront their own moral and bodily limits in the promise of progress. The resurrection is also their end. During the dictatorship of Marco Pérez Jiménez (1948–58), when *Caín adolescente* debuted, thousands of dissidents from the barrios were jailed and tortured.[10] As Juana and Juan confront their new surroundings, facing challenges that tear apart their small family, we are reminded that the ultimate betrayal is that of a modernizing state which has shut them out.

Betrayal is implicit in the title of *Caín adolescente*, offering complex portrayals of the *compadrazgo* networks that so many rely upon in their transition to city life. The brotherhood between Juan and Matías is betrayed first by Matías exploiting Juan's labor as a naive newcomer to the barrio, and is later fatally betrayed when Juan "turns his back" on their friendship. We might look further to Matías's betrayal of Carmen, Petra's betrayal of Juana, and Juana's betrayal of Antonio, a man she dates at the beginning of the play who is quickly replaced by her healer lover Encarnación. In the end, we confront a cycle of betrayals and blame that are systemically intertwined.

But there's another kind of betrayal as well in this play—the betrayal of memory and belonging. When times get rough, Juan implores his mother to return to their village, disclaiming Juana's insistence that the move, as Juan's schoolteacher had suggested, would help him "become a man." There's a sense of her inability to accept going back, as if she refuses the memory and reconstruction of her own past in the face of modernity. It is only in the final scene that we find out that a massive flood preempted their move. But for Juana, there is no compensation to return, only confrontation with the false promises of modernity that erase the path to go back; as she says, "The buses surely don't go in that direction" (Chalbaud 1991, 39). Coping with the reality of Encarnación's eventual imprisonment, Juana searches but finds no redemption in a world that does not heal. The play reacts to this condition of exhaustion in the infinite promise of modernization and the ultimate failure of the state to relieve those it has impoverished and displaced.

Chalbaud's plays reflected this critique of the state. He and many other artists of the era—including Ignacio Cabrujas and Isaac Chocrón—brought attention to the daily lives of barrio residents who were otherwise invisible in the media and lacked political representation.[11] One can imagine that when Luis Buñuel's classic film *Los olvidados* (1950) hit the small art-house screens of Venezuela, the buzz captured the attention of a young Chalbaud. As critic Rubén Monasterios states, "Highly polemic, Chalbaud from his beginnings—*Muros horizontales* (1953) and *Caín adolescente* (1955)—adopts a critical and demystifying attitude toward a society that was 'officially prosperous, democratic and sustained over a solid moral foundation' " (1990, 71). Chalbaud's work directly challenged the perception that democracy in Venezuela was stable, productive, and lucrative for all its citizens. As part of the "next generation" promising a new voice and politic, he exposed the fallacies of these official claims. Thus, for Chalbaud, to stage the barrio meant not only to expose that which was erased from public view, but also to condemn the conditions of worker exploitation and little access to health care and housing.[12] In this context, Chalbaud dedicated himself to recording the population explosion in his midst and, more importantly, to humanizing the stories of migrants and the situations they encountered.[13]

Caín adolescente and other works by Chalbaud tell a story of this migration in ways that centered barrio life into the popular vernacular of theater, film, and television. As his longtime friend and collaborator Ignacio Cabrujas writes, "The pieces of Chalbaud are like a personal map of Venezuela. It is a map that shows its validity, particularly, in the emphasis that it places on the decomposition of humanity and its conditions that surged in large urban centers. Since as much as Chalbaud is national, he is also urban, and as urbanity, he transformed a large part of the population that turned their backs on the countryside and came in to try to live in the hills and cracks of the cities" (Cabrujas 1981, 7). Chalbaud's plays and film productions from the 1950s reflect these transitions geographically and ideologically. Moreover, his work bridges a period of time in which barrio residents developed a critical and even militant response to the economic and political model of modernization promoted by the state.[14]

Chalbaud, who identified as a migrant in the early stage of the boom, sought to document the systematic erasure of migrant experience, especially in the national frame of the media. Few migrants and barrio communities appeared in the newspapers, on television, or on film of the time. In my study of two major daily newspapers of Caracas, *El Nacional* and *El Universal*, in March and April of each year from 1953 to 1955, I found that in the hundreds of images for each of those periods per year, perhaps unsurprisingly, there were only scant and peripheral references to the barrio and practically no images that featured ordinary working-class and poor people within the context of their communities and homes. It is telling that exceptions to this erasure were images of large and often indistinguishable masses of people celebrating the Semana Santa (Holy Week) fiestas.[15] Indeed, it seemed as if the very identity of the popular class was constructed through these images of fiesta.

Concurrent with the deprecating view of fiestas as disorderly, and the erasure of other aspects of barrio life in newspapers, the state's response to the growth of the barrio was eradication. State-controlled media considered the barrios unsightly for the ideals of a modern nation. Barrio residents faced a full-fledged anti-barrio campaign from the Jiménez dictatorship, including what was dubbed a "Battle Against the Rancho!" (Velasco 2015a, 33).[16] In his book *Barrio Rising: Urban Popular Politics and the Making of Modern Venezuela* (2015a), historian Alejandro Velasco looks at this campaign in detail, citing a technical report published in 1954 that states, "'housing construction in [working-class barrios has] been completely anarchic and in many cases clandestine,' amounting to an imminent 'threat' against 'morals, health, and safety'" (39). The campaign against the barrio continued in various guises both publicly and behind closed doors in the decades after the Jiménez dictatorship, when the space of the barrio was presented as blight and as both the waste product and cause of the economic failures of the state. The problems of the modern state were thus projected back on the barrio, while the work of *Caín adolescente* holds a mirror to this relationship, including the exploitation (and displacement) of labor and its impact on the people who live there.

Performance, in this case theater, became a crucial vehicle for this particular kind of visibility, and it humanized barrio life for wider viewing publics. I move with some caution, however, around the hope invested in visibility. As we know, that which is symbolically central is often politically marginal (Das and Poole 2004). For Foucault (1975), to be visible implies a greater degree of state control. I am curious, then, as to what made this form of visibility generative for those who lived there—how did the barrio in popular media, theater, and film of the late twentieth century contribute to residents' own advancement, or not? One answer is that it makes strategic sense if barrio residents positioned the space of the barrio as a fissure in the edifice of the state. To make the barrio public appear onstage as subjects dispossessed by the state was also to rupture the dictatorship's narrative of wholeness, of totality.

Perhaps there is an even more obvious answer regarding the effectiveness of visibility towards the formation of populism in the pre-Chávez era. Rather than peripheral to greater powers, the barrio was depicted as the center of Venezuelan popular culture, a space in which its residents, complexly defined, are contenders for political power. The space itself became a populist signifier of barrio law that would emerge as the political and populist foundation of the new revolutionary state. Unlike charity aimed from the urban center as the giver to the unfortunate, a model of "outreach" that reinstates power from the outside in, these performances established an important precedent of barrio residents looking from the inside outward and an even more important precedent of having a conversation within. To stage the place of the barrio with residents talking to one another, and building a place of their own was crucial. Centering the barrio onstage meant deconstructing the singular primacy of the urban city center. Like the *cumbe* or the *palenque*, the barrio becomes a center in its own right for an alternative politic. As no longer peripheral, the barrios therefore represent another axis around which a political culture of the popular class is developed, including forms of populism that are generated from within.

While making a space for the barrio onstage was of crucial importance to Román Chalbaud, I cannot help but wonder what kinds of representational strategies were more widely useful among barrio residents. The scholar and critic Pedro Eduardo Aguilera Vásquez describes *Caín adolescente* as a "poetics of the margins," one that opens a dialogic space between the characters of the play and its audiences (2014, 62). Next to, or as a source of, the poetics, there is a materiality of the space that invokes a kind of realism. As José Antonio Barrios Valles, professor of theater and economics at UNEARTE,[17] suggests, rather than directly imitating reality, Chalbaud's work re-creates the situations of daily life within a realist discourse (2014, 56).[18] The material links between the set onstage and the actual barrio construction reminded me of Paola Hernández's and Jean Graham-Jones's "theater of the real," in which props, images, costumes, and sets establish a shared materiality with the streets outside (Hernández 2015; Graham-Jones 2014). In this theater of testimony, they find a possibility of new witness by staging a trace of materiality that carries over between the space of the theater and that of the city.

I adopt this hope for the transitive power of materiality and place-making as it is viewed onstage, referring to the bodies, bricks, and mortar that were called into attention by the play *Caín adolescente*. Indeed, location and performance have arguably always been deeply connected. *Location* links to the root word *allocare*, or *allocatum*, "to place," which means to call out from, to praise, or to distinguish by place. This is a practice of place not found but constructed from within. In this case, the distinction between Michel de Certeau's places as toponymical, and stories as spatial trajectories can be useful (1984, 115). Between the daily life of the barrio and the theatrical set on the stage, Chalbaud's stories create spaces "cutting across," as "spoken language," a position from which one sees and acts and forms a sense of belonging as "delinquent" and transgressive, "the privilege of the *tour* over the *state*" (ibid., 129–30). Place is thus called up by stories through dispersals of top-down determinacy with "emphasis on the curves and movements of space" (ibid.). Boundary-setting, in these terms, may indeed be flexible but also firmly rooted in the evidence of place, coming from a people as place, in confrontation with acts of disruption and the denial of place.

Dislocation or displacement is therefore as much a response to a performed act as it is a condition. To displace is a practice that causes upheaval or, in Castillo's words, *el desarraigo* (uprooting). Projects by the Pérez Jiménez administration, while purportedly serving the city's need for low-income housing, disregarded the factors of agency and self-determination and in the process destroyed thousands of houses along with the networks of power that had built them. At a time when the media ignored or disparaged the depiction of poverty and the barrio, Chalbaud's theater brought attention to the realities and problems that barrio residents faced (Álvarez 2014; Barrios Valles 2014). Across a fifty-year period of time, beginning with *Los adolescentes* (1952) and *Muros horizontales* (1953), these stories linked evidence of being in the barrio to the flexibility of boundaries as they were tactically remade.

A concern with location (the set, stage, and frame) in performance maintains its interdependency with an epistemology of the body. The body, space, and time are organized in performance to point to material and social conditions in the same frame. In *Caín adolescente*, the body is evidence of exploitation and injurious harm. Juana hurts her hand on the job as a domestic worker. Matías's leg is broken when the rig at the mechanics shop falls on him. A young woman dies from an illegal abortion done by Encarnación, while Carmen faces the same fate. At first, it appears that the devil is the cause. In suspect sympathy, Juana's neighbor Petra urges Juana to go ahead with Encarnación's supposed treatment, saying, "You have to do it, Juana. Remember . . . the devil. . . . It can burn your whole body . . . it can burn you right to the soul . . ." (Chalbaud 1991, 36, ellipses in original). The devil here is a sensate force of damage and pain. It is a bodily harm that must be remedied, and it is also the provocation to convince Juana to part with the last of her meager savings.

There is another harm as well. For Juana, the social relations of the city contrast with her former life, adding the damaging effects of psychological alienation. When her neighbor Petra introduces Juana to another potential employer, Juana says, "[the woman] looked at me from head to foot as if I were something strange. . . . The faces of people here are different than the faces of country people. There is something strange in them. They are too far from one. The distances are so far. . . . How painful to feel so small within all of this. For down below us there are thousands and thousands of people and houses. They will never even notice Juan and I" (Chalbaud 1991, 51). Juana's experience of alienation clearly points to racial-cultural and class confrontation in the transition from rural life to the city. But what I find interesting is how the people and the houses in the city down below are strange to Juana as well: strange faces of distanced masses that are "too far from one." What Juana sees is well marked within the barrio looking outward onto an ill society. It is a view that links the dehumanizing gaze of the employer to the alienation between her and the city.

While, in one sense, Encarnación is depicted as a malignant force, one that manipulates Juana and divides the house, there is another, more complex reading of these characters (Álvarez 2014, 29). As Encarnación and Juana begin a process of healing, the very conditions of their mutual "imprisonment" in society are exposed.[19] At one point, Encarnación says, "I've been a criminal since I was born" (Chalbaud 1991, 87), reminding Juana and audiences that criminality is a condition of society, anchored in the unjust racialized systems that are capable of criminalizing a human being at birth. His eventual confrontation with the police becomes the pivot point on which both Juana and Encarnación tenaciously attempt to salvage their mutual love and humanity. What is important for our purposes here is that the play doesn't merely present troubled subjects seeking to escape the barrio; it centers the action—and the conflict, the healing, and possibilities of resolution—from *inside* the barrio, which becomes, as we will see in the second half of this chapter, an insurgent space.

As these characters transform, the spotlight shifts from their own shortcomings or failures to the flaws of a system that failed them both. Knowing that Juana will be in danger by harboring a wanted fugitive (whether he actually committed the act that he is accused of remains somewhat ambiguous in the play), Encarnación leaves the safety of Juana's house under the cover of a devil mask in the midst of carnival revelry. He is quickly discovered, and the police arrest him and send him to prison, propelling Juana into a downward spiral with alcohol. Meanwhile, Juan is facing his own issue as he falls in love with Matías's ex-girlfriend, Carmen, who is pregnant and dealing with Matías's denial and rejection. Thus, Juan and Carmen are faced with the dangers of a possible abortion or a decision to keep the child. In Juana's and Juan's parallel ordeals, the very real stories of a social-health crisis are on stage in this play, making evident not just a people in crisis but also a *system in crisis*, one that is ultimately as negligent as Matías, a father who refuses to take responsibility for his unborn child. In this sense the principal betrayal of *Caín* is not necessarily brother-to-brother: it is the endemic failure of the dictator state to deliver on its promise to serve the public good.

These realities of medical impoverishment continued through the decades following this play, past the 1958 transition to democracy known as the Punto Fijo Pact, and into the 1990s when 60 percent of people in Venezuela were living in poverty, with the great majority not having access to viable medical alternatives (Briggs and Mantini-Briggs 2007, 163). Residents of barrios such as the 23 de Enero and others who were historically marginalized, for example, felt excluded and "subordinated by the state and the privileged classes in Venezuela" (ibid., 166). Inequities in public health, such as conditions of deterioration, long lines, and virtually no accessible clinics in the hills of the barrios, and an increasingly expensive private system of health care, became a major political issue that brought about its own revolution of clinic takeovers and organized demands for a responsive and locally accountable health system by the time Chávez came into office (ibid.).

Fast-forward a generation after *Caín adolescente*, to an evening in late February 1989. There is a lavish banquet at the Teresa Carreño Theater in central Caracas. The event, televised on nationwide broadcast, features then-president Carlos Andrés Pérez announcing a package of neoliberal economic reforms that would privatize state interests, shrink social services, and result in even less protections for the majority poor.

The result was a 100 percent increase in fuel costs that triggered a massive uprising; thousands took to the streets sacking stores in protest. President Pérez declared a state of emergency and curfew, and ordered troops to restore order by force in what became known as the Caracazo. The official reports claimed that 276 people had been killed. In 1992, two human-rights organizations challenged this figure and reported 396 deaths. However, the discovery of mass graves in 1990, corroborated with testimony, indicated that as many as a thousand people had been murdered by the state.

In 1998, one witness of the Caracazo told me that, when he was a small boy, he looked out the window of his home in the barrio and saw a group of soldiers drag his neighbor out of his house, accusing him of looting. They lay him face-down on the ground and shot him in the head at point-blank range. If the pretense for state violence was to restore order, the military ultimately failed. As Sara Motta and Mike Cole describe, "The embodied and visceral rupture of the Caracazo signaled the emergence of cracks in neoliberal elites' ability to speak for Latin America's popular classes" (2013, 6). The repression of 1989 left an indelible mark on the national consciousness that would shake the neoliberal order and forge what many people imagined as a new attempt for democracy under Chávez's leadership.

A state that had propagandized the illusion of a democracy forged by a free people was, by the mid-1990s, in crisis. The image of Carlos Andrés Pérez from his 1973 presidential campaign—a populist leaping over a giant pothole, promising that the *hombre activo* (active man) of the people would fix the barrio—stood in stark contrast with the image of a man who had ordered epic violence against barrio residents in the neoliberal regime of his second term (Coronil 1997, 237–38). In the campaign poster, Pérez's confident stride leaping over infrastructural blight promises to extraordinarily overcome poverty and disrepair.[20] His followers look on in admiration. He is one of the gang—even more, he is the alpha man of the streets, unsoiled by the mud. This constructed image of the people contending with the material conditions of the space of the barrio served Carlos Andrés Pérez well; he wore it like a badge.

What made the irony intolerable was that the very same president would, two decades later, order troops to quell the Caracazo by killing the very activists who had organized the barrio (López Maya 2004, 128). As Fernando Coronil wrote, events such as the Caracazo "marked a crisis of the populist project that had defined the relationship between state and pueblo since 1936. With the shift to free-market policies . . . , dominant discourse began to present the people not so much as the virtuous foundation of democracy, but as an unruly and parasitical mass to be disciplined by the state and made productive by the market" (Coronil 1997, 378). People of the barrio were now openly depicted as an imminent threat. Thus, it should come as no surprise that the populist *hombre activo* of Carlos Andrés Pérez became a symbol of betrayal amounting to the ultimate Caín.

Fiesta and the Populist Imagination of Román Chalbaud's *Pandemonium*

About a decade after the Caracazo, just prior to Chávez's run for the national elections, Chalbaud released his hit film *Pandemonium* (1997), which is a story about three lover-friends who manage to steal dirty money from the unscrupulous matron-boss, Carmin, and her favored son, a military tyrant named Radamés. Unlike *Caín adolescente*'s sincere story of newly arriving migrants to the barrios, *Pandemonium* ratchets up the loss of all that is sacred with a grotesquely cynical response to the Caracazo and the failure of the neoliberal state. It is also a film about finality and the possibility of redemption, where fiesta resurfaces in two contrasting scenes that I will examine, following a synopsis, in order to see the continuity of fiesta politics in the barrios as it was projected to wider audiences. *Pandemonium*, like *Caín*, is a fictional representation of the barrio (and the fiestas in them), this time within the two-dimensional frame of the movie screen, and yet it carries a telling interpretation of the barrio as a pluralist and contentious space from which change will emerge in the Chávez era as an insurgent populism.

Among the film's outré characters of the urban barrio is Carmin's second son, a "subversive" intellectual and radio host named Adonai (Hebrew for "God") who is physically bound to his footless body, and is mobile only by a hand pulley that allows him to scoot himself over the piles of books that make up his bed. Literally immobilized on top of volumes by the likes of Pablo Neruda, Francisco de Quevedo, and José María Vargas Vila, Adonai, in white pajamas, flips on his microphone and, tinkling a small xylophone for sound effects, broadcasts his show *Radio Pandemonium* from the aqueduct basement that he shares with his mother Carmin, his grandmother, and Carmin's adopted orphaned house servant, Demetria. Adonai's mellifluous words of poetry are disembodied and godlike, cast across the small tin roofs and alleyways out of rigged-up bullhorns and spliced lines that the camera slowly traces from his basement lair to the world above. Attended by Demetria, his Persephone-like teenage muse, Adonai is heavenly and, at the same time, a fallen angel, banished to the underworld, with his severed feet pickled in a jar kept next to his bed.

Contrary to Chalbaud's later portrayals of "the people" as extraordinarily noble or morally righteous, these mid-career works rarely (if ever) depict barrio residents as heroic and uniformly "good." Demetria (a.k.a. *la perra*, "the whore") and Hermes and Onésimo (Demetria's boyfriends who, we learn later, are wanted for grave robbery) lustily frolic on a construction scaffold towering above the barrio closest to heaven. Carmin, like the boardinghouse matron Edicta in Chalbaud's earlier production *Sagrado y obsceno* (1966), embodies the hypocrisies of the pious and law-abiding middle class. She fawns over her first son, Radamés, an unscrupulous white-collar crook with "status," laughing heartily that if a revolution indeed takes power, she will merely switch sides to Adonai. Indeed, the movie is most condemning of the middle class, suggesting in the end that glib indifference in the face of violence, corruption, and devastating inequities make the middle class the bedfellow of evil.

Whereas in *Caín adolescente* the characters contend against an urbanity that would "distort/entangle one's view" (Chalbaud 1991, 42), in *Pandemonium* the evils of the state are exposed in terrifying new dimensions. From his penthouse prison cell, Radamés appears unscathed and complicit in the prisoner massacre in his compound while family members pound on the gates in enraged despair. Carmin, who sells Demetria to a perverted general for a bag of groceries, smugly steps over the dead bodies in Radamés's compound, clutching the suitcase of stolen cash that Radamés entrusted to her care.

Figure 8. *Pandemonium* (1997), a film by Román Chalbaud, featuring Adonai (Orlando Urdaneta) broadcasting his radio program with the devil in the background. Image courtesy of Román Chalbaud.

When Demetria and her two boy-lovers plot to steal the laundered money, their plan is foiled by Radamés's henchman Ram Ram, a former boyfriend of Demetria who, by the end of the film, kills Hermes and Onésimo, takes the money, and then seduces Demetria to run off with him to Miami, promising that she will meet the Little Mermaid at Disney World. Eventually, upon finding out that his mother no longer has the dirty money, Radamés delivers her to the gate of an enormous Gothic cathedral in the city center where she meets "her old friend," the devil himself. None of these characters are sacred. There are no perfect ideals.

Just as there are no ideals, there is a vacancy in the so-called democratic state, one that the notion of evil in *Pandemonium* points to. A false democracy occupies the place of evil whereas the barrio kids, who are marked as thieves, prostitutes, and subversives, a threat to the state, are the real angels. In a spatial reversal, Adonai in his saintly bed wrap speaks the truth from his underground while the real devil resides in a church at the center of the city.

These and a host of other absurd situations and characters portray the barrio with ironic bitterness and tremendous empathy, switching sacred and profane, inside and outside, heaven and hell. It is as if the barrio itself belches back the widespread, national complex of pandemonium, seeking both an epic sense of historical justice and some form of new beginning. Setting conventional sincerity aside, the film manages to locate the barrio as the site of possible redemption in which fiesta serves to envision an insurgent subjectivity of the barrio in the face of all-out pandemonium. I look at this further in the two following scenes, one in the middle of the film and the other at the end, to propose that fiesta, and the politics that surround it, enable an imaginary of insurgent resurrection.

First scene: after several screenshots throughout the film of people attempting to draw water from the dry public spigots at the entrance of the barrio, the public fountains finally flow. The moment is one of joyous occasion. People from all walks of life in the barrio (of various races, genders, ages) gleefully bathe in a collective baptism. A middle-aged woman runs out screen left with her arms outstretched, rapturously bellowing, "The water, *water*! Water is *life*!" (Chalbaud 1997). People run and skip into the frame, dancing into the flowing tubs, spigots on full blast. Several openly queer or trans characters shave their legs in revelry. People sing, splash, and wildly scrub their bodies. Demetria fills up two buckets that she hoists across her shoulder, with Hermes and Onésimo assuming their goggle-eyed courtship by carrying the buckets for her. The eruption of fresh water pouring into the barrio unites the multitudes in *pura fiesta*.

Second scene: at the end of the film the sounds of excitement outside compel Adonai to finally ascend from his underworld. Using a crate on a conveyor belt, he painstakingly hoists himself up through the roof to watch with wonder as crowds of people ascend from the city below back to the barrios with looted goods. He watches Demetria dance and skip, swimming through the waves of the crowd. The scene is absurd, sentimental, riding the edge of the gestalt of Adonai's envisioned revolution, yet clearly it is also a realistic overlay of actual events that happened during the Sacudón, the period of looting that directly preceded the tragic events of the Caracazo. Yet, the vision is ultimately betrayed when, just as Demetria is laughing and twirling, she encounters Ram Ram who convinces her to run away with him to Disney World. Demetria's distressing choice to ally with the assassin of her friends underscores the bitter ironies of reality for the poet. Yet, what I find most telling about this scene is the comparably positive portrayal of the crowd once juxtaposed to the fatality of the other characters. Multitudes of the barrio look resolute, hopeful, and peacefully eager to get home with their goods. Others are smiling and calling out to each other as they haul slabs of meat, appliances, and other merchandise of all kinds. There is no put-on hype; this last scene of the Sacudón is awash in daylight, in real time, where ordinary people of the barrio offer the restoration of hope in the film.

What we can see in these two scenes is that the film, as superlative as this genre permits, presents fiesta as hyperbolic, and also the only sane moments of the story. It is oppositional to the neoliberal absurdities of the 1980s' scarcity and austerity suggesting abundance and diverse expressions of humanity. In the processional return of basic foodstuffs and in the moment when fresh water finally flows, the barrio itself becomes the utopian ideal, moving from a camp-like dreamscape to the realist assertion of the people as protagonists of a political alternative.

Whereas *Caín adolescente* deals with people being bulldozed and ultimately buried in the procession, *Pandemonium* offers the last scene of the Sacudón as a phoenix-like moment that carries the thread of a historical continuity to the political moment of the uprising in 1989. As Roberto Forns Broggi asks of this film, "What purpose does this apocalyptic vision serve if not to enliven the search for a cultural alternative?" (1999, 167). The mayhem in *Pandemonium* not only damns a corrupt and perverse form of state and military collusion, but also points to fiesta as an alternative.

In *Pandemonium* we see the surfacing of these lines of continuity where the collective space of the barrio is again signified by fiesta. As in the fiestas of San Juan Bautista (St. John the Baptist), when people run through the river, in Chalbaud's film the barrio neighbors baptize themselves in the public watering hole. Adonai, Demetria, Hermes, and Onésimo reinscribe the carnivalesque into daily life, enjoying a sumptuous moment of feasting on street food and playing on the sidewalks before jumping back on the motorbike with a gorilla mask and short shorts. The cultural critic and historian Luis Duno-Gottberg called the motorcyclists a "return of the real" as a political subjectivity that shaped the historical emergence of Chavismo (2009, 145–46). On their motorcycle, they make their way through the city with extra-capable mobility—they are flawed and dangerous and yet ultimately equipped with a moral integrity to take care of their own which surpasses that of the neoliberal state. It is ultimately in these playful moments that Demetria, Hermes, and Onésimo extend this space of the barrio into the sidewalks, the demolished buildings, and other uncharted sites on the city streets.

At one point the trio sneak into a church that has apparently been ransacked by "subversives" who rebelled against a corrupt priest. Among the fallen beams and broken glass, Demetria, who is still in the white communion dress and veil that Carmin made her wear for the general, sits on one side of the confessional looking at her two boy lovers through the open frame. She asks seriously, "Are you good, or are you bad?" They are neither, of course. Sin and virtue are entirely skewed and irrelevant in this world. It is, as Adonai's mock radio ad for an English language school states, the Tower of Babel. "Torre de Babel!" he bellows across the airwaves. The destroyed church, like the unfinished apartment buildings that rise above the barrio, are remnants of an incomplete past, an unfinished state beset by confusion over the very different "languages" of how to run the country. Out of the confusion, it seems the only real hope of reconstruction comes from the unconstrained passions of the delinquent kids; as Onésimo says, "feelings are all we have" (Chalbaud 1997). Amid the corruption of the political world, these moments of feeling provide a space for an alternative historical continuity in tandem with the finality of the scream: this is the communal banquet in which the real goods come *in* to the barrio.

In a prescient example of historical continuity, *Pandemonium* reconstructs the nation over the grandmother's delirious recollections of the past. As if telling a bedtime story, the grandmother recalls Ezequiel Zamora, "general of the sovereign people," who rode into the village on a galloping horse, gathering with him her father and other men from the village who joined him in battle. "Down with the oligarch!" she cries out (Chalbaud 1997). Zamora was a rebel hero of the nineteenth-century Federal Wars who sought land distribution to compensate those who were unjustly enslaved. Without land, Zamora argued, the society's severe inequalities would persist. Zamora became a leading general of the Federalist army, which fought against the conservative landholding elites, before he was eventually killed in battle, allegedly by one of his fellow generals who had politically sided against him.

The grandmother represents a past that Demetria, who all along was desperate to get out of the barrio to go to Disney World, coldly refers to as already dead. Indeed, Adonai's dying grandmother, in an interview on *Radio Pandemonium*, breathlessly recounts a story of the nation in a message of finality. She recalls the cries of land and liberty, the cries for the end of slavery, and the slogans of successive, corrupt presidents until, gasping, she speaks her last words: "this country is a pure grito [cry/scream] . . . so many cries for nothing." And yet, just as her last words are lifted into the airwaves, ephemeral and fleeting, and her body is burned on a funeral pyre of Adonai's books, the past is resurrected in this film.

If Adonai's grandmother's corporeal death is a sign of finality and the death of the nation, then these moments of festive affection may point toward its springlike renewal.

In its most practical sense, analyzing the carnivalesque in *Caín adolescente* and *Pandemonium* presents a barometer for the ways in which artists understand the state at different moments in its more recent history. Chalbaud's depictions of fiesta in the pre-Chávez period appear symbolically as an organizing principle against the state. As Marita King (1987) points out, *Caín adolescente* is entirely organized around fiestas: each act of the play pertains to fiestas, respectively Christmas Eve, Carnival, and Easter. The very structure by which the drama proceeds—a structure tracing birth to so-called profanity to resurrection—encompasses an entire cycle of life in the barrio outside of the state.

Fiesta thus encompasses a kind of totality, not limited to the spatial confines of the barrio. Rather, the play suggests that the occasions of fiesta are a transcendent and unifying alternative to that which unnaturally divides people in the city. Chalbaud's use of La Noche Buena (Christmas Eve), for example, is explicit. As the indigent sage in the first scene says, "Tonight all the lights in the city will shine. Even the stars will shine. It will be born anew" (Chalbaud 1991, 23). The "birth in the manger" (simultaneously Juana's sexual awakening) radiates from both within and beyond her house. The unities of space outside by the city lights, the stars, and the barrio suggest an almost cosmic dimension of the entire urban arena. That which is born (on Christmas) brings a new centrality to inside the barrio walls, only to break out later during carnival as a means to transcend the territorial divides between barrio and city center.

Fiesta combines the ordinary and the extraordinary, the epic and the episodic, the cosmic and the footsteps of everyday life. In *Caín adolescente*, Christmas, Carnival, and Holy Week also encompass the seemingly ordinary in what the itinerant laborer Antonio Salinas describes, in the final act, as everyday miracles: "To be born in every sunrise. To be alive. To have hands and feet, eyes, a heart and a head. To be able to speak, to be able to read, to be able to feel. It's just that it's so common that people don't believe it's a miracle. But it is" (Chalbaud 1991, 110). To locate these everyday miracles in heightened but ordinary experience, to me feels different from the ludic adventures of Mikhail Bakhtin's Pantagruel in which we "enter a completely new order of things" (1984, 34). Fiesta is, according to Roberto DaMatta, a "rite without a master . . . where we generally encounter the masses who are on the margins of the socially accepted world" (1991, 16). But the way I see it, fiesta is integrated with the bodies and lives of *Caín*'s characters, signaling continuity with the very rhythms that govern daily practice and events.

For Bakhtin, carnival is an upending of the body, where the lower parts take prominence as the new order of carnival—carnival as an upside-down world. DaMatta thought of this slightly differently; in his view, the social-political inversion of carnival was interior to exterior where the house is turned inside out. That is, within Brazilian social life, DaMatta sees carnival as a time when domestic life (that which takes place in the interior patio where domestic affairs and intimacy apply) opens out onto the streets. There is a metaphorical airing of one's private "laundry" into the public space of the city, suggesting a public-domestic spatial binary rather than a lower-to-upper bodily reversal. In short, DaMatta's view of inversion is an inside out where Bakhtin is flipping upside down.

The key idea for both Bakhtin and DaMatta, though, is that the body and the house are disjointed. One space or body part replaces the other. The carnival experience is defined by the onset of a wholly different order, where the parts of a whole are stripped from their anatomy and dislocated from their place. I read the cultural portrayals of fiesta within Chalbaud's early works as consistent with the social order, a contiguous inside space that remains the place of futurity. Chalbaud's portrayal of fiesta "inside the barrio" is a proposal that situates the politics of fiesta in the actual building of the barrio networks and place. Recall that the binary between the domestic and the public is already fractured. In *Caín adolescente* there is a distinction between two exteriors and two interiors: the barrio and the urban center are two publics, and within the house the sheet splits the domestic into sacrosexual and familial spaces. Binary inversions of the interior patio versus the streets do not apply in this case. In *Caín* the spaces of the barrio, like the so-called good and evil in the characters, are not turned inside out. They are simultaneously exposed. They are all at once visible, a double visibility that becomes the remedy to invisibility and also a labyrinth of foreboding complexity. The simultaneous presence of outside (exterior) and inside (interior) reminds us of the ability of performance to capture the ambiguity and multiplicity of both just as it denaturalizes the false divisions between them.

In the case of *Pandemonium*, fiesta doubly inscribes these seeming contradictions and crossovers. Adonai, now god of the underworld, lives in his basement, past the dripping lagoon; where the river Styx is a protecting moat juxtaposed to the caped devil who resides behind a grand set of iron gates, up a regal stairway, and in the Gothic cathedral of the city center. Normalized state violence is thus pandemonium, which ordinary people in the processional return of the riot potentially remedy by bringing goods back into their space. It is a reversal of the stampede at the end of *Caín*.

This last scene of *Pandemonium* is, in a sense, a procession taking back Carlos Andrés Pérez's banquet that was televised during the announcement of his neoliberal reforms. The sacking of the city, in other words, can be seen in this double inversion as a *reasonable return* of what has been stolen from the people. Heaven and hell, sacred and profane—these are inverted just as the military-state's and the *pueblo*'s positions as arbiters of justice are inverted. Rather than acting as mere contradictions, in other words, inversions in this sense do the work of correction; they are a logical response to the world when it is already inverted, already upside down.

A formulation of carnival theory must then take into account the barrio in which the carnival is produced, with its geosocial locations of language, behaviors, and material demands. This fiesta space is at once the social life and materiality of the barrio public (and cosmos, as the barrio is notably attached to the full surround of the city lights and stars in the sky), as it is positioned inversely to the repressive state (the police), to the dehumanization of capitalism (Juana's employer, Radamés), and the prison (which takes away Encarnación). Performance, in this sense, calls attention to the presence of real bodies, real building blocks, and real spaces, like the alleyways, doorways, steps, and landings of the barrio. The evidence of materiality is in the very building blocks of the location that take shape through space, time, and the body. Fiesta does not occur in a purely domestic or covert individuated space; it is precisely about this materiality as it is defined and re-created through ritual knowledge, worldview, and everyday practices in public places.

To reflect on *Caín adolescente* and *Pandemonium* at a time when initiatives of the socialist government have gained traction around these ideas makes it possible to see the cultural constructions of endogenous populism. Populism changed from the post-dictatorship era toward Chavismo in ways that increased the mainstream acceptance, visibility, and insurgent collectivism of barrio activists. Unlike the populism of Carlos Andrés Pérez, which was buried by cynicism and mistrust of the state, the Chávez project developed populism from the inside; it built from the space of the barrio public and placed it as its center of discourse.

Current state-sponsored projects such as El Sistema (1975 to the present), a music program that was infused with millions of dollars in 2007, gaining international prominence, and Corazón Adentro (Heart Inside), a culture program reminiscent of the Cuban post-revolution literacy projects, are examples of this endogenous form of populism. Corazón Adentro, established in 2007, presents film, plays, music, and other forms of cultural expression in local neighborhoods, in metro stations, in public plazas, and on the streets of the hills surrounding Caracas.

Barrio Adentro (Barrio Inside) is a program that placed 33,000 health professionals in the hearts of low-income neighborhoods across the country. In accordance with Articles 83 and 84 of the 1999 constitution, the program sought to fulfill the state's new claims that "health is a fundamental right and obligation of the State, and the system of public health must be 'decentralized' and 'participatory,' integrated to the system of social security, guided by principles of gratuidad, universality, integrity, equity, social integration and solidarity" (as quoted in Briggs and Mantini-Briggs 2007, 163). The circulation of ideas such as these about social medicine that had emerged among thousands of working-class residents was important to the creation of the Barrio Adentro program (ibid., 172). Even more crucial, however, was the common demand among residents that the program be designed endogenously to the barrio. The Barrio Adentro program thus followed the ideological premise of a "health revolution," as one community worker said, "right here in the barrio" (ibid., 169). Its very name, Barrio Adentro (Barrio Inside), was chosen among community workers to affirm the "political symbolism of the space" (ibid.). It is precisely this symbolism of activism *inside the barrio* that I see reflected in its infancy in projects such as *Caín adolescente* and matured in *Pandemonium*; one could say that these ideas were incubated and amplified within these performance works.

While much of the work of public health, theater, and film and other forms of cultural production performed in the decades prior to Chávez's presidency is beginning to be documented, it's important to emphasize that the political subjectivity of the popular class did not emerge only from clandestine meeting rooms and underground leaflet campaigns. As George Ciccariello-Maher (2013) points out, even before Hugo Chávez appeared on television to renounce his coup attempt in 1992, offering the hopeful message of "*por ahora*" (for now) that brought him to national attention, the movement was already well underway. What is much less studied is the influence of culture and the arts within the second half of the twentieth century in bringing about that change within the middle class. Fiestas, theater, and film opened a space that brought the networks and relations of barrio-building to the attention of the middle class. This helped to shape the representation of the popular class in the national scope of political transformation at the end of the century.

What makes *Caín adolescente* and *Pandemonium* important to this era is that these portrayals brought attention to the Venezuelan popular class at particular moments when the national imagination was being freshly revised. Populism embedded in this imagination ultimately carried a torch to the dictatorship—not only did the visibility of individuals, such as the neighbor who goes unnoticed, increase, but there was also the amplification of a political culture and place that would ultimately be organized outside of institutionalized society. Theater and film contributed to this building of a populist sovereignty, one that had grown during the life of Chalbaud for over four decades prior to Chávez and was sustained through the efforts of many people.

Rather than featuring well-intentioned elites bringing culture to the poor and marginal sectors, public-health initiatives emphasize the idea of "from the inside [*adentro*]" and the bottom up and employ words such as "endogenous" and "nucleus." The utopian moments of *Pandemonium*, while "collective," are not uniform and almost always include multiple representations of race, gender, age, and body type. In another way, however, the ebullience of the multitudes masks the particular relational dynamics of real-life conflicts. The romanticism of *el pueblo* rarely does more than reauthorize it for consumption yet again. Yet what is important for our purposes here is to see the shift between these two pieces, where fiesta—grotesque, dangerous, and also utopian—transforms the collective expression of the barrio public into an act of political agency.

From this perspective, the concept of festive inversion more fittingly applies to the barrio public entering the urban political and economic center. This certainly does not limit dissidence to being rooted only in the barrio; importantly, dissidence has emerged from many other spaces of the modern nation and world. Nevertheless, the barrio space, as complicated and variegated and a place from which a political proposal emerges, has everything to do with populist reason.

In this regard, Laclau's (2005) critique of Gustave Le Bon's unreliable "crowd" applies, since the very premise of melodrama and the fiesta as the disorderly, domestic, or slovenly expression of "the people" must be revised. This view maintains a racialized and classist bias against the political as much as social expressions that are found in popular culture outside or on the margins of institutional society. Rather than stop there, it is the place to begin the recovery of what has been stored within the vilified mass: the multiple social and political forms of organization that are a part of fiesta—pluralism, the challenge to Manichaean logics, and locally based networks of participation that shape not only popular culture but also the culture of populism.

In tracing the arc over forty years of cultural production, we find the contrast between *Caín adolescente*'s characters, who remained relatively passive and accepting of their fates, and *Pandemonium*'s depictions of the popular, which correspond to a new form of political agency: an agency that seeks to further activate the multiple voices of the barrio. Fiesta in this case is one way for an artist like Chalbaud to draw attention to a potential liberation, one that would alleviate the pressures of those on the margins who were excluded from political formation. On these multiple levels, these performances broadcast an alternative voice of the barrio to wider audiences, perhaps like Adonai did. While arguably reductive in its melodramatic and parodic forms, the portrayal and visibility of the barrio public in these works by Chalbaud humanized the popular class during the decades following the dictatorship of Pérez Jiménez and in many ways symbolically attached this endearment of the popular class to a populist imagination.

So far I have argued that religious manifestations and fiesta, theater, and film—alongside public health, housing, and other demands—shaped the ideas and practices of populism. Referring to populism at the turn of the twentieth century, historian Charles Postel claims that rarely were so many men and women in the United States engaged in a political movement that occupied the "lecture halls, classrooms, camp meetings, and seminars or produced such an array of inexpensive literature, lecture notes, editorials, letters, diaries and minute books left behind" (2007, 4). As I mentioned in the introduction, if the early formations of populism in the United States were as a "reading party," contrarily, we can imagine populism's roots in mid-twentieth-century Venezuela in terms of performance. In Venezuela, the political movement leading up to and in the first decade of Chávez's presidency took place within popular performances such as in the work of Román Chalbaud, with embodied repertoires and cultural production as its record. Twenty-first-century populism left Ángel Rama's lettered elites behind and instead found its fullest expression through performance in the streets, in the theaters, and in media of various kinds.

In sum, if in the first chapter, performance was a practice of populism, this chapter extended that argument to suggest that populist repertoires constructed a space to reflect and envision a politics of the urban popular class. What we can learn from the works of Román Chalbaud is that there is a location and language rehearsed in that politic. If ideational populism considers the formation of a set of ideas, beliefs, and attitudes as the basis of populism, I believe those ideas are less about any intrinsic good versus evil and more a question of how position or place is articulated in the processes of making populism. Staged theater in the urban context showed networks of place-building and fiesta, where the production of the barrio space projected a particular kind of visibility staged from within the heart of the barrio. The idea of "inside the barrio" is thus spatially and materially defined, serving as a powerful example of the expansion of populist imagination in theater and film.

Since 1999, when Chávez officially took office, filmmakers, musicians, and playwrights such as Chalbaud have taken up the task promoted by state entities to "rescue" historical figures that had been ignored by previous regimes. New sources of funding and the explicit support of and by the state opened the floodgates in the revolutionary theater of Venezuela, mainly in cultural performance and projects to "recuperate" public space and history. Figures from the past whose struggles were left out of official history began to take new prominence in state-artist initiatives. Performances about these historical figures in theater, film, and dance, as well as in circus arts and public art murals, proliferated through cities and small towns across the country. Whereas the first half of this book focused on populism in performance, the next two chapters dial up the role of leaders and public office to focus on performance in the populism of the revolutionary state.

Chapter 3

✦

Florentino and the Devil

Campaign Populism as Performance

In September 2006, Hugo Chávez lambasted then-president George W. Bush during his speech to the United Nations with what some considered an outlandish comparison of a head of state to the devil. Holding Noam Chomsky's book *Hegemony or Survival* in his hand, Chávez addressed the assembly: "Yesterday, ladies and gentlemen, from this podium, the president of the United States, the gentleman to whom I refer as the devil, came here, talking as if he owned the world. Truly. As the owner of the world."[1] Chávez continued, "As the spokesman of imperialism, he came to share his nostrums, to try to preserve the current pattern of domination, exploitation and pillage of the peoples of the world." He made the sign of the cross, and put his hands together as if in prayer. Each gesture was deliberate. In what followed, Chávez spelled out a trenchant critique of U.S. aggression and urged for a shift in the allocation of resources to the challenges of climate change ahead. The response in the room was resounding; representatives who had been standing in the hallway flocked into the room when he began, and, by the end, the room full of delegates heartily applauded, standing again for a lengthy ovation.

The response from U.S. officials, on the other hand, was terse. Secretary of State Condoleezza Rice said the address was not "becoming of a head of state." John Bolton, then U.S. ambassador to the United Nations, dismissed the speech, claiming, "We're not going to address that sort of comic-strip approach to international affairs."[2] Given President Bush's own slogan of "Axis of Evil" in reference to Iran, Iraq, and North Korea, politics and comic strips have hardly been oddities. Yet to dismiss the performance aspects of this speech means to disregard the deep and broad influence of popular discourse on contemporary politics. Candidates and elected officials in all types of democracies—liberal, direct, and participatory—are no strangers to the art of grabbing attention with visual or verbal language borrowed from popular culture. Political posters, radio jingles, slogans, and entertainment have long served the interests of politicians as mainstays in U.S. political discourse.

We may consider, as the popular culture and politics scholar John Street does, that in one way, "politics is being packaged in ways that harm democracy." But, as Street argues, this conclusion obligates us to examine further "the character and quality of the packaging process, . . . the meanings it supplies and the responses it elicits" (1997, 59). In other words, the question of benefit or harm to democracy depends on a more fully developed account of how political cultures borrow from popular cultures. How does this borrowing operate, and whom does it serve? Perhaps the speech impressed more at-home viewers than initially were interviewed or would admit, but mainly, in the United States, it became fodder for critics to wildly dismiss Chávez as a populist. The hype—and the populist critique—however, stayed at the tip of the iceberg, missing a vast reserve of meaning under the surface.

This chapter approaches Chávez's "devil speech" at the United Nations as a missed opportunity to peel back the "packaging" of the performed dimensions of populism in the Venezuelan revolutionary state. In Venezuela at this time, performance such as folk ballads, puppetry, rap, and poster art all became a successful modality of political—and democratic—participation.[3] To disregard performance was to leave out a vital component of participatory democracy, and whether wittingly or not, to corroborate in a much more menacing campaign against it.

To begin, we need to go back two years before the UN speech to a pinnacle moment of the Chávez era: the recall-election campaign of 2004 in which millions of people in Venezuela took to the streets as chorus and protagonist of a popular legend known as "Florentino and the Devil."

Florentino and the Devil

The story of "Florentino and the Devil" is about a plainsman of humble origins who battles the devil to defend his land and people from exploitation and ruin. In 1940, Alberto Arvelo Torrealba (1905–1971) recorded the first published version of this widely known legend, which had been performed among people in the great plains of Venezuela as a musical ballad for at least decades beforehand.[4] The plot is quite straightforward. While riding alone on horseback across the vast drought-stricken *llanos* (plains) of west-central Venezuela, humble Florentino is challenged by the Devil, a man on horseback wearing a long black cloak and a hat covering his eyes. The Devil sings out a *reto* (a challenge) to Florentino, threatening to force him off of his land.[5] When Florentino realizes that the stakes are life and death, he accepts the challenge, and they agree to duel in the village of Santa Inés (in the state of Barinas), which was the site of one of the most famous battles of the federal wars in the mid-nineteenth century.

"Florentino and the Devil" first appeared as a ballad played out through song and improvised riddles in a traditional Venezuelan musical performance of the *jaropo*. The *jaropo* is a cadent and mellifluous music somewhere between the *vallenato* and the sounds of the marimba, played mainly with a harp and maracas, with soaring and at times mournful vocals. As the story goes, the Devil presents a rhyming riddle—in song—to the young Florentino that he must solve or face forfeiting to the Devil. Florentino solves it, remaining in rhythm, and then presents his own riddle back to the Devil, and so forth. The lyrics consist of these riddles, which are in effect coded to local knowledge and colloquial expressions; to plants, animals, and the land; and to the way of life among the poor, rural inhabitants of the *llanos*.

The musical showdown takes place with the entire village of Santa Inés as witness; young and old stand in wait, most playing instruments, all in anxious anticipation as the battle plays out. In Torrealba's version, after a long bout, Florentino's unwavering, sustained voice finally defeats the Devil at dawn, at which point Florentino and the villagers force the Devil to flee. As important as vocal virtuosity, however, is that Florentino issued a riddle so subtle and with such unmatched poetic sensibility that only those with a practiced local knowledge living close to the land could answer it, giving credence to the proverb that "the one who works the land knows it best." Hence, we see in the story that (1) the performance is derived from local knowledge and experience; and (2) the fact that Florentino's fellow villagers share in the stakes bears consequence as a collective act.

The musical performance of "Florentino and the Devil" recorded by Torrealba includes a back-and-forth form of verbal jousting between two singers called a *contrapunteo*, or what Venezuelan ethnomusicologist Teresa Espar calls "a dialogic duet" as a form of "participatory communication." With its large musical entourage, which includes dozens of people playing instruments and observing the showdown, the *contrapunteo* is a contest involving a network of relations and meanings that are more than a simple duel between two individuals. According to Espar, the *contrapunteo*, by the act of creating and solving riddles, creates a kind of social "contract of knowledge-power and doing" (1998, 59). This knowledge-power of the riddles suggests the import of relationships to place and belonging, while the repertoire carries this power into rehearsed participation. Moreover, the *contrapunteo* centers this contest on the ritual performance of unscripted lyrics, improvisation, and the vocalists' creative ability to win each *copla*, or musical phrase. The win, therefore, is determined by the singer's ability to use their virtuosity in combination with their wit to challenge and solve the riddles within the improvised moment. The song lasts as long as the singers continue to perform, and whomever performs the most enduring, captivating, and musically impressive *copla* wins the duel.

The story of "Florentino and the Devil" was first published as *El reto* (*The Challenge*) during a period of transition and antiauthoritarian sentiment soon after the death of dictator Juan Vicente Gómez in 1935. Gómez had forcibly maintained executive powers from 1908 to 1935. Then activist (and later president) Rómulo Betancourt called him "the instrument of foreign control of the Venezuelan economy" (1979, 43), and his ruthless secret police earned him the title of "tyrant of the Andes." When Gómez died, his successor, Eleazar López Contreras, who had basically been appointed by Gómez, succumbed to pressure by mass protests and immediately released hundreds of political prisoners who were being held in Maracay (see Martz 1964; Coronil 1997). During this post-dictatorship period *El reto* became one of the nation's most celebrated literary works (Espar 1998). Through the 1940s with Betancourt's successor, the novelist and later president Rómulo Gallegos, and others such as the writer and politician Arturo Uslar Pietri, Venezuela ushered in a new democratic nationalism of literary giants.

Torrealba was writing throughout this tumultuous period in an exploration of the regional language and the customs of his home state of Barinas, which he later governed from 1941 to 1944. The majority of his writings were derived from his devotion to *llanero*, or *campesino* music. He recorded several *corridos* (ballads) during his lifetime, including *El reto*. He published two subsequent versions as epic poems titled "Florentino y el Diablo" in 1950 and 1958.[6] The 1958 version, the most widely recognized, coincided with another push toward democracy following the regime of Marcos Pérez Jiménez.[7] Later, the same year of Torrealba's hit recording of "Florentino and the Devil," the country moved to a formal "transition to democracy" known as the Punto Fijo Pact. The Punto Fijo Pact solidified the power of three moderate parties: Acción Democrática (AD), the Comité de Organización Política Electoral Independiente (COPEI), and the Unión Republicana Democrática (URD). According to the proponents of the pact, the agreement stabilized Venezuela's democracy. However, in their attempt to install a liberal democracy, the elites of the Punto Fijo Pact in effect alienated radical groups and ultimately created weaknesses in the democratic viability of the parties that took control (Myers 2004). By the time Chávez was running for government, Torrealba's "Florentino and the Devil" had already become a populist repertoire in the country's political history of the twentieth century.

The popularity of the ballad-poem of "Florentino and the Devil" surged at these key moments in the turn toward democracy over a tumultuous century. From the mid-twentieth century, when Torrealba first recorded the poem, to the post-dictatorship, the story of humble Florentino harbored great hopes for change. The 1958 Punto Fijo Pact, however, locked out a major sector of the majority rural poor from the national political process, opening the way for yet another appearance of Florentino in the Chávez era.

The Campaign

Well before he came into the international spotlight as president of Venezuela, Hugo Chávez gained national attention as the commander of an attempted coup in 1992. The events that precipitated the coup began in 1989, when then second-term president Carlos Andrés Pérez of the AD party signed into law a controversial package of neoliberal reforms that caused the widespread disruption and protests of the Caracazo.[8] As described in chapter 2, Pérez's response came swiftly and forcibly: he ordered the army to suppress the demonstrations and shoot suspected looters. Though morally objecting to the Caracazo, Chávez and others began to organize inside the military to oppose the government. By the mid-1990s, after years of work (beginning in the 1980s), Chávez, who was born in the state of Barinas, was able to create a political movement within the armed forces, drawing on his many years as a lecturer and working between various factions to consolidate both moderate and radical demands for change (Jones 2007). The painful memory of the Caracazo propelled this movement, making it possible for Chávez to persuade several key members of the armed forces to carry out a plot to overthrow Carlos Andrés Pérez in 1992 (see López Maya 2003; Ellner 2008; Trinkunas 2010). The plot failed. As its principal author, Chávez was captured and imprisoned for two years; he was released only after a pardon by the transition government of Rafael Caldera in 1994.

During this time, Chávez was recognized by many as a national hero. In a famous moment, he acknowledged the failure of the coup on national television, leaving one of the most enduring memes of the Chávez era. The moment was widely viewed, as all of those who had wondered about the mystery man who dared a military coup were finally able to catch a glimpse of him. The self-assured voice of Chávez did much to convince people that the intent for a regime change was serious, as was the possibility of its future. The responsibility was clear: "We failed to reach our objective," he said, adding after a half-beat pause, "for now." According to Ryan Brading, author of *Populism in Venezuela*, "The coup d'état failed; nonetheless, in a one-minute surrender speech, Chávez's *Por ahora* became an empty signifier that spontaneously captured the imagination and support of antagonized social sectors" (2012, 60). Those two words, "for now" (*por ahora*), came to stand in as a refrain for the movement, one that gave people hope for its eventual return.

During the two years Chávez spent in prison, the *contrapunteo* was performed for and about the commander-hero who had made history. As he served his sentence in a federal prison in Yare, just south of Caracas (coincidentally, home of the largest and best-known dancing-devils *cofradía* in the country), old song-poems were revisited and new ones were invented. At this point, however, popular support for Chávez was still an undocumented story. The Venezuelan historian María Eugenia di Benedetto (2000) explores this "unofficial" history of the mid-1990s. Di Benedetto describes the *contrapunteo* (again, the poem-song genre from the *llanos*) as a form of popular support and exchange. Songs about Chávez were also performed during this period to communicate directly with him, and to share an attitude and opinion about him and his actions (Di Benedetto 2000). Although few of the pieces from this period were recorded (most were improvised), it is important to keep in mind that this form of communicating support preceded Chávez's campaign for the presidency. Thus, by 1998, when he ran for the national elections, this form of popular cultural expression surrounding Chávez was already established—it wasn't a spontaneous result of Chávez's demagoguery. Thus, populist agency, and one could say, populist repertoires, had developed and gained traction among Venezuelan citizens in ways that were uncharted and well under way before Chávez became president.

Chávez certainly strengthened a broad-based popular movement in the course of his electoral campaign in 1998, galvanizing his support among the popular and middle classes. Running on a coalition-party ticket, Chávez went from town to town across the country in a whirlwind campaign that resulted in a solid win of the presidential elections with 56.2 percent of the vote.[9] One year later, he won the Constitutional Assembly with 59.8 percent, which essentially gave him free rein to rewrite the constitution.[10] His new constitution added many substantive claims to the revolutionary program, such as health care as a human right (articles 83–85); guaranteed political representation; land rights for indigenous groups; land reform; and environmental protections. While it is considered one of the most progressively "advanced" constitutions, it was also controversial for increasing presidential powers and reducing the two-chamber legislative body to one.

The new constitution of 1999 further consolidated Chávez's goal of situating Bolivarianism, which bore the name and memory of the national liberator from Spanish colonial rule, Simón Bolívar, as a twenty-first-century "revolution" against the neoliberal fiscal constraints that had been deeply resented during the Pérez administration. The Constitutional Assembly directly opposed the agenda of the dominant parties, AD and COPEI, and sought a political opening for the needs of the majority poor in the areas of health care, housing, local microeconomic development, agricultural reform, literacy, and education (see Ellner 2005).

Despite a clear victory at the polls in favor of Chávez in 1998 and again in 2000, the coalition party against Chávez, Coordinadora Democrática (CD), formulated a plan to depose the Chávez government and thus end the revolution.[11] The plan included two major events: a coup in which opposition leaders would remove Chávez by force from the Palacio de Miraflores and, as backup, a national strike to paralyze the oil industry and thus force regime change by inducing economic instability.

The coup against Chávez was a highly scripted plan. It opened with a concerted denunciation of Chávez's right to govern. Several military and business leaders called for Chávez's resignation. National media, including the major television networks, newspapers, and radio programs firmly controlled by the opposition, repeatedly called for demonstrations against the government.[12] Finally, a bonanza rally by the opposition set a course to crash into a pro-government rally. The result was a deadly collision that most global media reported as sufficient rationale for the president's removal, supposedly for the protection of the people. What they did not realize was that an independent documentary team was already in the Palacio Miraflores filming as the events transpired. Their film, *The Revolution Will Not Be Televised*, showed a very different narrative than what was reported by the global media. The film thus created an unexpected wedge in the credibility of the events that followed.

On April 12, 2002, opposition leaders carried out a military coup to depose Chávez. Among the coup leaders were chief strategists Pedro Carmona, then-president of the Venezuelan Federation of Chambers of Commerce (Fedecámaras); Gustavo A. Cisneros, the head of Venevisión; and Marcel Granier, the head of Radio Caracas Television (RCTV); and including Leopoldo López Gil (board member of the newspaper *El Nacional* and father of Leopoldo López, a major force in the *guarimba* street protests of the present day).[13] Armed guards locked the gates and took control of the presidential palace, while the president was taken by helicopter to an unrevealed location (see Cannon 2004; Wilpert 2012). During the events of the coup, it is fascinating to note that two of the largest media channels owned by Carmona's supporters (channels 4 and 23) aired reruns of cartoons, a move that infuriated viewers from across the political spectrum. Despite the confusion on the ground and a media blackout involving literally Looney Tunes, within hours the White House spokesman Ari Fleischer reported to the international media that Chávez had suppressed a peaceful demonstration and then resigned.[14] The United States immediately recognized the Carmona coup, lending the coup legitimacy in a moment of uncertainty and suspicion. On the streets, however, the word was getting out that the president had been kidnapped, and people began to gather at the Palacio de Miraflores. And here is where the script began to falter.

As soon as news leaked out that Chávez had been kidnapped, thanks to motorcycle-messenger brigades that began calling people to action up and down the streets of the barrios, mass groups of protesters stormed the gates of the presidential palace, demanding Chávez's return. Eventually, one of the armed guards opened the gates (reportedly he was sympathetic to Chávez), and the protesters physically took over the presidential headquarters. As crowds of people occupied Miraflores, Chávez was returned by a rescue party.[15] Eventually the crowds began to go home, but the consolidation of "*el pueblo*" around these events did not dissipate. Over the next several years, the plaza became a permanent installation of independently organized pavilions in memory of the people's defense of the president.

In the aftermath of the failed coup, the country's former oil executives launched their backup plan to oust Chávez by leading a two-month oil strike and lockout that severely debilitated all operations of the state; losses ran to roughly US$7 billion (Buxton 2005, 333). Executives and employees of the state oil company who sided with the opposition refused to open buildings, stopped all oil production, and ceased shipments in and out of the country's ports over the month of December.[16] Their rallying cry was "2002 without Christmas, 2003 without Chávez!" (Jones 2007, 377). Meanwhile, the international organization Human Rights Watch, which many considered to be biased against the Chávez administration, issued a formal statement imploring the opposition to cease its violent action and use legal means to oust Chávez from the presidency (see Human Rights Watch 2008; Tinker-Salas, Wilpert, and Grandin 2009; and Leech 2013).

In 2003, with businesswoman María Corina Machado at the helm, the main opposition group Súmate petitioned legal channels for a midterm referendum election. If the referendum petition obtained a sufficient number of signatures, a new election would be held for the presidential office.[17] After several unsuccessful attempts to undercut the administration in the years prior, Machado adopted this legal mechanism of the referendum, a mechanism that Chávez had sponsored that was designed to structurally enforce the terms of participatory democracy during the constitutional reforms of 1999 (Hellinger 2005).[18] In May 2004, a coalition of opposition groups (including Súmate) under the umbrella name of Coordinadora Democrática gathered and submitted to the National Elections Committee (CNE) the petition to initiate a recall referendum. While many groups contested the validity of the signatures and the legality of open funding by the United States's National Endowment for Democracy, Chávez eventually accepted the recall process that was negotiated in part by the Carter Center and stated his resolve to lead a campaign against the referendum, declaring on national radio that the election would "demonstrate to the world where the majority really stands."[19] On June 8, Francisco Carrasqueño, president of the CNE, announced that the election would be held on August 15, 2004, just two months after the petition was ratified.[20]

The showdown was officially on, and political handlers started to unveil their ideas for how to approach the campaign. Minister of Communication and Information Jesse Chacón said that Chávez had initially envisioned announcing the referendum election from an outdoor location in the Plaza Bolívar. Despite his intentions, Chávez was persuaded to deliver the speech in his office to facilitate what Chacón described as his desired effect of a "close connection between the people and the president" (see interview in Francia 2005, 53). Chacón arranged for a camera lift to be installed in the presidential quarters in order to allow for broader camera movements. Outside, large screens were set up in front of the *palacio* with scaffolds and speakers broadcasting the speech across the Plaza Bolívar.

As Chávez rehearsed his speech in his office, a detailed account by Néstor Francia (2005) tells us that the president marked his delivery by referring to the objects in the room.[21] He gestured to a small statue of Christ in the corner, saying, "Let's start over here, with Christ." Then he signaled to the portrait of Bolívar. "Then we'll move to Bolívar and later to the Sucre. When we're at Sucre, we'll begin to talk numbers since Sucre was actually an engineer, a statistician."[22] Then he motioned to a bust of Ezequiel Zamora that was on his desk. "We'll put Zamora in this corner," and at that moment he summoned an aide to retrieve Ignacio Pérez Arcay's historical account of the Federal War (1859–63). Chávez opened the book to the strategic map of the Battle of Santa Inés (1859) and discussed with Chacón the concept of analogizing the referendum campaign to the battle. Moments later he asked for the text of "Florentino and the Devil" by Alberto Arvelo Torrealba. Although Chacón remembered that Chávez had referred to these analogies before, nevertheless, as he describes it, it was remarkable for him to watch Chávez assembling the material only a few hours before an address on national television. It was a performance, an improvisation, and one that Chávez insisted would be live. Not live to tape, as advisors had suggested; he preferred a simultaneous delivery.

Notwithstanding these unconventional and seemingly remarkable methods of preparing the national address, I want to suggest that these are not so much spontaneous acts, but rather evidence of the repertoires that make up populism, the practiced and patterned connections and stories that did not only belong to Chávez, but that existed in a realm of popular beliefs and customs.

By midmorning, people had begun to gather outside the *palacio*. Many who favored unseating the president were already celebrating what they thought would be an easy road to victory. Chávez supporters, on the other hand, were discontented with the president's appointed committee, Comando Ayacucho, which they felt had been too quick to dismiss the reports of the opposition engaging in fraudulent practices in collecting petition signatures. Chávez had not done enough, in their view, to curb the ruthless tactics of the opposition. The president had been too lenient in accepting the petition, caving in to political pressure from the opposition and international observers. As political scientist Sujatha Fernandes observes, "Some activists wondered if perhaps Chávez had brokered a deal with the opposition. Others said that the Comando Ayacucho was simply incompetent. In a series of local assemblies in La Vega, 23 de Enero, and other barrios, community leaders emphasized the need for self-organization, saying that barrio residents could not rely on the government and officially appointed committees to organize 'on their behalf' " (2007b, 18). Many Chávez supporters were disillusioned by the referendum vote because to them it represented a conciliatory and unwarranted concession to opposition pressure.

Barrio residents had already been mobilized to count and verify the votes, taking up the duties of state to officiate the elections.[23] Therefore, when Chávez spoke, it was a particularly charged moment, full of anticipation and divisions among both supporters and opponents of the Chávez administration. Some people placed their televisions outside their houses to watch with neighbors from the comfort of a front yard. Viewed on giant screens set outside of the *palacio* and aired on three major channels, Chávez's speech

Figure 9. In the corner opposite the Palacio de Miraflores, and in several other locations, pavilions such as these facilitate public discussion and debate. Author photo, Caracas, 2008.

reached people in living rooms, in cafés, on streets, and in plazas on the evening of June 3, 2004.

We are thus reminded, as Ngũgĩ wa Thiong'o wrote, that the performance space is not empty; rather, "it is constituted by the totality of its external relations to these other centres and fields" (1997, 13). In Caracas this history was palpable on streets and in plazas such as the downtown Plaza Bolívar, where the public's memories of the Caracazo (1989), Chávez's coup attempt (1992), Chávez's election (1998), and the Carmona coup (2002) had produced participatory action. In 2008, the plaza still had several small pavilion tents in its corners that offered chairs, tables, television viewing, and sometimes lunch (see figure 9). Presently, people gather in these spaces to hear speakers and debate the issues. These primarily Chavista corners, each representing different ideological leanings but all generally in support of the president, are stations in the plaza that remind people of the last decade of political change and of the participatory movement surrounding those historical moments. These installments in the Plaza Bolívar exist as evidence of the embodied memory of populist repertoires.

For example, let us return to 2004, on the night of Chávez's announcement of the referendum, when several thousand people gathered at the Palacio de Miraflores. The memories associated with this site include ordinary people occupying the plaza for long periods of time, claiming the space as their own, singing songs en masse, and communicating both through and outside the regulated media. Supporters of the Bolivarian Revolution had already rehearsed these populist repertoires during the coup attempt of 2002, which still reverberated in the political spaces of the campaign.

I view the two-month recall referendum campaign of 2004 as a historic moment in which Chávez and his supporters assumed the role of Florentino in a full merger of performance and populism, one that would activate a broad-based constituency and set the terms for participatory democracy in the country. This was not an example of the president's personality or outward-facing "style" bowling over an unwitting public in the political moment; there was a very different dynamic at play. In the next section, I examine some of the complexities in the president's speech to illustrate how performance communicates differently off the written page as an improvised act and a form of charisma mutually generated by actor and audience. I argue that the speech (and the campaign) were performed in ways that carried its production of the *contrapunteo* along with it—the improvisation, the cultural practice, and popular occupation of the Plaza Bolívar.

During his address to the nation on June 3, 2004, Chávez set up the recall-election campaign as a reenactment of the battle of "Florentino y el Diablo." With deference to the CNE, which would determine the rules and parameters of the referendum, Chávez began by telling the story of King Pyrrhus, who lost more in victory than he would have gained in peace. "This is a reflection," Chávez said, "for those who sing victory to remind them of the process by which they claim that victory and the value of their own achievement" (Francia 2005). The process of democracy must prevail, where the referendum itself was a victory for a more fully participatory democracy.

Savoring the irony at the end, to capture the bittersweet moral of Pyrrhic victory, Chávez reminded his audiences that the process of democracy was at stake: would the opposition minority accept the policy changes that the majority freely endorsed? Chávez then segued to how he saw his current political position as analogous to the federal wars of the mid-nineteenth century, specifically the Battle of Santa Inés. He told his audience how in 1859 the rebels led by General Ezequiel Zamora had retreated into the irrigation ditches of the village of Santa Inés in the state of Barinas. They established positions with four lines of defense and waited for the federalist forces to attack. The idea was that each line of defense would fall back, luring its opponents into the innermost and strongest rebel position. After the conservatives appeared to have won, their troops found themselves caught inside the rebel perimeters and unable to penetrate the long lines of trenches that had been dug by the villagers of the town. The conservative forces were then overwhelmed and surrounded by the sheer numbers of rebels in the trenches. Chávez's supporters knew that, like the Devil that challenges Florentino, those who lack local knowledge—in this case knowledge of how to navigate the geography—are eventually forced to withdraw. The Battle of Santa Inés was known as a decisive victory for the rebels. The popular majority overtook an enemy that was better equipped and better trained by drawing them into its home turf.

In his national address, Chávez described the victory of Zamora, "the general of the sovereign people," as "a model of how an adversary force is handled: it is denied advance and brought to a definitive battle." He compared his own campaign to Zamora's military campaign: "This seems to me so similar to the battle of Santa Inés, so similar that today I announce to all Venezuelans that I will lead the command of the campaign of Santa Inés from today to the final vote of the referendum" (Francia 2005, 18). Embedded within the performance of the speech, as Chávez recited the story of Santa Inés and "Florentino and the Devil," were also the proposed terms for inclusion and exclusion of the social body of the revolution: the election process was the deciding factor that represented the trenches of Santa Inés; the majority poor were at the center of the revolutionary program (as a participatory democracy); those with *el pueblo* would be metaphorically in the trenches to vote, while those who chose to sabotage, or otherwise not respect the results of the election, would be exposed on the open field and ultimately be forced to resign.

The analogy between the referendum and the Battle of Santa Inés could not have been stronger. For Chávez and his supporters, the recall campaign had mobilized already-organized groups to claim and defend their national political space. For these groups, after the events of the previous five years, the main issues were the right to govern and democracy itself. Most of Chávez's supporters worked long hours at low-paying jobs, believing in the possibility of advancement through the electoral process. After decades of disillusionment, the scenario of the Battle of Santa Inés provided a strategic blueprint to visualize and rehearse the capacity of the poor to overcome what they saw as an intervention in a legitimate democracy.

From the conceptual battleground of Santa Inés, the president's speech then turned to Alberto Arvelo Torrealba's epic poem based on the legend and ballad of "Florentino and the Devil." Chávez contemplatively took Torrealba's book in his hand and read aloud the opening passage. "*El coplero Florentino, por el ancho terraplén*" ("The poet-singer Florentino, on the wide sloping plains"), he began. "It was six o'clock in the afternoon when the *catire* [blondie] Florentino was retracing his steps on the great plains when he realized he was being followed by a mysterious horse rider who suddenly came up beside him." Chávez stepped out of the narrative for a moment to comment: "Listen to what the legend says. Listen to the devil that went past with this black hat, and you couldn't see his eyes, and then he sings out to Florentino *el reto* [a challenge] and he says, 'If you dare, my friend, come see me in Santa Inés, for I'm looking to sing with you.' The *catire* Florentino stays perfectly still, frozen by the horror of what he saw. But when he recovers, he makes the sign of the cross." Chávez crossed himself with careful precision and then continued reading: "One for my soul, and one for faith in God, I will stop and respond" (Francia 2005, 76–77). Chávez paused and looked up from the book: "Like today, I . . . respond here in this broadcast. To those who have challenged me: to Santa Inés! The *coplero* said it then, and now today I say it to those who challenge me: May this shady singer know that I follow through with my word, and since I've sung with everyone I have to sing with him as well." He continued to comment off the page, "May this mysterious singer/*coplero* know that I follow through with my word, and I have won seven elections and will win the eighth as well in the land of Santa Inés!" (Francia 2005).

With these words, Chávez harnessed the dramatic force of the poem to his campaign—the victory at the polls would be the Battle of Santa Inés again, with the voters as the protagonists of their and his story, their and his own Santa Inés. By remaining almost entirely true to the text of "Florentino and the Devil," he did more than bring literary history and readings into the elections. On the one hand, he created a situation in which the reading of a familiar story of a struggle against tyranny brought the current political moment to new clarity. The pairing of these two concepts made sense to people, convincing millions that, like Florentino, even when Chávez was faced with unknown or incommensurable odds, his election would mean an epic victory over perceived tyranny. His victory would be not just a victory of his right to represent the demands of many; it would be the victory of many to defend their own democracy. There was also something about knowing the two stories, one an allegory of traditional meanings and the other a yet-undetermined political moment, that resonated or made sense together. The speech performance thus became the medium through which this pairing of the elections and "Florentino" could take place.

On the other hand, the speech also suggested that the opposition was closer kin to the Devil than to Florentino. Where the story of "Florentino and the Devil" played off the binary forces of good and evil, the speech also seemed to carry this binary logic into the context of a national campaign. As if aware of the implications of aligning those who had signed the referendum petition with the Devil, Chávez was careful to clarify that by "evil" he was not speaking generally of the forces of the opposition. He said, "I'm not referring to those Venezuelans who fight in the opposition; rather [I refer] to those elites of the conspiratory opposition, this opposition that has fallen into coups, terrorism, and, more recently, paramilitarism. This has much to do with this devil, this devil that casts a challenge. I accept it" (Francia 2005). Here Chávez qualifies the story to ensure that the law-abiding opposition should *not* be categorically associated with the Devil. Recalling the discontentment among supporters over the fact that the referendum had legitimized a group (Súmate) that had been directly affiliated with the coup, the oil lockout, and mass street disturbances, the election was already controversial for both sides (see Hellinger 2005). Again, Chávez asked both the opposition and his constituency to respect the results of the referendum and the rules of participation that the CNE, as a neutral body, had procedurally established in partnership with international observers (Carter Center 2005). Furthermore, Chávez invited the referendum to build a newfound unity, a triumph in which democracy would prevail.

Yet for some Chávez's speech triggered a very different response. Many among the opposition to him felt that his speech undermined the democratic process of the referendum. Despite his clarification, the speech story appeared to conflate the million-plus signees of the referendum petition with the *reto* of the *Diablo*. Those who disagreed with Chávez felt that the speech maligned their interests. The criticism seemed legitimate, considering the story-logic of "Florentino and the Devil"; the story, taken as a binary, produced a residual alignment between the oppositional minority and the Devil. What is interesting is how much the story, in some ways, overshadowed Chávez's attempt to qualify the speech. How did Chávez's variation of the story register across the ambiguous terrain of those who simply disagreed with the president's agenda of reform and were exercising their democratic rights to support his recall, versus those individuals and interests that were deeply invested in preventing the majority, by forcible and illegal means, from exercising their democratic rights to bring about political change? Chávez made a necessary shift by clarifying what may have felt ambiguous. Interestingly, this is where the story in turn was performed by a chorus, or among various contending publics, in different ways. Where the original written text of the poem emphasizes a binary, Chávez's speech (and, for that matter, the performed musical ballad) actually *pulls back* from attributing evil to all members of the opposition and instead begins to qualify the terms "good" and "bad," again using the opportunity to delineate the very terms of democracy.

For his part, Chávez clearly searched for a way to reconcile the tensions between the democratic principles he espoused and the real challenge the recall campaign presented to his administration. In some ways, his speech attempted to capture the holistic ethos of democratic ideals, and using the story-logic he abnegated his own role as a contender, relying instead entirely on "the people" as protagonists. It was clear that Chávez himself could not stand in for democracy, yet, as critics pointed out, he conflated his revolutionary program as synonymous with democracy. Thus, whether Chávez intended it to or not, the performed speech to accept the recall election opened an important space for and even a reliance on a third role of "the people" to ratify his vision of a new democracy.

At the end of his speech, Chávez sought direct contact with the crowd outside of the Palacio de Miraflores, as if, by the presence (and transfer) of his body, he would suture the divisions that he had just created in the speech. To be assured of reciprocity between himself and the crowd, he interrupted himself to ask, "Are you seeing me from out there? Raise your hand if you see me and hear me in front of the Palacio. [Applause can be heard.] That's great! I too am seeing you; a kiss and my love for all of you and a hug from this Hugo that belongs to you in body, soul, life, and heart." In the closing of his speech, he said, "You, the Venezuelan people will demonstrate, one more time, that the people of the South American liberator are capable of stopping an oligarchy that pretends to again take over the homeland of Bolívar. And this government and this one, your humble servant, has a sword and a heart ready to love you and defend you and always unite us" (Francia 2005, 226).

According to Néstor Francia, who was in the crowd, the speech provoked a "radical turn in the attitudes of the people" (2005, 55). But the turn that Francia refers to is one from a radical rejection of the referendum among supporters who saw it as a continued effort to undermine the government, to a renewed commitment to honor the democratic process. The speech also resulted in the paralysis of the opposition. Chacón explains: "Before the president spoke, people were asking for the heads of the members of the Comando Ayacucho. When the president ended his talk, it was quite a different thing. And when he threw his tie up over the crowd of people, the change was total. . . . The march of the opposition that was planned for the following Saturday was demoralized, and the Chavista demonstration the day following on Sunday the 6th overshadowed that of the opposition by hundreds of thousands" (quoted in Francia 2005, 55). What seemed to signify this radical turn, according to Francia, was the symbolic act of Chávez throwing his tie (the mark of his official status) into the hands of the people, signifying to a broader base of constituency—not just to his supporters, but to all—the principles of democracy to which Venezuela should aspire.

In his book *It*, Joseph Roach meditates on this question of how an actor exudes "it," the extraordinary quality of magnetic personalities that charms with an irresistible allure on stage and screen. This quality is not just about looks, he argues, and it is not even necessarily what an actor projects. In his analysis he points to the accessory—the hat, the tie, the purse—as a kind of effigy that restores life, "useless for all practical purposes and yet symbolically crucial" (2007, 55). Roach sees charisma as speaking through these seemingly trite objects to reveal what he calls the available body of the celebrity star.

> To accessorize is to make a useful sign out of a practical superfluity. The word accessory suggests not only a surplus or an excess . . . but also an oblique yet significant instrumentality. . . . The less practical the accessory item is, the more it means: even today, a tie—that refunctioned atavism of the nobleman's sword—is required of gentlemen because it has nothing useful to do . . .
>
> . . . It works as a prop to support his performance as he fights his way across the threshold of gentlemanly status and claims the social spaces beyond as his own. It makes him visible to himself and to

> others as what he wants to become. Therein lies its magic. In such charmed rites of passage, accessories are to implements what stages are to altars. (Roach 2007, 51–53)

In this insightful passage, Roach describes how the tie, replacing the sword, in essence is a symbol for a complex and richly social recognition of absence or of loss. The tie is more than "the one for the many" (Roach 2007, 53); it is an invitation or a sign of availability for "the many" to occupy the social vacuity that it actually represents.

If, in this case, the tie stands synecdochally for the presidential office, Chávez performatively transfers, as Roach would say, this "effervescence" of the accessory by throwing his tie to the crowd: "in that charmed puissance—the power publicly to imagine the whole by making visible the accessorized part—resides the theatrical foundation of modern enchantment" (Roach 2007, 54). This speech by Hugo Chávez, particularly its embodiment, with Chávez standing in live contact with thousands of people in the plaza, referencing the sword of Bolívar and throwing his tie to the crowd, reveals the very nature of what it means for one to become available for the many and highlights the nature of the relationship between the people and the state. The act of transfer is precisely the point. The emphatic, passionate, or heightened experience of this contractual exchange between the people and the state is an explicit language in itself; while the sober debate has its moment, so too does this ecstatic exchange in which the voices of millions echo through the available body of Chávez, carrying the sword (tie) in their hands.

Although popularity for the president soared following his speech, I want to return to the issue that critics were concerned about, that Chávez's rhetoric in the campaign maligned the opposition. Even more moderate members of the opposition wondered if they would have a space of dissent if the Devil was the only other part in the dramatic metaphor besides Florentino. What was missing from this critique, however, was acknowledgment of the pressure among the organized Left, which (as described in chapter 2) had been organizing on its own terms since the post-dictatorship period. What can be seen from the campaign is how Chávez dug deeper into the historical record in an attempt to rationalize and also mend these divisions. On the surface these populist references to specters of the past may seem to disguise the struggles of the present day, but Chávez set up these historical figures and situations as a kind of theatrical forum in which the roles and disputes of the current moment could be explained and played out, to his advantage, in historical debate.

In the 2004 recall election, the framework of campaign politics became a performance of national historical reenactment replete with action figures and plot lines. The campaign committee was named Comando Maisanta after Pedro Pérez Delgado, the rebel figure (and Chávez's great-grandfather) who opposed the Gómez regime (see Tapia 1974). Combined with the symbolism of "Florentino and the Devil" and the Battle of Santa Inés, the animacy of historical reenactments no doubt ruffled the feathers of those who wanted politics as usual. Indeed, it was a different way of performing politics, one that abandoned the advice of professional political handlers and moved instead, unabashedly, into a realm of cultural performance. Chávez personally directed the anti-recall campaign. The team he appointed to run his electoral campaign included few political cadres; instead, it "was dominated by artists and academics with little previous participation in politics" (Jones 2007, 409). They organized "electoral battle units" (UBEs) of five to ten members, each committed to convincing ten other people to vote against the referendum. According to one observer,

> many UBEs organized themselves street-by-street or building-by-building. Others focused not on where they lived but where they worked. They proved to be an effective electoral tool: an estimated 1.2 million people, or 4 percent of the population, joined a UBE. Many were activists in long-standing social movements or land and health reform committees. But for the majority it was their first experience in political activism. (Jones 2007, 409–10)

It is important to remember that the state did not control the major media during the election of 2004. Four of the five national networks (RCTV, Globovision, Venevisión, and Televen) were owned by opposition members who were fierce critics of the Chávez administration: a former correspondent for CNN in Latin America notes that "owners and managers of the private television stations in Venezuela have been openly aligned with the political opposition to Chávez for years."[24] Their political biases were apparent in their stations' broadcasts, which contained outright misrepresentations and racism directed at the president and his followers (Delacour 2004; Duno-Gottberg 2004, 2011). Virtually shut out of Venezuela's major televised networks, the Chávez campaign sought effective ways to maximize its visibility. Short, inexpensive, and effective advertising was necessary in order to reach large numbers of people in limited allotments of television time.

Once again tapping into popular cultural tropes of the Devil, the campaign developed a series of animated video clips that featured a Wile E. Coyote-inspired *Diablo* and a sombrero-clad Florentino, the latter playing out the Chávez position on political issues surrounding the election. Additionally, thousands of small groups of Chávez supporters generated their own versions of posters, handbills, mural art, and other locally distributed materials to support the campaign. The scenario of "Florentino and the Devil" was reactivated by artists and supporters performing in multiple expressive genres.

Within a few weeks after the onset of the campaign, popular participation erupted in multiple forms throughout the country. The Florentino song was played at large public events and even turned up in cell-phone jingles. People sang the *coplas*, both familiar and improvised verse, at demonstrations and public gatherings.[25] Demonstrators on the streets portrayed "Florentino and the Devil" in puppetry and street theater. A hip-hop rap song by MC Arena y MC Robex put the battle of the humble *campesino* and the Devil in an urban context; their version, which included samples from Chávez's speech, reached the top of the Venezuelan music charts.[26] People improvised their own lyrics for the song-poem and created new music to express their political views in direct support of the president (Valencia Ramírez 2008). In these examples, popular performance became more than just an initiative of the campaign organizers; it was a co-creation among artists, activists, and the state and a voice for active political engagement. Perhaps growing beyond what Chávez could have predicted, the kinds of agential politics that emerged from music, dance, theater, and street art were largely outside the scope of politics as usual.[27] Performance, in this case, became a medium for populism, broadening the field of who was participating in national political discourse. Extending beyond an idea of good versus evil, populism seemed to flourish as performance. Not only did Chávez's speech ignite its immediate audience, but the aftermath of artists and groups of people mobilizing on their own illustrates this powerful mix of populism and performance.

But was there any truth to the idea that Chavistas and the participatory democracy of Chavismo had entered an authoritarian discourse by promoting a battle against the Devil? Or would this performed media produce a different kind of consequence, perhaps one pointing toward a more fair and free society? There is a political answer. As María García-Guadilla has pointed out,

> the adjective "participatory" leaves open the question of whether liberal or radical democracy will be the main axis of orientation between civil society and the state. Which tendency emerges as dominant depends on whether participation develops as a complement to or a substitute for representation, on the type of criteria used to select the subjects or actors allowed to participate, on the extent to which the participation of minorities was permitted, and on whether the right to participate was defined by objective or partisan political criteria. (2003, 194)

These were essential questions for determining whether the state was likely to end up, as García-Guadilla puts it, "'kidnapping' preexisting sociopolitical actors and repeating a cycle of political exclusion familiar in Venezuelan history" (ibid.). The concern, it seemed, was that those previously privileged would be persecuted, and thus the pendulum would dangerously swing to threaten a minority that formally held power, or that once assuming power, the state (now in a new guise) would once again exert its influence against the majority poor.[28]

In this discussion, there is also a cultural equation to consider. Traditional music, the portrayal of the Devil, and the stories in Chávez's speech were perhaps vehicles of communication that were unsuitable or, as John Bolton and Condoleezza Rice claimed, "inappropriate" as means of conducting politics. The limits of civil society's inclusiveness therefore ran up against the very culture of the campaign.[29] These questions bring to mind the politics of the devil dances. If, as Chantal Mouffe argues, "society is always politically instituted . . . and it is never neutral" (2007), then were we not witnessing the crash of opposing hegemonic constructions that unfairly privileged some political cultures over others? To embark on this inquiry, we need to closely examine so-called proper and familiar political conduct to first delink what is not a neutral form but one highly constructed, learned, and also performed.

In this highly polarized society, a society that had been fractured over centuries of unequal distribution of wealth and unresolved trauma in the national collective psyche, political cultures contrasted. Edgardo Lander, a sociology lecturer at the Central University of Venezuela, says that before Chávez arrived on the scene, Venezuelan politics were "like an upper-class party in which everything was very refined and educated and cosmopolitan" (as quoted in Branford 2004, n.p.).[30] Conforming to the conventions of the professional class, campaign posters rarely deviated from clean, smooth lines, using polished headshots or sometimes a midrange shot that was careful to include a well-tailored suit and tie. In the 1998 election, the former beauty queen Irene Sáez was represented by a smiling image of blue eyes and flowing blond hair framed by kelly green, the COPEI party colors (she initially ran in her own party, but was endorsed by COPEI in the run against Chávez).[31] Few campaign posters varied from the head-and-shoulders view of a suited candidate with party-color endorsements.[32]

By 2004, the political culture of Venezuela had shifted considerably, and audiences accustomed to certain norms were confronted with a very different style of communication. From the perspective of conventional campaigns—even in Venezuela, where populist and dramatic speeches are more often a convention—Chávez's "Florentino and the Devil" speech was over the top. Chávez's actions—bringing a book into his speech, reading from it spontaneously, and throwing his tie into the audience—contrasted with the pre-Trump sobering officiality of campaign politics in the United States. The political culture of Chavismo was decidedly different, prompting concern and even alarm among those of the previous government establishment who had leveraged the idea of performance to discredit Chávez's administration as unruly and clownish.

Yet the question remains: Did Chávez's performance generate an exclusionary political style, or was it a mirror held up to the exclusionary logics of the political establishment? Could it have been both? Where some saw the speech as demonizing the privileged opposition and opening old wounds, others saw a condemnation of injustices that was part of a spirit to heal the open wounds of historical injustice and violence. The speech was one of Chávez's most successful and certainly most memorable political performances. Was it Chávez's skill as an entertainer, the smoothness of his transitions in and out of the text, and the particular style or quality of his poetic reading that made the Florentino narrative convincing? If, for Laclau, populism is based on a chain of agreements, how did the performance of the speech fray or secure those bonds?

While the performatic elements of the speech—its theatricality, flow, and dramatic technique—certainly contributed to its impact, I believe this particular moment was also affected by a much more profound dismantling of the distance between the state and the people affected. This was a dismantling of a particular hegemony of secular political conduct, the same measure of proper conduct that dismissed ritual performance as political. This was a shared presence in communication that dethroned liberalism in search of a political autonomy, a continuity of the "we" that has remained in the national, collective psyche from the independence wars to the present day.

In the next chapter I will examine this last point further and from a different direction. For now, I will turn to two examples from the campaign to explore how performance factors in to the urban populism of this high point of the Chávez era. In the first example, I look at short ad clips featuring "Florentino and the Devil" that were produced by campaign organizers, and in the second I examine a controversial poster produced by an ad hoc student group and union.

The "No" as an Icon of the Popular

One of the most striking performances of politics in the 2004 recall-referendum campaign can be seen in a series of fifteen- to thirty-second video clips produced in support of Chávez that feature animated "Florentino and the Devil" figures fashioned in the likenesses of the 1948 Warner Brothers Looney Tunes characters Road Runner and Wile E. Coyote. Illustrated in the bright yellow, blue, and red colors of the Venezuelan flag, these characters engage in various episodes of conflict about issues raised in the campaign. The title of the series, in folksy block letters, is a line taken directly from the poem "Florentino y el Diablo": "*El Diablo pasa trabajo*" ("The Devil is taken to task"). These short videos, which offer a catchy jingle and clear, precise concepts, animated the demands and agenda of the Chávez constituency during the referendum campaign.

In this television campaign, the Florentino figure projects the humble *llanero* of Arvelo Torrealba's poem onto the Chavista platform. The campaign video shorts feature Florentino with his characteristic cowboy hat and red kerchief humbly facing up to a wily and nefarious gray Devil who surreptitiously makes away with natural resources and financial markets. In each of the clips, Florentino foils the Devil's plan and returns the public services of health care, education, land rights, and job opportunities to the people.[33] In one typical scenario, as a gloating *Diablo* (Devil) presides over an oil field, a multitude of sky-blue Florentinos, all wearing colors of the Venezuelan flag, waddle in unison over the hillside to take it back from the *Diablo*, all to the background tune of "Florentino." They quickly send the Devil running for cover, overwhelming him with their numbers, and thus reclaim their rights to the petroleum industry.

In another of the video clips, the Comando Maisanta team shows the *Diablo* figure being confronted again, but this time by the ubiquitous messaging of the "No," suggesting popular support for the "No" vote against the recall of the president. In the first frame, the *Diablo* drives a large gray convertible with flashing red tail fins and a giant set of horns attached to the front fender. The Texas-longhorn hood ornaments reappear later on the fence posts of the *Diablo*'s gated mansion, perhaps a reference to the greed of oilmen. As he drives along, the *Diablo* sees an enormous billboard at the top of one of Caracas's high-rises that features the word "*VenezolaNO*" (meaning "Venezuelan") with the "NO" in large type and blazing red. Shocked, the *Diablo* continues, only to find other signs sporting the word "NO" as he moves across the cityscape. When he enters his mansion, the television screen features the words "*Aló CiudadaNO*," a play on the name of an opposition-led television show, "Hello Citizen," hosted by Leopoldo Castillo as the counterpart to the president's own live weekly broadcast of "Aló Presidente" ("Hello President"). The *Diablo* is ultimately overwhelmed, unable to escape the proliferation of the NO.

The "No" component of the campaign frequently appeared as a red word on a white background inside a red dialogue bubble, like those used for print comics.[34] This "container" for the "No" provided a particularly effective vehicle for communicating the act of voicing "No" as a live speech act. By saying "No" to the recall referendum, the message not only rehearses the political act of making one's voice heard, but also says "No" more broadly to the previous political establishment and to the current one that had rallied to revoke Chávez's term in office. The ideas voiced within the dialogue container of the comic strip became the new politics of the revolution.

There was also a public memory of taking up the negative in defense of the revolution prior to the recall campaign. One of the principal rally tunes of the Chávez contingency during the referendum debate months earlier was a song that included the line, "*Uh, ah, Chávez NO se va*" ("Oh, ah, Chávez is *not* going"). This became a ubiquitous refrain during the campaign. The "No" was also used in the phrase "*No volverán*" ("They're not coming back"), referring to the return of previous leaders of state. The "No" enunciated resistance to a powerful elite in the opposition party. Chacón describes the importance of the "No" to Chávez supporters: "We're contestational, we're always opposing something [he laughs], we say 'no' to things. Of course, whoever was managing the publicity logistics considered it difficult to strip the 'No' of its negative connotation, to convert it into something positive. But we assumed that it would be that way and we had to work on the issue" (quoted in Francia 2005, 55). To convert the "No" into something positive meant more than just creating a positive outcome for the president. In some ways, campaign organizers discovered that the issues they faced in converting the "No" into support for Chávez pointed precisely to the fragility of state hegemony.

With national and international media generating what Luis Britto García (2008) calls the "media dictatorship," it is important to emphasize that the state did not control the media at this time. Arguably there was no hegemony of the state, and the revolutionary government lived in constant threat of being dismantled even though its leadership was democratically elected. The campaign was not about policy; it was about whether Chávez and the majority who had supported him in previous elections had a right to govern at all. It was a challenge that, in the end, Chávez supporters embraced judo-style with the refusal expressed in "No." It was also built upon layered repetitions of populist repertoire.

Like the story of "Florentino and the Devil," the "No" campaign went viral. It turned up in posters, on billboards, on hats, and in digital graphics and became a symbol of visibility for Chavismo throughout the country. The flexible wordplay that associated "VenezolaNO" with "FlorentiNO" became the center of one of the promotional pieces that was aired on television, and was a common motif in the print materials, posters, and banners that appeared in nearly all the campaign materials. There were huge demonstration murals with the word *NO* printed at the top of one of the largest housing projects in Caracas. In the city of Mérida, the letters *NO* were visible on a mountainside, created with sacks of chalk that farmers reportedly arranged in a clearing. According to Francia, these variations showed that each region added its own reality and idiosyncrasies to the "No": "The simplicity of the NO corresponded with the great creativity of our people, and although our campaign command was centralized, we wanted to combine this with the freedom for people on the streets to construct their own developments." Key to the functionality of the "No" was the capacity of this "freedom of the street" (Francia 2005, 57). And indeed, supporters brought their own ideas and actions to the campaign. The cartoon dialogue bubble turned up as hand-painted signs on houses and in shop windows. The word "No" was painted on and etched into the walls of urban buildings and on other surfaces of the cityscape. Hats, T-shirts, and other materials were produced in such huge quantities that the country experienced an unexpected shortage in material made of the color red. As Francia states, the overwhelming response even surprised the members of the Comando Maisanta campaign team. Most of the "No" materials, affirmed Francia, were produced by organizations and individuals on their own accord, independent of the official campaign team.

During the recall-election campaign, the choice to identify with the "No" vote was an expressive branding of Chavismo. Even though voting for Chávez in previous elections had meant ticking the "Yes" side of the ballot, his campaign team was able to effectively and definitively change that for the recall election. In that election, Chávez and what he stood for was clearly associated with the assertion of "No." Because audiences were familiar with the story of "Florentino and the Devil" and its relationship to the political messages of the moment, they had a point of entry and a voice they could use as coproducers of the meaning of the campaign. Thus the campaign opened a space for people to express visible local engagement (voice and action) with the issues and the election, this time as protagonists of the process who, to a certain degree, exercised operative control over the campaign.

These populist repertoires of the recall-election campaign aligned with a broader and more inclusive genealogy of popular struggle. It reactivated historical figures associated with major issues of racial equality, the continental union, and sovereignty. From Bolívar to José Leonardo Chirinos to Zamora, these figures grounded certain issues within an extended philosophy of Chavismo in 2004. Chávez and his supporters sought to align the Bolivarian Revolution with a twentieth-century struggle to democratize the country in order to include voices that had been excluded from previous regimes. "No" was one of the expressions that most aptly conveyed the idea of resistance to the "shrines of power" in the media, military, economy, and state that situated the people's resistance within a larger historical and geographical framework.

The cartoon version of "Florentino and the Devil" also did a particular work of infusing humor and irony in ways that I will argue ultimately diffused a good-versus-evil dualism. First, in the cartoon's limited fifteen- to thirty-second format, the same action is repeated over a dozen short scenarios in a continual cycle. The effect is to bend time in what could be seen as a cycle of futility. The Coyote—in this case the *Diablo*—is the emblem of this futility. Comparing the Road Runner to Sisyphus, Douglas Bruce writes, "Both Sisyphus and Wile E. Coyote exist outside of the cruel, binary logic of the life-world, the logic of one or zero that postulates the only choices as dead or alive, yes or no. . . . Theirs seems to be a world whose logic is fractional rather than binary. In such a world, there are infinite possibilities between one and zero. There is always a smaller fraction between the two numbers, always another opportunity to roll the boulder up the hill, or to organize and fail at another chase" (2001, 239). This fractional world seems to be the very framework of debate that exercises and expands the antagonistic frontier of populist decision-making.

If we see the antagonistic frontier as only the result of sorting roadrunners from coyotes, or saints from devils, then we are missing the acts of deliberation, the sticking power of allegory, and the fractional logic that undergird these processes. We are once again obliterating the history and extensive production networks that go into identifying the variable meanings at the heart of the democratic process. This is the problem with viewing populism only through text instead of through a much wider range of media.

Moreover, the idea in these cartoons is also to "take the Devil to task" in which the videos served as a kind of public record of accountability.[35] To take the Devil to task meant contrasting the unacceptable behaviors and political proposals of the "Devil" with a set of principles and a moral prerogative toward a program defined in the ad clips as an ethical stance of humanism. In such a scenario, the cartoon campaign spots are not merely a reenactment of an endless battle, but also a renewed opportunity to lay out the stakes for Florentino-Chávez's program in health care, education, transportation, and food justice.

Wile E. Coyote's attempts to usurp or surreptitiously take control of resources or public opinion are always met by the matter-of-fact simplicity of Florentino, who consistently dodges the increasingly complicated schemes of the *Diablo*. Just as the Road Runner foils every plan that Wile E. Coyote devises (with the ever-confounding technologies of the Acme Corporation), Florentino defeats the *Diablo* every time by letting him trip on his own devices. If the *Diablo* is an opposition that has access to the major media, millions of dollars of U.S. aid, and the polished skills and resources of the "professional" class, it is precisely his morally questionable uses of these technologies that render him helpless. In the end, these films cut down to size what was once an untouchable and dominant oppressor. The message is clear: this devil can be defeated.

Thus, the cartoon was one way to reduce the threat of an otherwise indomitable order. Laclau's notion of the underdog historical agent involves a process, where the act of consolidation into the "yea" and "nay" is an end result rather than a cause of populist reason to confront a political adversary. Fractional moments open a space for negotiation within the logic of dualism; this is the space of the performed animative. To recall Taylor's description, the animative might be seen as the "ruckus in the stadium," which is unlike the officiating power of the referees (Taylor 2007). To be populist and animative in this sense joins Chantal Mouffe's understanding of the "core of a vibrant democracy" with what she calls an agonistic struggle (2007, n.p.). The public space that Mouffe envisions is neither an authoritarian populism with officiating discipline, nor a mob politic, which is tersely reductive; this public space is "always plural" and functions through a variety of articulations. Much of this aspirational understanding of public space and democracy surfaced in the campaign. As one analyst describes, "In political terms, Chávez lured the opposition into his territory for the 2004 recall referendum—that is, into democratic territory, and away from coup mongering—to inflict a crushing defeat at the ballot box on the Venezuelan opposition" (Blough 2006). For Chavistas, the devil was not to signify the opponents of the referendum, nor the debate among difference, but precisely the opposite of the referendum itself: the foil to democracy, the coup that would squelch the debate.

In his 2004 speech, Chávez called on the framework of dualism but pushed against its boundaries; he turned back from labeling every opponent as the devil. In some ways, it can be argued, he merely reframed dualism as a struggle between the rich and powerful baddies and everyone else as the goodies. More importantly, though, as I'll be examining in the next section, Chávez invoked this Sisyphean myth or cosmic struggle and brought it into the political realm with the cosmology of the dancing devils, which actually operates not just as a shift from Manichaeism, but as its antidote.

Here performance breaks altogether with the binary logic associated with populism. The fractional logic of the *diablos* was a way to transform Manichaeism that was imposed on them. If Chávez was for some a polarizing figure, it was only because he was bringing to the surface the long-hidden dualism that had been carried forward through the centuries of the devil dances. To expose this logic is to embark on a much broader project of handling competing definitions of good and bad and competing definitions of how to deal with good and bad, within the legacy of civilization and barbarism. In the last section of this chapter, I turn to an example to continue this argument that what appears on its surface to be dualism in populist iconography contains within it a broadened episteme of issues and subjectivity, of history and historical memory, and a process of deliberation and exchange as performance.

Reversing Scenarios of Conquest

One example of the participatory production of the Comando Maisanta was a poster that was produced by El Tano Yea, an artist and leader of a student group and a member of and collaborator with a farmers' and longshore workers' union (see figure 10). The poster features Chávez bearing down on a tiny devil figure who is wearing festive horns and an opposition-party (CD) cheerleader outfit while waving a U.S. flag. Animating the devil even further, a bubble caption appears above it in which the devil claims to vote *¿Zí?* in favor of removing Chávez from office; a *Z* replaces the *S*, emphasizing a put-on lisp as if to parody peninsular Spanish.[36] At the top of the poster, a rainbow cascades into the squat and puffy letters *N-O*, recalling the 1988 Chilean referendum against Augusto Pinochet.

The central image resembles a page from the playbook of Saint James the Moorslayer (Santiago Matamoros): the figure of a patriarchal saint/state on a white horse bearing down on a diminutive subject. Scenarios, according to Taylor, are "portable, flexible frameworks for thinking and doing" (2016, 137). The scenario is not mere duplication. It is a reactivation. In Torrealba's story, young Florentino wields only his voice to defend himself against a much more terrifying, nefarious power. Later, in the cartoon, we see the equalizing effect of Wile E. Coyote and the Road Runner in an endless and

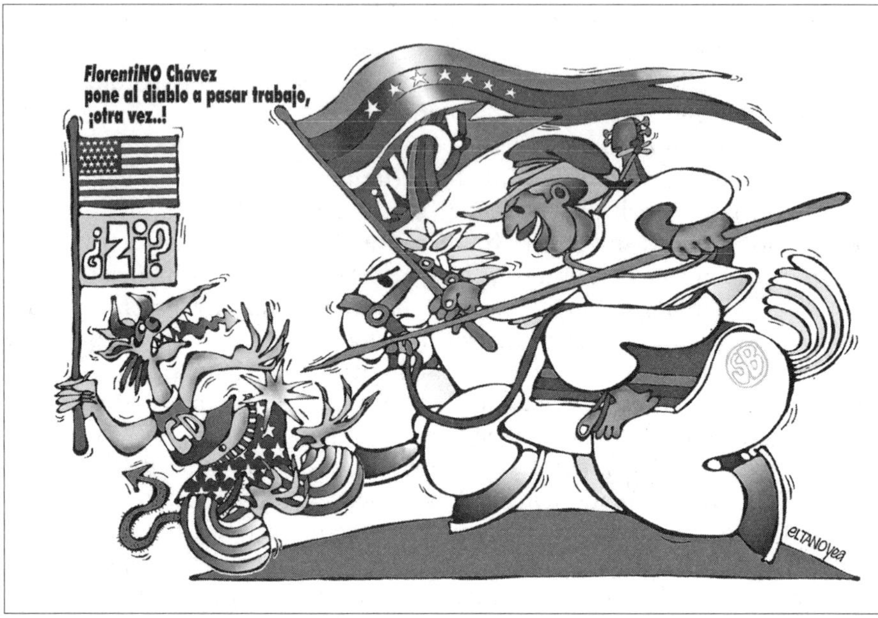

Figures 10 and 11. *Top*, a 2004 recall-election campaign poster. Image courtesy of the artist, El Tano Yea. *Bottom*, Santiago Matamoros (Saint James, the Moorslayer). Anonymous (Cuzco School), eighteenth century. Pedro de Osma Museum, Lima. Image courtesy of Hemis / Alamy.

repeating "cosmic struggle." But had Chávez as Florentino on a horse with a lance gone too far? Here the colonial scenario of Matamoros/*indios* serves with a campaign that had ostensibly sought to eradicate the colonial legacy of social and economic injustice. The poster provoked a new set of questions about the limits of the colonial scenario of conquest, models of liberation, and the revolutionary verve of the popular state.

In the scenario of conquest elicited in the poster, the conquistador saint-knight slays an abject figure, placed as a dragon and replaced over the centuries with infidels, devils, "moors," or *indios* depending on the context of the Christian avenger (see figure 11). The idea was to depict the saint as trampling unwanted subjects of church or state under the hooves of his horse, with sword in hand, to slay the beast and save the town. However, upon a closer look at the poster we see that the embodiment of Chávez is quite unlike the colonial knight; the person charging on the horse bears little resemblance to the usual conquistador. The bare toe in the stirrup isn't the shiny black boot of conquest or military dictatorship.

Chávez more closely resembles a traveling troubadour with a *cuatro* guitar slung across his shoulder. He rides with only a traditional saddle blanket and *llanero* cowboy hat. His Afro-indigenous features are pronounced, with the color of his skin emphasized as brown.[37] Images of Santiago Matamoros and Saint James the Dragonslayer typically epitomize a white heroic figure jockeying the horse. Placing the nonconforming body of Chávez in the saddle of colonial power does more than swap a mixed-race man into the seat of white power. It speaks more to the scenario than to any literal interpretations of the act.

While the poster seems to replay the story of the conquistador knight and the devil as a scenario of conquest with a new body in power, the symbolic disruptions in the performance of Chávez as the slayer of the opposition party-Devil should not be ignored. In the framework of this scenario, the medium itself has changed: actors are no longer singular bodies; they are like a net, towing the relationships, the histories, and the symbolic order into their orbit.

But first, does the poster perform? Susan Sontag suggests that "the poster-object itself may be viewed as a kind of instant visual theater in the street" (1970, 4) or "a quotation from life" (16). Not only does the poster contribute to a symbolic scripting or sequence of action, it also engages in a temporary way with the environment. Posters go up; posters come down. They capture a short clip of action that plays in the imagination. The knight and devil in the poster act out a scenario of power *as if* this were a performance, one that is well rehearsed in the iconography of saints and devils. Two very different symbolic memories of power (conquistador and liberator) cross in what Néstor García Canclini calls a "path of reformulation" (2005, 204). In the poster, Chávez the liberator is on the horse as the conqueror, and, in this case, the CD party has clearly become the devil.

Indeed, for some, this poster demonstrated an implicit (or even explicit) violence in the Chavista movement, serving as an example of political culture that drew this path of reformulation squarely back to a scenario of "good" versus "evil." I read the poster as a parody of the scenario of conquest, one with a bite. But ultimately one that skirts the edges of a danger zone where its effectiveness as parody relies on the unequal power relations that are reversed from actual political life. As Taylor points out, the scenario is not a fixed container; it is flexible and also capable of disruption. Through a "cultural masquerading or a strategic repositioning" players can subvert the message or produce alterations, parody, and other forms of distortion to original meanings (Taylor 2003, 39). There may be some retrieval of the victorious saint, but Chávez departs from the colonial embodiments to join another genealogy of popular religiosity.

By these strategic repositionings the saint-knight has been reworked by popular imagination and practice to alter its meanings. Many years after its arrival in the Americas, Santiago Matamoros transformed from offender to a protector of indigenous rights, at one point knocking down and trampling the conquistador Pedro de Alvarado for his cruel mistreatment of indigenous people (Sulai Capponi 2006, 254). Others see Santiago Matamoros as syncretic with the Yoruban *orisha* Ogún or Oké; Illapa, the thunder god in Perú; and Huitzilopochtli in Nicaragua (ibid., 267).[38] But is this image in the context of the campaign poster flexible enough to withstand the double articulations and transitions of the *diablo* and the horseman? It would seem that the poster invokes Chávez as a syncretic figure, which pushes against the colonial-knight origins, staging it once again only in order to disrupt it.

What did people see in that message of taking the devil to task? On the one hand, the devil is cut down to size. Chávez is now in the seat of power wearing two hats: the *campesino*'s hat and the red beret of revolution. He bears down on the small figure of the *diablo* that is holding the flag of the United States, thus claiming national sovereignty that had once been denied. On the other hand, critics to Chávez both within the revolution and against it were deeply bothered that they were maligned and linked to foreign intervention. But there is more. The *cuatro* on Chávez's back carries a dual message. He is the poet-troubadour Florentino, and he is also the *cuatrista*, the protector of the devil dances. Rather than expulsion of the devils, the poster suggests a new totality to include these playful antagonists, subsumed within the totality of democracy that the state sought to uphold. When Chávez is on the horse, he is in the stirrups of a steed with the brand "SB," the very horse of Bolívar that I will discuss further in the next chapter. When he is not on his horse, his bare feet are literally on the ground. So, in one way, Chávez is the underdog man of the people, the one who could defeat a Goliath–CD party and a longtime political establishment. In another way, he assumed both the role of candidate and/as a symbolic fusion to the state itself. On both levels, this poster reinforces Chávez's power as a leader who could effectively wage the battle and win.

The motto of the poster, "take the devil to task," underlines the work of this campaign as a sequel to Florentino's battle with the Devil during the 2002 coup d'état. It acknowledges the continued negation of the political victories of Chávez and the drive to discredit the agenda of the people who elected him. Not only did the *llanero* hero prove victorious in the first electoral battle; now he would demand accountability from this devil and demand acceptance of the reforms and transfer of power to the majority in a meaningful way.

When the festive devil enters the poster, parody enters as well, but it is a parody that relies on the fanciful and festive devil. The plumes and blazing tongue of the poster devil recall the fierce masks and playful gestures of the dancing devils of Venezuelan popular culture discussed in chapter 1. This devil is a figure whose presence is at once endearing and familiar. The devils guard family members against illness. The devils in the present-day Corpus Christi fiestas visit houses to offer blessings, not curses. These popular manifestations of the *diablo* transform the demonized devil figure of the church into a known figure who is part of the fabric of the community. The devils of the devil dances convert an unspeakable enemy to a familiar and even endearing foe. In other words, in Venezuela, the devil symbol is not fixed to one meaning. The devil in the poster evokes more than one scenario, and any political interpretation of that figure must account for these multiple roles and the moving play between them. Chávez and the devil are again playing out the cosmic struggle, but this time it is a struggle that is similar to and informed by the performance of the devil dances.

As my last point about this poster, I must note that I was struck by the way it surfaced on the internet so quickly in 2004 as evidence of Chávez's authoritarianism. El Tano Yea's poster was just one of thousands of posters produced by ad hoc groups, unions, and other unregulated sources. In analyzing the image, I realized that there were entire aspects of its production that needed to be uncovered: one was the rapid reflex of social media in opposition to the government, and second was the relative decentralization of the campaign from within. While in some ways Chávez's political powers became more centralized during the campaign, this example of the campaign poster discloses a level of production that was horizontally distributed, decentralized, and ad hoc. Relatively few controls were exercised on how information was used and circulated by the many nodes of production within the movement. Hence, posters like this one were part of a polyphony of political messaging by artists that reflected the pluralism of the Chávez movement. The movement was not a solid bloc of the good against the bad. In fact there was, as the rainbow cast out of the "No" on the poster suggests, a wide diversity of voices reflected in the campaign. The rainbow, like that of the Chilean plebiscite, sought to include a broader diversification of popular support.

In May 2010, during the talks of the Union of South American Nations, when Chávez took the floor he spoke of a persistent strategy on the part of Europe, North America, and interests within Latin America to divide the growing movement toward unifying the South by defining a "good left" and a "bad left." Chávez explained: "There was a desire to present Lula as if he were the 'good left' and 'Chávez as if he was the devil—it's a systematic campaign in Europe, Latin America and North America." Chávez and the other leaders of this convention agreed to increase their public visibility by meeting every three months in order to deflect attempts to isolate Chávez from the other South American nations. Chávez was saying that visibility is an essential antidote to the West's political demonization of the Left that he, Evo Morales, Néstor and Cristina Kirchner represented. Persistently associating himself with other like-minded Latin American heads of state would work against the isolation tactic that was necessary for demonization to take hold. Chávez was trying to transfer the lessons of Santa Inés: do not stand alone.

The campaign's mobilization of the "Florentino and the Devil" narrative, the contestations of the "No," and the popular production of politics that followed represented a trend toward altering the language of politics in Venezuela. Instead of endorsing a politics that took place behind closed doors, these tactics of the Chavista Left borrowed and created a politics of visibility on the streets, in the plazas, and on the airwaves, furthering a claim that the people owned the public spaces of the nation.

The campaign and the political culture that supported it certainly tell us something about the potentials and pitfalls of "comic-strip politics." The devil was a recurrent trope in the Chavista discourse that generated new forms of participation while surfacing a deeper set of issues that uprooted the very foundations of Manichaeism. In 2010, I sat in a small café in Brooklyn watching the image of Hugo Chávez on a CNN broadcast. Boldface capital letters under his image read "LEFTIST MENACE." Other reports systematically maligned the president, calling him "mentally ill," a "would-be dictator," and, in one case, a "killer clown."[39] These labels seemed more menacing to me than the 2004 campaign, or even Chávez's "devil" comment at the United Nations. In the presumed neutrality of the network broadcast was a much more dangerous circus than the performed tropes of the "Florentino and the Devil" campaign.

Whether Chávez's reforms were denounced on a CNN broadcast or cheered on by crowds on his television show *¡Aló Presidente!*, they stirred up what critics and supporters alike describe as a hurricane. In just six years from the time he was elected in 1998, the movement reached what some called maximum intensity during the presidential recall-election campaign.

Of the many factors that contributed to the success of the campaign, the legend of “Florentino and the Devil” provided a score to which millions of people organized and claimed political space in a victory that radically impacted the political history of the continent.

Chapter 4

✦

The Symbol Keeps Performing

Three Populist Turns of the Horse of Bolívar

"The symbol keeps writing," lament the desperate rebels as they defend their short-lived insurrection in the capital city of Bogotá. This is the last scene in the 2002 Colombian film *Bolívar Soy Yo* (Bolívar, I Am) directed by Jorge Alí Triana, in which Simón Bolívar, a.k.a. "the symbol," ducking out of the actual fight, feverishly writes letters at his desk while soldiers storm the gates. But rather than the actual life of Simón Bolívar, the movie is about an actor turned real-life impersonator of the nineteenth-century Liberator who unwittingly sets into motion a modern-day social uprising to unite the continent. Outfitted in the general's famous red and blue jacket with gold-tassel epaulettes and riding through the city streets on a white horse, the rogue actor transforms his fictional identity as Bolívar in a popular telenovela into a lived-out version of the revolutionary ethos of modern-day Colombia. Along the way, he meets all kinds of people (garbage collectors, children, politicians), gets a job in a parade, upsets a convention of self-serving statesmen, and ends up in the crossfires of a civil war, with the actor at one point telling the Colombian president, "You take care of the theater, and leave the politics to me" (Triana 2002).

Simón José Antonio de la Santísima Trinidad Bolívar y Palacios Ponte y Blanco is known as "the Liberator" of six modern countries of Latin America: Venezuela, Colombia, Panama, Bolivia, Ecuador, and Peru.[1] One of the most lauded figures of the American wars of independence from Spain, Bolívar has been revered by successive presidents in Venezuela, from right-wing dictatorships, to the neoliberal regimes of the Punto Fijo period (1958–98), to the leftist socialism of Hugo Chávez and Nicolás Maduro. His image is printed on paper and coin currency, stamps, billboards, playing cards, brochures, and posters. Nearly every town in Venezuela—and indeed, many towns throughout Latin America—has a central plaza named after Bolívar (including Ocumare). Statues of the commander general are located around the world, one at the south gate to Central Park in New York City and, famously, one in downtown Caracas, where the bronze figure of Bolívar on horseback commands the center of the plaza in front of the Palacio de Miraflores.[2]

As monumental as Bolívar's petite frame could appear (he was 5'3") rising above the plaza, his image has been transformed by popular culture into something grandly beyond the sanctioned story of the state. In prolific ways, the popular religiosity surrounding Bolívar remakes the authoritarian general and visionary hero of independence into a saint figure that graces home altars, fiestas, and street art. One of the preeminent scholars of this religiosity of Bolívar is the Venezuelan anthropologist Yolanda Salas de Lecuna, who argues that "[Bolívar] is not so much about a character that lived in a moment of historical time in the world of memory, of what was, and of his glories, rather his powers and forces are actualized by people who pray to him, who call him and who ask from him. In this way, Bolívar as a saint, redeemer and benefactor is also a cult object for a wide sector of the national population" (1987, 89). This "cult object" of Bolívar is also very much a living body that continues to perform its own imaginaries, as the actor in *Bolívar Soy Yo* comes to realize. The embodiment of one person ultimately fulfills multiple dreams, in which "everyone has their own Bolívar" (Triana 2002)

In this way, Bolívar, the figure of state, doubles as what Jean Graham-Jones calls a performing icon, as "cultural agent *and* cultural product" (2014, 5). As agent, Bolívar enacts a particular set of ideals in the social and political environment, affecting and creating the world in which it appears. As product, Bolívar appears on street murals, in enactments onstage, in film, and in active debates over the historical record in the contemporary moment.[3] The icon of Bolívar remains an animate force of interpretation and debate, "collectively made, unmade and remade" (ibid., 7). This chapter is about the icon of Bolívar performing as saint, liberator, the state, and the people in ways that compose a uniquely Bolivarian populism. For the performing icon of Bolívar, there is no one Bolívar; rather, multiple Bolívars are enacted simultaneously, with each proposing different directions for the nation and continent. Well, sort of.

You see, instead of centering on Bolívar's life and legacy, my approach to the memory of Bolívar is more about his horse. To explain what I mean by this, this chapter starts with the 2006 redesign of the bicentennial coat of arms that put the horse in the middle of a public controversy. The controversy brought attention to the symbolic representation of the horse of Bolívar in tandem with its phantom rider. I reconstruct that representation here as an interpretative schema of the populist state. In it, I examine the horse's physical turn in the redesign as pointing toward three different scenarios of the relationship between the people and the state. Each turn represents a different valence of political power: the first is the official state, in which Simón Bolívar is the preeminent father of independence; the second invokes a multicultural liberalism in which Bolívar, portrayed as a mestizo, is aligned with the majority indigenous and Afro-descendants in Venezuela; and in the third I see a radical turn, where a shift in the reproduction of Bolívar's historical memory structurally transfers the power belonging to who tells history.

Figure 12. Venezuelan coat of arms. *Left*, the version from 1863 to 2006; *right*, the newly inaugurated version from 2006.

In 2006, Hugo Chávez unveiled a new version of the national coat of arms for its bicentennial commemoration. In the previous version (figure 12, left), the horse runs on a green pasture, turning its head to look behind (to the past) with a light step forward (to the future). Yet, for Chávez and the bicentennial committee in charge of the redesign project, the horse was caught in ambivalence. It appeared conflicted and tentative, with the head in one direction and its body moving in the other. The 200-year anniversary of the flag provided an opportunity to propose a new design, which was approved by Venezuela's congress and adopted in 2006. In the new version (figure 12, right), the horse bolts to the left with its mane and tail flying in the wind. The hesitant prance is replaced with a gallop, where the horse appears to be in midair, off the ground, leaping toward the symbolic terrain already marked as the past. At its inauguration, Chávez said, "The white horse is now liberated, free and vigorous, galloping to the left as a return of [Simón] Bolívar and his dream" (Mazoch 2006, n.p.).

Rather than a unifying moment, however, the flag became, for some, the center of controversy in the spring of 2006, just prior to the elections in the fall of that year. Vociferous critics, whose comments were picked up by major global media, claimed that the new flag was a sign of "totalitarianism, autocracy, and communism" (BBC News, March 13, 2006).[4] To them, it was a waste of money, uncalled for, and merely a "whim of the president," whose offhanded comment that the new design was inspired by his daughter suggested to them that the new version violated due process (NBC News, March 13, 2006).[5] To those opposed to Chávez, changing the constitutional symbol that had consecrated the nation at the end of the Federal Wars in 1863 became emblematic of a deeper conflict around discretionary powers. Opposition leaders campaigned against the flag. They boycotted the new version, tore it down on several occasions, and hung the previous flag at various high-profile events. Even Miss Venezuela carried the old flag on stage with her during the crowning ceremony to symbolize her disapproval of Chávez.[6]

While there are indeed many questions that surround the bicentennial redesign, my focus is on the symbolic reversal of the horse of Bolívar as a somatic performance of state inscribing a broader program of historical redress. The horse's turn and its gallop toward the symbolic terrain of the past perform on multiple registers, not least of which is the social corpus that Bolívar's horse invokes as the national body. The turn is a metaphor of change, revolution, and return. In looking beyond the metaphor, we can see the antagonisms between each turn and how the multiple performances of state—whether intentionally or not—dismantle universal narratives, while at the same time reworking them for a new order. The way I see it, the icon of Bolívar is very much alive, as is his legacy and the demands that people enact through it. With the decision to change the direction of the horse of Bolívar on the national crest, the performing icon seemed to somatically buck those who previously saw (only) themselves in the saddle.

The multiple Bolívars land differently throughout the hemisphere. They inspire different prayers, different altars, and new versions of Bolívar's representation. In a performance-centered approach to the icon, the simultaneity of these visions of Bolívar suggests that multiple forms of populism overlap and interact to debate the ideas of what would fulfill Bolívar's unrequited dream. In Graham-Jones's words, "present in iconic performances and their reception is a shared ambivalent mythopoesis, in which our 'historical' need to make the myth flesh runs up against our 'critical' desire to demystify the flesh through mediation and appropriation" (2014, 7).

As a practice, populism enters this space of the ambivalent mythopoesis, where it mediates and also appropriates the memory of this prefigurative celebrity of Bolívar in an active endeavor to historicize and broaden contesting claims for legitimacy. His memory in film, street art, and popular storytelling includes Bolívar's arrival on the shores next to Ocumare de la Costa. In this chapter, I consider how Bolívar and his horse are reproduced in an ongoing saga around national and continental history. History in this sense is far from having reached its end. In short, the power of the symbol is "still writing" in ways that point to multiple and simultaneous populisms that still perform.

First Turn: The Head of State, One for All

The first turn of Bolívar is a state turn, a gesture of scientific "officialism," but not without its own mythologies. It enforces an established narrative of

Simón Bolívar as the father of independence that bows in deference to an official and now opened past. In this regard, we could imagine this horse of Bolivar as bearing similarities to the one in the previous coat of arms with its head tossed back to the left while prancing slightly to the right. In this populist repertoire of the horse, it is unclear if it is possible to bring about real social change, or if ceremonial reinstatements of the patriarch will ultimately render the revolution like the regimes of its predecessors. An authoritarian rider will surely return.

In Chávez's political project, the centerpiece was Bolívar. The day after his 1994 release from prison, for example, Chávez visited Bolívar's memorial at the National Pantheon, as is now famously narrated. Just as Rómulo Betancourt and his fellow student activists had done in 1928, Chávez placed a wreath beside Bolívar's grave, a symbolic beginning to his series of travels around the country, which he called the "Bolivarian hurricane."[7] In the new crest of arms that Chávez put forward, the vigor in the horse's gallop is a vision of the state running ever more deliberately in one direction. Yolanda Salas de Lecuna (1987) points out that every Venezuelan president since 1842 has openly pledged his loyalty to the symbol of Bolívar.

What is interesting is that Hugo Chávez invoked the Bolivarian ideology more intensely, and, in so doing, he shifted the emphasis of the statesman from an empty icon to a revolutionary politics, and a radical reenvisioning of South American unification. The political movement in Venezuela over these first ten years of revolution openly adopted Bolivarianism in order to reconstitute nationalism. But more importantly, perhaps, a new officialism of his image helped to embolden a diplomatic push for transnational alliances among neighboring countries of Latin America.

Let's consider a dream. It's a dream of a free America, and "not one just for white men, for all men." It's a dream of a united America, supported by the people: "we are all children of America." These are lines from the biographical epic film *The Liberator* (2014) by Alberto Arvelo, grandson of the writer of "Florentino and the Devil" (1940). The first scene opens on the commander: the camera is behind him as he enters the palace. He lays his sword and his jacket into the arms of a waiting servant. He ascends the regal stairway and throws back the grand doors to where a woman is waiting for him. It is Manuela, the beautiful and faithful woman with whom Bolívar would survive to fulfill his defeat of the Spanish imperialist crown. The film truly is a melodrama, glorifying patriarchy and saturating the gritty underside with heroic virtues of racial equality to forge brotherhood among Venezuelans, and also (especially) Colombians, a dream that the movie contends was ultimately betrayed.

In 2010, Chávez announced an official inquiry into the cause of Bolívar's death. The inquiry culminated in the disentombment of Bolívar to determine whether there was foul play. A highly public and formalized act, the exhumation of Bolívar was a spectacular moment of state performance. Soldiers stood erect as doctors in lab coats systematically, quasi-religiously opened the coffin on a televised broadcast. Chávez narrated a video of the event on national television, calling for respect, and all those in witness as the children of Bolívar. The political opposition had a field day, in one instance featuring a white woman as a shamanic healer on Univision discussing the spiritual implications of violating Bolívar's grave, calling it witchcraft, a sacrilege, and so forth. Symbolically, however, the exhumation functioned to reinvigorate the debates. With his body eviscerated to the bones by the embrace of widely divergent political platforms that claimed to function in his name, Bolívar once again became the ultimate empty signifier.

But is it entirely empty? According to Ernesto Laclau (2005), an empty signifier is the hegemonic expression and constitution of a popular subjectivity derived from the differential logics of heterogeneous (plural) demands. Wearing a slogan, printing a symbol, or practicing gestures, and so on are thus expressions of shared beliefs and actions, but when invested with an even more meaningful (and emotive) quality, they become popular signifiers. Populist repertoires, in this phenomenological sense, by virtue of their becoming, *perform* an intermedial role between what people *do* as collectives to the chain of equivalential political logic. People perform their approvals or disapprovals, enunciating their stances in relation to others using gesture, timing, movement, and utterance. As a chain of agreements takes shape, symbols gain power, stretch or consolidate. Through the complex and sometimes subtle details of this logic, once identified, the empty or floating signifier then becomes more than a disconnected ruse. The empty signifier becomes one of the very mechanisms by which popular identities can be conferred and accumulated toward signs, symbols, or a cause.

The forensic exhumation straddled a line between the official state and a subaltern alignment of Bolívar. There was a perceived missing piece in history in which Bolívar was wronged. Bolívar must, in this view, be "freed" from the past, a past that has bridled his memory in a manufactured story. But what other kinds of evidence did the exhumation reveal? Compared to the thin and even wavy depictions of the face of Bolívar in previous limnings, the new rendering of the Liberator's face (in figure 13) is noticeably wider; his jaw appears more prominently, his forehead protrudes. The fact of the esteemed forensic scientists that produced the image from skull data adds another layer of officialism. But this time the state becomes the rider, where the image as product of a ceremonial exhumation rivals only the profound scientific and mystical union of the nineteenth-century nation-building enterprise. In light of the new design of the national crest, the turn of the horse seems to be galloping with firm resolve to evoke an authoritarian reinstatement of a patriarchal order.

This populist repertoire emboldened an authoritarian state with his recollections of Bolívar, recasting Chávez's own body, or voice, as the magician to procure forensic evidence from a bygone era. For some, he effectively

Figure 13. The official 3-D facial reconstruction of Simón Bolívar based on skull data from the exhumed skeleton of the Libertador. Image courtesy of Visualforensic P. Froesch, 2011.

embalmed the socialist state in a coffin of the past, as if desperately seeking a foundational order on which to build the socialist state. For others, however, it was a noble pursuit of truth, quixotic perhaps, but again, not without its own histories and social alignments. I believe, once its layers have been revealed, that it shows a much more complex portrayal of the state and the revolution in the Chávez era.

This takes us to the second turn, which examines the possibilities of a subaltern alignment that goes beyond Bolívar's bones in his grave. The exhumation engaged millions of people in a historical quest, in which the brave and faithful steed (read: the people) would discover the truth of the independence wars and the stakes of those battles in the political debates over land and resource distribution today. In other words, the horse of Bolívar gallops to the past to pick up the pieces of what was left behind.

Figure 14. Pavel Égüez, *La Patria naciendo de la ternura* (Patriotism Is Born from Tenderness). Mural on the Avenida Baralt in downtown Caracas. Author photo, 2010.

Second Turn: Remaking Bolívar as the Popular State

The second "turn" in the making of Bolívar is one that projects him as an integral part of the expression and spiritualism of the popular class. In the mural shown in figure 14, featured prominently on a municipal-services building on the Avenida Baralt in downtown Caracas, Bolívar is positioned at the center with his accomplice and companion Manuela Sáenz. The two ride together on the horse with several groups of indigenous and Afro-Venezuelan subjects surrounding them. They all seem to ride the horse at a gallop, turned fully to the left, and are closely placed together as if they all fit in the saddle at the same time, one body sprouting out of another. Simón and Manuela outstretch their hands in the same direction as the others, just as the hooves of the horse are lifted out of the multitude against a cobalt-blue sky. People are shaded in different colors, some with houses fleshing out their bodies, their various painted faces accented by a mosaic of eyes and hands of Afro-descendant and indigenous *pueblos*. Two faces are turned upward at the top, with mouths open, recalling Cubist abstraction or the Lucumí-inspired paintings of the Cuban artist Wifredo Lam. Others are holding masks or shown in profile. Some eyes are seeds or leaves, as if they too grow from the corn plant that rises up and arcs toward the horse's braided mane. No longer is Bolívar the white *criollo* (native-born Venezuelan of Spanish ancestry). No longer is Bolívar the sole commander in the saddle of governance.

In the remakings of Bolívar, he appears to be fully absorbed into an indigenous America, like in the mural on the Avenida Baralt. In various other depictions and portraits, he also appears as *moreno* (brown) with an Afro or a full curly beard.[8] The very body of Bolívar goes *raza*, bordering obvious misrepresentation and appropriation. But the question remains: Who is appropriating whom? When Chávez was asked to respond to the Spanish king Juan Carlos's rebuff at the Latin American Summit in Chile, he famously replied, "I'm not going to shut up, and they won't shut me up because I'm not speaking for myself, I am speaking for millions, the millions who are the children of Bolívar, the millions who are children of Guaicaipuro and Manuela [Sáenz], José Leonardo Chirinos, and all of those who the Spanish murdered, ambushed, and slaughtered here" (quoted in Carlson 2007, n.p.). In the mural, these families, having clustered and crossed over, one into the other, ride together on the horse. Street art and speeches leverage Bolívar's memorial power as an indisputable figure of state to reach across national lines, to affirm indigenous and Afro-descendant struggles for rights and vindication.

Yolanda Salas de Lecuna wrote prolifically on these popular remakings of Bolívar in what is known as the "Cult of Bolívar." Her book *Bolívar y la historia en la conciencia popular* (1987) records dozens of interviews with people on the northern coast of Venezuela, in which they relate stories they heard about Bolívar. Among them is a story that Bolívar was the child of a black woman enslaved in the town of Capaya in the western state of Barlovento (25). Others believe he was a descendant from the lineage of Guaicaipuro, who was one of the first indigenous leaders to fight against the Spanish in the early colonial period (41). Still others claim he was born in the state of Aragua, in San Mateo, La Victoria, or El Consejo (41, 47). In these multiple origin stories, Bolívar begins to resemble the transculturated layering of the state's appropriation of Afro-descendant and indigenous identity.

In some ways, this phenomenon also appears to be occurring the other way around. Though buried, Bolívar remains visible and emanating from and *as* the saints and martyrs of Catholic popular religious manifestations. For Salas de Lecuna, what this means is that for those who identify with the newly composited saint of Bolívar, there is an act of elevation and re-vindication that goes beyond passive identification *to participate in the naming and identification process*. As she sees it, "in these examples, it is difficult to speak of an ideological hegemony by part of this dominant sector in the formation of the popular cult of Bolívar" (Salas de Lecuna 1987, 39). In other words, if the first turn of Bolívar is top-down officialism, in this second turn the remaking of Bolívar is very much from the ground up.

In this view, Chávez invoked Bolívar in the name of a new political project that incorporated previously excluded working-class and indigenous groups. Asked during an interview what Simón Bolívar meant to him, Chávez described the liberator as an embodiment of those he sought to empower: "[I see Bolívar] in the face of the Yukpa and Yanomami Indians, trampled by the dominant sectors of our country; in the working class of Caracas; in university students and in schools" (quoted in Bercovich 2014, 62). The biographer Bart Jones writes, "Chávez's Bolívar was an expansive figure, sufficiently vast and heterogeneous to encompass a broad new coalition" (2007, 24). Whereas in the first turn the charismatic leader overshadows the people's voice, in what is in some ways an authoritarian move, now in this second turn Bolívar shares the space with the people, who have ratified the Bolivarian project and presumably share its principles.

Again, I am not attempting to prove that one turn exists over the other; to me, all three turns—and perhaps more—are happening at once with important intersectional relationships. By virtue of their differences and overlaps, these various ways to restore and imagine the figure of Bolívar contribute to its pluralism, ultimately working both with and against the hegemony of an "official" story.

Before concluding that a pluralist politics is made possible through the empty signifier of Bolívar, however, more of the religiosity or spiritism of Bolívar must be taken into consideration. As Salas de Lecuna notes, the popular consciousness of Bolívar is both "epic" and "messianic," which echoes the critiques of ideational populism made by scholars and others who are skeptical of precisely these terms of an "epic" and "messianic" influence in democracy (1987, 205, 209). Messianism suggests a fervent or passionate belief in one to lead, a danger that the Western philosophical tradition has long argued is associated with fascism and totalitarianism.[9] Giorgio Agamben's idea of the state of exception is, of course, predicated on the idea that messianism delivers an exceptional state to the law. As an epic and messianic signifier, Bolívar transfers religiosity to the *patria*, powers that presumably transcend a law shaped and interpreted among members of mortal society.

While the terms "epic" and "messianic" arguably offend the secular political tradition, still others see Bolívar as existing outside of politics for other reasons. One person that Salas de Lecuna interviewed claimed that Bolívar is "antipolitical." "Politics," as Salas de Lecuna argued in the 1980s, "is no longer the art of governing the people, rather it is to disintegrate them, and the 'antipolitical' character of our hero translates as a protecting function although one of action . . . that becomes patent when the spirit of the Liberator descends and materializes in a medium" (1987, 83). Thus, Bolívar's symbolic transcendence was a way to confront political illusion (and hypocrisy) through action. In other words, his messianic virtue materializes in order to restore a collective right to "rule," bypassing one system of legitimation by appealing to another. In a populist model, the medium and those who participate in the materialization of this medium are embedded within a larger network to confer on Bolívar that which makes him godly.

In these recorded histories, Bolívar's horse is central to the performance of the symbol of Bolívar. In another interview documented by Salas de Lecuna, Bolívar was identified with his white horse: "[His white horse] was a way of distinguishing him from the others because almost all the other men were tall, 'recios,' and Bolívar no, he was small, a little short. It was the horse that made Bolívar" (1987, 57). In Salas de Lecuna's view, the horse of Bolívar lent an external divinity to Bolívar, where the horse became a "supernatural force of external protection incarnate in the horse" (58). She sees this belief as rooted in a messianism of Bolívar where the much-repeated iconography of the white horse announces the liberator. Stories documented by Salas de Lecuna also suggest that an old woman, often described as a black woman, had set aside a young colt for a liberator who would come; the horse was born on the same day as Bolívar and mysteriously disappeared the day he died (58). The horse was his guardian angel, according to another, never leaving his side (60–61). The white horse was Bolívar's "sixth sense," said another (61). One person who was interviewed said her grandmother Trina and another woman were witness to Bolívar being gifted a horse in the town of Mamporal. Others say the horse was from the state of Aragua (62). If the horse is what lent this messianic quality to Bolívar, it is conferred on him by this popular sector.

Given these decades' worth of documentation, it seems to me that the story of Bolívar's horse complicates the messianic gesture. The hybrid man-horse, or spirit horse, takes up new meanings in a non-Western worldview. The stories of the messianic and of deliverance have to do with a spirituality lived on the ground. The notions of savior and salvation have much to do with the process of belief-making, which gathers its information from ancestry and a continuum that exists between the political and the spirits of the dead. The body of Bolívar is bound to the body of the horse, and in that sense there is a durational force, an assemblage of real spirit that is reactivated. The messianic quality of Bolívar (and Chávez) that Salas de Lecuna observes is flattened into a story of an authoritarian state, overriding the internal tensions and distinctions between the top-down established power of the first turn and the heterogeneous popular remaking of Bolívar in the second. The term "messianic" thus splinters into differentiated qualities that raise larger questions about the erasure of religious difference and about a continued bias toward dismissing "magic" and "bad religion" within the scholarly critique of populism.

Nevertheless, after studying various images and performed examples in each of the first two turns—the official Bolívar statesman and the subaltern composite body—Bolívar, as patriarch, still remains at the center, riding the horse. It may indeed be that the plural subjects of embodiment live within and around the statesman as a model of a more inclusive democracy; yet, in both the first and second turns, Bolívar ultimately and literally holds the reins of state power. As a populist iconoclast, Bolívar's aura still seems to overwhelm.

Third Turn (*en Ruta*): Bolívar in the Historical Archive

The third turn gravitates around an actual moment of Bolívar turning his horse, a moment with historical repercussions that still resonate. I'm referring to Karl Marx's scathing account of Bolívar famously recorded in the *New American Encyclopedia* of 1858. In it, Marx describes how Bolívar, receiving news of a possible ambush, turned on his white horse and fled from the very same coast of Aragua in Ocumare, leaving behind several hundred troops to face the Spanish royalists on their own. As a consequence, Marx argued, Bolívar ultimately failed to deliver liberty to those who remained; his cowardice meant that he betrayed the revolution and the promises that were contingent on its success.

In this section, I analyze Bolívar's letters and other correspondences and accounts of what took place when Bolívar sought to win over Ocumare and what he called the "heartland" of Venezuela. With the aid of Haitian president Alexandre Pétion in July 1816, Bolívar landed in the tiny port of La Boca, about three miles from where the street mural in figure 15 was commemoratively painted along the main road through Ocumare de la Costa; I discuss the events leading up to this landing. Finally, I consider these archived materials in relation to the performed repertoire of a tour-based history project organized by residents of Ocumare in order to situate the legacy of Bolívar and his expedition alongside the popular demands of Afro-descendant cultural producers of the region.

Where the first turn of Bolívar's horse (for 200 years) dismissed the Afro-descendant struggle against colonial rule as merely a footnote to the independence wars, and where the second turn sought to ride forward with Bolívar representing this struggle, the third turn of Bolívar reflects on the historical reproduction of this figure in order to claim the rights of new storytellers of the revolution both then and now. A shift in the terms of history telling to a model of participatory production works in tandem with this last turn of the horse to reveal a broader range of possibilities for historical redress. The third turn of the horse is therefore a radical turn that attempts to reconcile conflicted stories of Bolívar himself.

La Boca literally means "the mouth" and refers to the small cove and fishing port straight down the main road from Ocumare to the ocean. Among the fishing nets and small lean-tos, which have scales to weigh each catch that comes in from the fifty or so fishing boats that venture out each day, there is a large block statue featuring a plaque that marks precisely where Bolívar sought to enter the heartland of Venezuela to win popular support for the revolution. This is the same place where small boats from different towns along the coast bring their respective saint figures of San Juan Bautista into the harbor of La Boca to visit the annual fiesta on June 24. Here in La Boca, on the Aragua coast, and among the Afro-descendant "red" (a network that extends throughout the Caribbean), the past is active terrain for a discussion about the principal protagonists of the revolutionary wars, statehood, and emancipation.

To illustrate some of these debates, it is important to start before Simón Bolívar, with José Leonardo Chirinos (see figure 15, on the left in the mural), who led a rebellion against the hacienda elites in 1795 near the town of Coro on the same coast, just west of Ocumare. Chirinos worked for a merchant marine on a boat that delivered goods to Haiti and other parts of the Caribbean. As an enslaved man, he was well aware of the conditions that a majority of Afro-Caribbeans faced on a daily basis in plantation society. After learning of the Haitian Revolution of 1791, he was also aware of the possibility of successful insurrection and a free black state. Chirinos and several hundred other black abolitionists rose up to fight against the *hacendados* (hacienda owners of European descent), successfully pushing back the Spanish and *criollo* elites into the fortresses of Coro. When military reinforcements arrived for the Spanish, however, Chirinos and others were overpowered and eventually captured and killed. In a spectacle of terror, the *cabildo* (local municipal governments) ordered that Chirinos's hands be nailed to the front gate of the hacienda where he had been enslaved, and the movement was repressed.

Nearly a generation later, an army of mixed, indigenous, and black *campesinos* was mobilized across the *llanos* of the south; they were led by the Asturias-born *caudillo* José Tomás Boves. Of course, by this time *criollo* elites were protesting the taxes and laws obliged to the Spanish and had started their own revolutionary war against Spain, splitting the factions of white landowners in the region. Between the revolutionary rhetoric of the *criollo hacendados* and the promises of protection by the royalists (who were allied with the Spanish Crown), mixed indigenous and black abolitionists were the pivotal future of the revolution of independence. When Boves, much feared by the *hacendados*, died in battle in 1814, and Spain repudiated the Unborn Child Act in 1816—which would have granted freedom for children in utero of women in slavery—the political alliances among black and mestizo *campesinos* shifted in favor of Bolívar to join forces and fight the Spanish.[10]

Meanwhile, Bolívar went to Jamaica to enlist aid from the English, who rejected his appeal. He then headed to Haiti, where President Alexandre Pétion supplied Bolívar with ammunition and a printing press on the condition that Bolívar declare the abolition of slavery.[11] José Marcial Ramos Guédez (2004), a prize-winning researcher of Afro-Venezuelan studies, notes that Bolívar's commitment to the campaign against slavery was questioned by those opposed to the project both historically and presently, and yet it is clear that he advanced two important decrees, one on June 2, 1816, and the other a month later in Ocumare de la Costa on July 6, 1816, both to end slavery.

Bolívar thus began his campaign for popular support, planning to eventually take control of the region by entering the "heartland" of Venezuela through Ocumare de la Costa. It's important to recognize that up until Bolívar embraced the issue of the emancipation of slavery in 1816, first in Cumaná and later throughout the Caracas province, he had not been a viable candidate in the eyes of the popular classes who would ultimately determine the result of the war. Two years earlier, he had been essentially driven out of Venezuela by the royalists, who had successfully enlisted mostly enslaved and recently freed people—mestizos and disenfranchised whites who were perhaps more committed to fighting against the ruling plantation-owning oligarchy (*hacendados* and *cabildos*) than they were to fighting on behalf of the Spanish Crown.[12] One must also remember that, in 1815, so-called *pardos*, or mixed-race elites, were completely militarized, and their demands for equality had deepened after five years of war (and more). Their grievances toward the *criollos* with respect to slavery and racial divisions were in many cases not allayed. The royalists used this to their advantage, in some cases feeding a rumor mill that the Spanish monarchs had discontinued slavery and it was the *hacendados* who did not obey the new law (Klooster 2011, 402). It was also a strategic choice on the part of the *pardos* to leverage the powers of the monarchy to rid them of an internal exploitation. Hence, in some ways, both the *pardos* and the Spanish were engaged in a strategic relationship against what they saw as a greater enemy, the *criollo* elite.

Perhaps by looking at the actual terms of the revolutionary project as it was envisioned by the *criollos* at the time, we can see that for most black families in the region, whether "free" or enslaved, freedom was extremely provisional. Both sides in the war threatened equally high stakes for not enlisting: any man between 14 and 60 years of age who failed to enlist would be punished by either a lifetime of slavery for him and his family or death. Anyone caught hiding or assisting draft dodgers would also be subject to penalty of death. Hence, in some ways there was little difference between the laws of the new *patria* (patriotism/homeland) espoused by Bolívar and that of the former slave state. Additionally, no citizen could move or transport themselves or any goods without a signed document from the commander of the district. Although Bolívar "officially" read the proclamation of emancipation in Ocumare in 1816, it was highly conditional and was then dismissed by urban *criollos* who supported independence but not abolition until almost twenty years later in 1838.

What exactly happened over the summer of 1816 on the coast of what is now the state of Aragua near Ocumare has generated long-debated questions about the alliances and betrayals of the revolutionary wars. On July 6, Bolívar arrived in La Boca with thirteen vessels and Pétion's investments of arms and ammunition and the printing press, which his small and tired crew unloaded onto the shore. It was there on the coast of Ocumare that Bolívar issued a decree of the emancipation of slavery. Several days later, Bolívar traveled through the area by horseback, soliciting support from the few sympathetic landowners there. During his campaign, Bolívar reported that he successfully enlisted 800 recruits from the area, but even that figure was likely inflated by as much as double in order to mask his position of weakness in the valley.

Turning to Karl Marx's understanding of events in that summer, the picture becomes even more critical toward the commander. According to Marx, during Bolívar's southwesterly advance toward Valencia, most likely up the very footpath that Gómez would later build through impossibly steep gullies over the coastal range, Bolívar "met [the royalist General] Morales at the head of about 200 soldiers and 100 militiamen, the skirmishers of Morales having dispersed his advanced guard." Marx then recounts an "eyewitness record" that claims Bolívar "lost all presence of mind, spoke not a word, turned his horse quickly round, and fled in full speed toward Ocumare, passed the village at full gallop, arrived at the neighboring bay, jumped from his horse, got into a boat, and embarked on the Diana, ordering the whole squadron to follow him to the little island of Buen Ayre, and leaving all his companions without any means of assistance" (quoted in Marx 1858, n.p.). Admonished by his peers, especially the black, mixed-race Curaçaon general Manuel Piar, Bolívar had led a disastrous incursion to Ocumare. The Bolivarian Revolution of "La Gran Colombia" (1806–17) reached a geopolitical turning point as Bolívar withdrew from his original plan of attack against the Spanish in Ocumare and instead retreated to the sea.

The aftermath is no less indicting. In May 1817, just a year after Bolívar's failed expedition to Ocumare, Soublette, his right-hand man, accused Piar of conspiring with Alexandre Pétion to start a revolution of mestizos and blacks intent on forming their own state. Soublette himself read the order of general desertion that called for Piar's execution. With generals Santiago Mariño and Luis Brion presiding over the court-martial, the newly constituted revolutionary state of 1817 passed the penalty on October 15, and Bolívar signed it the very same day. While the official record describes these actions as addressing matters of loyalty to the state, there is another story here where race is the pivotal question of the revolutionary struggle. Statehood, in other words, was very much a racialized project, and although white, mestizo, and black revolutionaries may have had a common word of "freedom," inequalities from this period were left unresolved.

Today, a pro-Chávez website reminds us of this history in a three-part fictional essay by Eligio Damas (2007) entitled "El General Manuel Piar opina sobre su fusilamiento" ("General Manuel Piar Opines on His Execution") that became important in the debate, raising the issue of vindication for the assassination of General Piar.[13] It is no coincidence that the debate was raised in the era of Chávez, a president who has self-identified as mestizo and black. The debate also tore at the presumptions of the Bolivarian Revolution—the glorification of Bolívar as a hero to the movement, in my opinion, initiated a healthy skepticism as to the possible misgivings over a figure like Bolívar. Eligio Damas's piece, written in 2007 during Chávez's second term in office and published on a popular pro-Chávez news source, demonstrates the flexibility of the revolutionary political culture of this moment. While there were no doubt many who took issue with the article, Damas took Chávez's discourse as an invitation to examine the historical events of the independence wars with emboldened scrutiny and debate.

There is of course another side to Marx's story. It was known that Boves had an army of 7,000 men before his death in 1814, so perhaps it is conceivable that General Morales, the royalist, whom many of Boves's forces still rallied behind, would have wielded as great a force (Falcón 2006, 128). Soublette sent Bolívar a letter from an advanced position inland, misleading Bolívar in his tactical decisions. Most of Bolívar's tiny squadron had fled and the boats had already left the dock.[14] Bolívar was therefore forced to abandon 1,000 guns and 60,000 bullets on the beach and rally once again to victory the following year. Strategically encumbered by the arms that were still unclaimed and facing sure defeat by a much more powerful army, Bolívar may have seen retreat as the only possible option. Nevertheless, the loss was substantial, and the exit strategy was clearly a disaster.

There was, however, perhaps an even greater loss that neither Marx nor Bolívar fully recognized. As Susan Buck-Morss notes, an entire framework of history-making would privilege the passing of "revolution" from one white regime to another (2009, 12–13). In this sense, Ocumare was a crossroads of two major revolutions of the nineteenth century, and how the people of Ocumare and other Afro-descendants of Venezuela are historicized today has far-reaching repercussions for who claims the Bolivarian Revolution, whom it serves, and what new frontiers of racial equality in the Americas may be achieved by its success. As Jesús Chucho García, a Venezuelan historian and leader of an Afro-Venezuelan network, argues, "long before the French decreed liberté, egalité, et fraternité, Africans imprisoned in cacao, sugarcane, and cotton fields in the Americas were already revolting against their exploitation" (2007, 286). For García, Chirinos's rebellion in 1795 began the revolutionary wars for independence, a battle that was, for many, defined more by emancipation from slave society at home than by emancipation from the tax and property levies that tied Venezuela to Spain. With corporal enslavement, land rights, and resource distribution at stake, for the mestizos and Afro-descendants of Venezuela the war was waged on two sides, with the threat of oppression and exploitation coming from revolutionaries inside the country as much as from abroad.

García writes that "reconstructing this other history," a history of Afro-descendant struggle in the revolutionary period, "also meant elaborating strategies to demystify the erasure of the Africanity of Venezuela's national formation" (286). As García reminds us, even at the inception of Bolívar's abolition, the cause was bound to a conditional freedom: "Soon after the wars of independence had subsided, previously enslaved people were re-enslaved. Provoked to indignation, they increased their *cimarreonaje*. Reneging on abolition during the independence era was consistent with the Eurocentric notions of Venezuela's white creole 'paladins of liberty,' who could not accept the insurgent and more complete ideal of liberty contributed by the African and Afro-descendant rebels whose quests for freedom had helped to destabilize and defeat the Spanish colonial regime" (García 2007, n.p.).

The task of the revolution today is therefore to recognize the many forms of knowledge production that were absented from or continuously discredited or devalued in national education: this included the arts, songs, music, poems, and dance. As told through oral historians in the region around the independence wars, these discredited histories include stories of healers such as Cocofío, who inspired José Chirinos's rebellion in 1791, broadening networks through his council among *cumbes* (self-liberated spaces) and other villages on the coast.

To emphasize the significance of these histories that are often buried in the written archives, let us take a look again at the symbol of the horse. The icon of the white horse of Bolívar has its own history that reaches far back, even before the independence wars in the Americas. In what was known as the Kongo and Luongo Rebellion of 1749 in Caracas, it is recorded that a "sergeant of the free blacks" prophesied that "a bishop who was coming from Spain, escorted by four black crusaders on horseback, would arrive carrying the emancipation decree" (Klooster 2014, 416). Could the celebrated white horse of Bolívar be a surrogate, in Joseph Roach's use of the term, for the black revolutionaries from a generation prior to Bolívar? More than arguing for a corrective to the historicity of revolution, García and other activists point to a lineage of black emancipation to raise foundational debates in the nation and throughout the Caribbean about accepted narratives from both then and now.

This third turn of Bolívar's horse thus keeps generating new questions. Was Bolívar tricked? Or did he turn and run from the battle in cowardice, betraying those who risked their lives to follow him? Or was this the turn of his spirit horse to whisk away a war hero from sure ambush? Although Bolívar occupied a symbolically central role in the Chávez campaign, this ghost of a conflicted past remained unresolved. In Chávez's own words, at the time of his choice to build a political campaign, he saw Bolívar as a symbol of unity and compromise, a figure that would be incontestably received by both radical and conservative forces. The choice to include Bolívar was, in a sense, Chávez's way of seizing the flag itself and claiming the right to nationhood by upholding and, in essence, grafting his program on the very symbols that defined the nation at that moment in time. For Chávez, Bolívar was a strategic container for unification that stretched with each passing reassertion to the historical debates.

These are just some of the circumstances surrounding the year 1816 that present perhaps a more layered picture than the official profile of Bolívar as a symbol of absolute power. Moreover, the Venezuelan wars for independence and the Haitian Revolution, two contested roads of emancipation, remarkably intersect in Ocumare, where oral traditions have taken up thousands of possibilities over thousands more conversations on the plaza, on the streets, in scholarly discussions, and at events.[15] Thus, it should come as no surprise that the Venezuelan flag—the coat of arms being central within it—became the object on which these two different conceptions of the nation would play themselves out. The reversal of the white horse, its leaping return, quite possibly sought to rescue and in some way resolve this troubled historical disjuncture between two versions of a leftist revolution: one that would uphold an authoritarian stance of state, and another that would vindicate the wrongs potentially committed by Bolívar himself.

For many communities like Ocumare, the reversal of Bolívar's horse in this third turn embodies a return to the demands of emancipation while also rescuing Bolívar—both historically and presently. The key distinction between the second and third turns is a matter not so much of what Bolívar embodies but of who is telling the story. The following section analyzes the contemporary Ruta Afrodescendiente project in Ocumare, suggesting that local historians are making their way with and through the overlapping populist promises of the state to envision their own futures and participatory roles in the making of the revolution.

Rutas from Specter to Spect-actor

Carmen Zulay Echenagucia and Jorman Valera, local historians and educators, pulled up two chairs in the middle of a small cultural center on the corner of the Plaza Bolívar in Ocumare. Carmen and Jorman had initiated a project called La Ruta Histórica (The Historic Route), one component of a comprehensive education project celebrating the bicentennial anniversary of the Revolution of Independence, unveiled at around the same time as the new version of the flag. Rain pounded down on the roof. Puddles of water pooled up around the steps that surrounded the wide front entrance of the room, open to the street through a wall-length garage door. A few stranded people dove under the doorway for refuge on their way to the library across the street.

La Ruta, Carmen and Jorman told me, is a program in which local historians lead mainly students through seven historical sites in the area of the Ocumare coast. Jorman showed me photographs of about twenty young people standing in a circle around the Plaza Bolívar and at the beach of

Figure 15. Another component of the Misión Cultura education project is the creation of murals such as this one, created for May 10, Day of Afrovenezolanidad, on the main road through Ocumare de la Costa. *Left to right*, José Leonardo Chirinos, Simón Bolívar, Hugo Chávez. Author photo, 2010.

Playón approaching La Boca, the famous landing site of Bolívar in 1816 and of Francisco de Miranda ten years prior. Located between the major port cities of Puerto Cabello and La Guaira (nearest Caracas), Ocumare was at the center of the wars of independence and, in many ways, continues to play a central role in the current political moment. Carmen and Jorman were slowly getting the word out about their history tours to other regions of the country and internationally, with some help from the Misión Cultura to pay for their brochure and publicity.

I first met Jorman Valera in the Misión Cultura meetings in 2007, some time before the La Ruta project was started, so on this return trip to Ocumare in 2010 I was very interested in finding out what Jorman and Carmen had been up to. So much had happened in a few short years. Their brochure was entitled "Afrodescendant Bicentennial Route: Bolívar and *los Afros* in the History of Emancipation from Key Coastal Towns on the Aragua Coast."[16] As I paged through it, Carmen and Jorman told me the logistics of the program: students from the nearby towns of Maracay and Caracas were all invited to participate in the tours. They had also created a Facebook page to promote the project. The government has aided them in this process, but decisions about the content of the tours are handled by members of the local Misión Cultura. According to the group's website, "The Ruta Pedagógica 'Bolívar y las y los Afros' is a project that vindicates a civilized group that over years has been marginalized and excluded in the struggle for emancipation in the Americas. This revolutionary process allows us today to include Afropolitics in the law and constitution of the Republic."[17]

In *Silencing the Past: Power and the Production of History* (1995), Michel-Rolph Trouillot argues that history is partly shaped by what is told in the creation of sources, in the making of archives, in the accepted past of our collective imagination. What is silenced may remain as evidence but requires the tellers of history to make visible what has been buried or erased from view. Attention to the production of meaning is precisely the work of the La Ruta project. Cultural producers insist on tours that are face-to-face, locally rooted, and led by Afro-descendant historians. The tours are part of a more comprehensive education program that spans from early childhood to adulthood, involving oral history projects and mentorship. The tours are open to school groups nation- and worldwide and include site visits to places like the cacao cooperative, the landing site of Bolívar in La Boca, and the town of Cumboto.[18]

Setting its two major achievements in the passing of two constitutional laws, the Law of Liberational Education and the Law against Racial Discrimination, the Afro-descendant history project was as much about law and policy in government as it was about restructuring the way history is taught on the Ocumare coast. I include here a more substantial excerpt from the group's website (accessed in 2010) in order to stay true to their own words about how they developed their project.

> It is in this revolutionary transformation and the search for our real national identity that the Ruta Bicentenaria was born, "*Bolívar y los Afros en la Historia de la Emancipación.*" Along this route, historical evidence untold in official histories will be explored, including the great support of the people of Haití that unconditionally gave to the occasion of this bicentennial commemoration of Independence. The route includes the site in which Francisco de Miranda fought in the first naval battle in the history of independence in 1806, how Alexandre Petión supported the Bolívar expedition that arrived at the Aragua coasts ten years later and the Haitians that accompanied him. On this path, you will not encounter the history that you would normally find in books or the Internet. This is a social construct, a product of collective efforts of the Cumbe Afroaragueño. In the old educational model, it was not possible to approach these issues in our institutions but now, in these first years we have been working to bring these histories to our communities. (2010)

To illustrate the political significance of Afro-descendant rights as an issue that led to the La Ruta project in the Chávez era, Eubel López, a spokesperson for the Afro-descendant movement, unequivocally backed Chávez's successor President Nicolas Maduro, saying, "We are fully with the Bolivarian Revolution, because through it we have been made visible, with great achievements such as the Organic Law against Racial Discrimination."[19] The same year I visited Jorman and Carmen, the second annual *Afrodescendiente* festival brought together upward of 10,000 people, with 34 cultural-performance groups convening on issues of history, creation of knowledge, and building community networks. The *cofradías* and conferences in Aragua are building stronger alliances. Activists are strengthening existing networks and creating new ones. A stronger demand exists to bring forward these stories, to reflect these deeper pools of historical memory, and to continue to define new directions for the revolution through groups like the Afro-Red, a prominent Afro-descendant transnational network.

Fernando Coronil pointed to this very question of history in the Venezuelan state in one of his last writings: "What comes out of the Magician's Hat is now different: not elements of history, but History itself. And it is a history not for the whole nation, but for part of it. A radicalization of the narrative of History itself: what comes out of a hat is not cars, factories, hospitals, schools, or even a cosmogony, but history itself, a different history" (2008, n.p.). Here is an understanding of history *as* the magical state itself, once again, blasting open the distilled effects of totalizing forms of "official" histories and the limits of periodization and authorship that those entail. Rather than accepting that Bolívar initiated the struggle for emancipation with the reading of the Proclamation of Emancipation in Ocumare in 1816, we can see that the act was only one milestone in a continuum of emancipation efforts. Rather than co-opting history, these symbols of state offer a means to open history up and reexamine what was left behind. Rather than extracting a story as a resource for the state to exploit, this approach to historical reactivation is about performed face-to-face experience. The Ruta project allows for the production of history to remain in the oral tradition networks so that those in the region can decide how they will tell the story—as one of betrayal, of reconciliation, or of both.

The initiative of the Ruta Histórica challenges conventional historic accounts of the Revolution of Independence as a battle fought solely between Spain and the primarily white *criollo* oligarchy and instead asserts the Afro-Venezuelan political and cultural perspective within the construction of the new nationalism. The tours, led by local historians, including Valera, cover eight locations of historical interest. Among them is La Boca, where Francisco de Miranda attempted to raise the revolutionary flag in Venezuela to declare independence from Spain on April 28, 1806, before he was beaten back to the sea (Bushnell 2004). This is the same site where Bolívar would attempt the same incursion into the Venezuelan "heartland" ten years later.

As we sit in the open front room at the Misión, Jorman relates the importance of Bolívar's expedition in terms of the support received from Haití. "Haití," he says, "has been erased from our history, yet it was one of the most important countries to the foundation of independence in Venezuela. In 1816 when Bolívar landed in Ocumare, he came with the support of André Pétion under the condition that Bolívar support the emancipation of slavery." Jorman goes on to explain that the dates are extremely important; 1806 and 1816 mark the history of a struggle for independence in the region. These dates for the region of Ocumare bookend the official date of the bicentennial of 1810. "We are still in this struggle of independence," Jorman says to me as he points my attention back to the brochure (Valera 2010, interview).

Another important figure for the creation of the La Ruta project is Jorge Guerrero Veloz, an intellectual and activist who at the time of writing this represented Venezuela as a cultural ambassador in New Orleans.[20] The brochure for the Ruta project includes an essay by Guerrero Veloz in which he spells out the connections between Miranda, Bolívar, and Haití as the principal motive for creating the tours. According to Guerrero Veloz, the 200-year celebration of independence must take as its point of reference Haití and the emancipation of slavery. He argues that Haití played a much more important role in the history of Venezuela than what has conventionally been accepted by historians. He also suggests that this support from Haití must be considered central in the account because on two separate occasions the Haitian leaders Jean Jacques Dessalines and Alexandre Pétion made it possible for Miranda and Bolívar to carry out their expeditions to Venezuelan soil: "[It is] an historical debt that we maintain still today with this generous country" (Guerrero Veloz 2001). Quoting Toussaint Louverture, he continues, "What we want is not a liberty of circumstances conceded to ourselves alone, rather the absolute adoption in which all people who are born red, black or white can not be the property of another" (ibid.).[21] The adoption of a version of independence that is based on the Haitian model of emancipation and the rights of all men countered the interpretations of independence encouraged by the *cabildo* powers that sought to expel the Spanish while retaining the rights of property and slaves for the *criollo* minority.

To vindicate this claim for historical independence on the basis of the Haitian model means to correct previous distortions of history. It reaffirms this national claim on the basis of an ethics of rights for all as opposed to only the few. It also upholds a genealogy of independence within the black abolitionist and black independence revolutionary traditions, suggesting an altogether different alignment of power that supports activists and cultural producers on the Aragua coast—like those developing the bicentennial history tours—who have taken up these issues both within Venezuela and internationally.

The bicentennial route is one created, planned, and guided by a group of cultural activists from the coast of Aragua. Projects by these cultural producers are about historical recovery, and, interestingly, they are very much defined by performance in face-to-face interactions. I agree with producers that projects such as the bicentennial history project create a liberated space, like the *cumbes* themselves, within which participants define their own forms of modernity that have come to influence and in many ways define a politics of the Bolivarian Revolution. Like the Barrio Adentro program, these projects emphasize the value of endogenous production networks. The production of politics happens in these spaces through the habits and processes of production in everyday life.

Indeed, the history project integrates fiestas and other cultural productions of the town, such as the devil dances, as centrally important aspects of their work. In 2010, Gio and I followed the fiesta Virgin Saint, who traveled down the street, to the church, and then to the day care center the next day. The Comunas and Misiones (collectives) repeat themselves through the continual display of elections on the plaza and the ongoing visibility (literally, with their garage door open to the plaza) within the Misión Cultura. A few years earlier, the former hacienda of one of Gómez's mistresses was renovated to become a cultural center on one corner of the plaza, which later became headquarters for the devil dances and various educational initiatives. The Ruta Histórica has its own planned route through various sites of historical interest. Together, these places are strung together to make a path, in a sense another processional route, where each place on that path opens up more possibilities to map a historical and contemporary redress of power, of who tells history, and of how that story is told.

Populism practiced through performance influences local and national politics within a proliferation of changes and new kinds of agency in Venezuela. Cultural producers engage in an active symbolic language, a language that is easily overlooked as hegemonic and yet thrives in populist politics. The controversy over the bicentennial flag points to a populist intervention in the symbol of state, one that presents a particular function of redress. Rather than being a sorcerer that covers up and obscures history (creating a theater of illusion), the state becomes, in Augusto Boal's terms, the "joker," taking on the role of facilitator, mediator, and provocateur, even at times taking the position of the "devil's advocate," not to merely agitate, but as a means of opening up possibilities where they seem to stalemate. In Augusto Boal's Forum Theater, "spect-actors" are spectators who enter the stage to take up roles, usually through improvisation, in order to use the staged moment as a laboratory in which they reconstruct problems and experiment toward finding solutions.

Representational theater, perhaps like representational democracy, is for Boal a form of coercion. Perhaps we are accustomed to a theater in which spectators are passive and actors portray scripted characters on stage. For Boal, theater is a weapon that must be wrested from the hands of the dominant class, which has used it as a mode of coercion, and reinstated toward the struggle for liberation. This reinstatement implies a radical transformation of the structure and practice of theater from an Aristotelian model that pacifies its audiences (ultimately inhibiting them from taking action in societal conflict) to that of a participant drama comprised of ordinary people who partake in a theatrical modeling of real-to-life situations. As populist repertoires, these staged events move from a participatory politic where one becomes witness and protagonist to a process of making collective identity as a political act. For Boal, nothing is outside of politics. Alienation and apathy, and even our inhibitions are, by the very idea of being thrust on stage, products of the Aristotelian notion of separating the actor from the real world, separating the production from the staged scene, and separating a political subject from the subject's own process of resolution. For Boal, the key is a transfer of the mode of production in the theater, where the actor is the creator of the theater, and the ordinary person is the creator of the actor.

In my view, the transfer of production is that which transforms Bolívar from the classic model of "one for all," where *one* leader defines the agency of others, to a model in which Bolívar becomes a loose-fitting and even arguably disintegrating meshed frame that gets redistributed and mobilized in fiesta politics. In this case, within the face-to-face retelling of Bolívar is where the deeper negotiation takes place, conducted by and within networks of cultural producers that directly include Jorman, Carmen, those local networks that produce the dancing devils of Ocumare de la Costa, and so on. The work of the "state" is also being handled, produced, and told from within these networks, which, like the *cayapa* (cooperative labor system), were for a long time held outside the state. This is not to say that Bolívar is an ideal or even necessary aspect of this negotiation. It is indeed possible that Bolívar's primacy is diminished in the process. What is significant for our purposes here is that the telling of history potentially enables many visions of futurity to exist through and beyond Bolívar. The key here is that Bolívar is not just handed over to the network of fiesta politics. Instead, perhaps the most fruitful possibility of revolution is when Bolívar and the state are appropriated by the fiesta rather than the other way around. In any case, the story is not ending, not with Chávez's untimely passing, nor as the state enters another phase of contestation.

The three turns of the horse of Bolívar enable a broader schema in which to identify the possibilities of the populist state. The first turn is representative of a top-down officialism in which Bolívar is the good father and the people are protected children; statesmanship is assumed in all its totalizing and patriarchal ways. In the second turn, however, the symbolic function of Bolívar moves toward trying to redefine and equalize that patriarchal figure in relation to a greater social body. The emphasis in the second turn is the state's composite constituency; at the same time, the remaking of Bolívar hangs in the balance between what people believe that image to be—a belief-effect of representation—and the reality falling short of that belief, a reality where only the strategic redistribution of power would allow the substantiation of that representation. The second turn separates itself from the "officialism" of Bolívar's portrait that conflates this larger social body to a degree of appropriation between state and *pueblo*. The third turn moves toward a structural shift in which the very reproduction of the history of Bolívar moves into different hands, where the meaning of state itself is carried and reworked by an entirely new set of producers.

As I have argued in previous chapters, people have already been producing their own local histories vis-à-vis performance. A move toward sharing the local perspective in a national history project like La Ruta is a potential game changer. It means shifting the symbolic position of those previously "on the margins" so that they can take a central role as producers in the historical-national story where the very site and subject of state recenter (and re-create) themselves within what Buck-Morss (2009) calls "constellations" of history. These are histories that open up that which was previously unseen, the multiple pasts and multiple acts of telling that are obscured by the imposition of "one for all."

If, as Fernando Coronil (1997) wrote, the "unseen forces" of the state still exist within the realm of "magic," then the close historical reading of Bolívar's actual encounter in the region of Ocumare de la Costa turns those unseen forces of the revolutionary state into a deliberate form of political negotiation. The process does not seek closure to the debate; it opens up the power of the past and present. In this sense, return is also a "re-turn," where going back implies a repetitive turn or somatic reversal to historical redress. Performance in this case offers an opening and a space in which to consider the various "forces" that enter a symbol of state. Performance lets us explore these forces that suggest a new (and old) political order and, importantly, help to make way for the potential future directions of a different story and storytellers in the guiding myths of revolution.

In addition to approving the revisions on the bicentennial coat of arms, the same bicentennial commission, produced by the Ministry of Popular Power for Education, issued a series of publications that analyzed the roles of Miranda, Bolívar, and José Antonio Páez in avoiding, and in some cases being complicit with, the perpetuation of slavery in the independence wars. These publications were widely distributed among the country's population. So when the media covered the right-wing opposition to Chávez that protested the turning of the horse, they missed these deeper ways in which the government's bicentennial commission—and, as I have argued in this chapter so far, the galloping horse itself—potentially opened, rather than closed, a discussion as to the very definitions of the nation and of transnational alliances among subaltern groups that are perhaps the broader issue at stake in the revolutions of the twenty-first century.

From the beginning of this research, I wondered how Bolívar (and the embodiment of his horse) were potentially speaking to a wider sensibility about the nation. The opposition's hyperbolic response to the new flag indicated just how much there was at stake, to claim a political space through symbols such as the horse of Bolívar. In the wake of the 2004 campaign (discussed in chapter 3), which had been all about historical revivals of figures from the Federal Wars, this question of a return to history in the pursuit of a revolution came up again. Unlike Cuba's revolution in 1959, which celebrated the "new man" and the "new woman," the Bolivarian Revolution at its outset was all about resuscitating the past. This political expression of populism wasn't just Bolívar and the multiple dreams he embodied, however; it was also a particular annexation and agency of "the people" that was reflected in the embodiment of his horse. The transformed body of the horse indicated deeper tensions among contending political futures.

The galloping horse may indeed be an extension of Coronil's (1997) magical state, a state made possible by the interaction between revolutionary hope and the oil industry's subsidized illusion of modernity. However, there also is a kind of demystified state embodied by the reversal of the horse on the national crest, which offers a means to sort out the seeming contradictions between national and local narratives of power through the performance of state. Rather than seeing ambivalence in the direction of the horse's gait, I conclude that the horse's return opened the way for a historical redress of Bolívar that became useful to reframe revolution. The shift from specter to "spect-actor" adds the dimension of participation, broadening the production network in ways that proliferate, populate, and even bust open the discrete and fixed container of the available body in which a future can be envisioned. As this chapter has demonstrated, Bolívar is a symbol of layered futurity in which the multiple competing embodiments of both horse and phantom rider point to the potential directions of the revolution. Along with its rider, the performing icon of Bolívar's horse continues to generate new debates over the revolution and its future that extend beyond nationalism in Venezuela to the political cultures and populism of América Latina.

CONCLUSION

The idea for this book first came out of the campaign poster of Hugo Chávez discussed in chapter 3. The cartoon image of the president jousting a squeamish, festive devil while astride a puffy white horse—branded "SB" for Simon Bolívar—struck me as a bold assertion of the revolutionary campaign. Chávez played the part perfectly, a comically rendered Saint George slaying the dragon with the lance-like sword in his hand. The image of the horse and rider reflected a reenactment of the colonial scenario—the hero-saint beating down the pagan and diabolical subjects. Yet the image was also an entirely transformed embodiment which seemed to parody that colonial act and even the campaign itself.

Given the history of news coverage on Venezuela, I knew to be skeptical of what was reaching the United States in mainstream media. But the poster was circulating on a private blog, and I wondered: What limits might it reveal about the socialist humanism espoused by the new, democratically elected government? Did the poster imply a threat by the president and his administration to minority subjects of the state? Was it an indication of authoritarianism in the name of a greater social good, as the liberal press maintained? But there was something peculiar about the image. The saintly horse was just too fierce and the devil was cutesy, even frivolous. The horse plodded forward, down to earth. Chávez's bare toes in the stirrups and the guitar slung over his shoulder qualified the image's militancy, reminding me of Alí Primera and Victor Jara, who fought against dictatorship with songs as their armaments. Nor was this image merely a swapping of swords between oppressor and oppressed, a reversal of David and Goliath. To me, there was something vaguely reminiscent of the perennial fiestas of *Moros y cristianos*, battle reenactments depicting the so-called conquest of Mexico (see Lamadrid 2003). Here the poster seemed to hold the same irreverence for the actual conquest, as if its replay of the charging horse in itself undermined the very pretension that conquest was ever final (ibid., 26). As I reflected, I saw that the poster was working on several levels at once to convey a cartoonish informality, even a sense of humor—one that mocked the depiction of the devil, the horse, and the rider all at once. I wondered what claims were being made in its parody, to whom it was being circulated, and how viewers were using it to frame both the existing government and the ongoing debate.

It was only then that I noticed what had been so glaringly obvious that it was easy to miss: who produced it. Printed on the original poster (not pictured) were the icons of the fishermen's union, a student group, and a neighborhood association lined up along the top; these left-wing civic groups were the producers of this campaign. In fact, it was not clear whether Chávez had anything to do with the poster image at all. And, after hearing testimonies by and having many conversations with activists and artists, I realized that the question to ask was not about what the *state* was doing to invent and exert campaign pressure, but rather about what people—some not even directly affiliated with the state—were doing to re-create the state. While the performance of state seemed to be dominated by the charismatic figure of Chávez, simultaneously Chávez was just as much a useful part in a play produced by others, an instrument of the complex cultural and political arrangements that moved through him.

Several years later, I had a chance to meet the poster artist El Tano Yea in his modest living space in one of the central barrios of Caracas. He had since been hired by the state for various projects, including printing educational information and messages about cultural diversity on the sides of government-distributed bags of powdered milk. Amid a world of tiny model ships, walls decorated with colorful comic posters, and cats, we chatted about how he developed as an artist while he was a student at the Universidad Central de Venezuela, his past as a survivor of the Chilean dictatorship of Augusto Pinochet, and his memories of the economic war that sought to blockade the government of Salvador Allende. During that visit, he showed me another poster he created of Bolívar's horse. Only this time the horse was trotting with flowers in its mane and birds above it, with hearts dotting the background. Chávez is accompanied on the saddle by the playwright and poet César Rengifo and the folk singer Alí Primera, in honor of the thirtieth anniversary of Primera's memory after his death in 1985.

Much like other forms of support for Chávez, the poster was an act of bottom-up production—in a way, *artivism*, a term used by Chela Sandoval and Guisela Latorre (2008) to indicate the merging cultural production between art and activism (2008, 81). In this case, different voices in the social movement were responsible for the proliferations of campaign material that riffed off themes and stories central to Venezuelan society. This is not to say that there were no directors or leaders who skillfully played a part in shifting the rules of the dialogue and in determining who was at the table. El Tano and many other artists were consulted on how to build revolutionary materials and communication and, in some cases, they enjoyed some benefits for their labor. Ultimately, however, throughout the ten years of the Chávez presidency (1999–2010), through the broader networks of artists, the hundreds of televised hours in improvised broadcasts, and the thousands of funded neighborhood and workplace groups, the question of how populism was reproduced went beyond Chávez to include a much wider network of people who chose to retrieve and re-create their own visions of a collective society.

Whether one agreed with Chávez is, in some ways, beside the point: the poster, like many of the performances discussed in this book, was indicative

Figure 16 El Tano Yea, *Con Alí a 30 años 2015 de su siembra*, 2015. The image shows Hugo Chávez accompanied by the Venezuelan theater artist César Rengifo on a white horse, along with other musicians, poets, and artists, such as the famed singer Alí Primera. Image courtesy of the artist.

of a particular brand of populism in the Chávez era. It was a populism that generated a responsive, radical democracy centered on what is referred to as governance in the streets. Much like the participants in the procession of the devil dances, the various contingents of the street rallies in Caracas made their own altars, small centers of agency and production rallying behind a banner or a rainbow-colored parachute. In symbols, signs and songs, posters, and performance, revolutionaries continuously sought open-air forums for public expression and debate.

Democracy, after all, was originally conceived as the power of the people to produce their own governance. As the political theorist C. Douglas Lummis argues, we forget this simplicity (1996, 15). Instead, we are barraged with false assumptions and myths about democracy in mainstream media: that democracy is primarily about electing competent leadership, where the *demos* or "people" of democracy are equivalent to the middle class holding a peg at the center of the left-right spectrum; that democracy is contrary to communism; that democracy is the right to protest (ibid.). The list goes on.

Yet the radical implication of democracy, according to Lummis, is that *demos* + *kratia* means "people power," or the power of the people to rule themselves.

A participatory democracy is thus ultimately a question of this popular power at the level of production. The fact that a union and a neighborhood association had come up with the poster demonstrated their commitments to the political process. Moreover, the poster was one of hundreds of images, many of them radically different in design and content, suggesting that their creation was more than an accidental slip of controls. This mode of production was very different from a top-down, streamlined campaign with handlers, political action committees, and central financing. It pointed to a radical restructuring that had been entirely obscured by the centralization of state in other arenas and by the charismatic and unifying discourse that Chávez had created as its counterpoint.

This ad hoc production of the campaign reflected a hodgepodge of interest groups instead of one centralized and centralizing force. Touching the state from this view meant encountering a relatively unregulated and diverse field of cultural messaging, and networks that run across and through the state and constituency. We were looking at populism as an archipelago, as Benjamin Arditi calls it, rather than as a singular source with radial rings of influence (2007, 145). In the streets of rural and urban neighborhoods, posters, murals, films, and theater were produced by so many different voices; this profusion of voices, styles, and modes of expression was perhaps most strongly expressed in performance.

The first main argument of this book is that populism is a performed act. As I discussed in chapter 3, by tapping into a performance practice—quite literally a story, song, and dance—the recall campaign proliferated new meanings among a broad base of constituents. As a performed act, populism manifests as political culture expressed within embodied performance practice.

Populism is indeed about the body. Unlike other political formations that deal with organizational power in relation to other entities, populism takes us right to the person-to-person interactions that originate in the body. Populism's concern is not necessarily with individual identity, but rather with how individuals connect to a collective. This does not sacrifice the I of the we; as Kamau Brathwaite (1974) understands, there is a "mwe" possible in this collective identification that retains individual will. Perhaps in reverse, Chávez, as the iconoclast figure of state, becomes this collectively made "mwe." But in this case, the body of state performs first, and one's role as witness, supporter, and detractor is then refiltered through one's relationship to these cultural perceptions of the collective nation. To focus on populism as a dimension of political cultures was in this way a deliberate choice to flip what felt like a standard preoccupation with cultural politics, or the politics of cultural exchange among individuals. Populism can simultaneously mean difference and a composite body. It is a strategic commitment to create a union of individuals *to* a collective will that is forged and re-created wherever bodies meet: at the kitchen table, in the streets, at the bus stop, and so forth. Populism refers to the political process that enables individuals *to make* collective power. It is the performative *doing* of politics, outside of parties or other formal organizational mandates.

It is important to be clear that the politics of performance and the performance of politics each point to very different questions and outcomes, yet they also rely on a fundamental interdependency of terms. The politics of performance is about what goes into the production of a performance, the political acts that surround the making of a performance event; while the performance of politics refers to how politics, policy debates, or displays of political power are performed, *as if* they are a performance. In the introduction I defined performance as a series or ongoing set of actions or events that are witnessed and framed as an act of showing, and politics as the influence or interplay of power.

Politics can also engage that power by artifice, or an art of illusion. In a theatrical sense, whether the political act is true or not, the show ends and when the curtain is up there is another world outside. Onstage, anything goes—as long as the audience is convinced. What is expected of politicians as actors, then, is a heightened skill of illusion. As Timothy Raphael (2009) argues, statecraft becomes stagecraft where the performance of state is ultimately a synesthetic art. Populism, like politics, is so often conflated as an art of illusory promise in which platitudes and clever memes supplant the criteria of substance. As the grandmother in *Pandemonium* laments, in the end, they mean nothing.

Whereas "good" performance is judged on its efficacy to maintain the illusion, populism claims to deconstruct the distance between audience and actors. Populism reorganizes the relationship between the spectator and the stage. Populism breaks down this theatrical fourth wall, or the imaginary barrier between the audience and the stage, to forge continuity between the production of politics (staged, framed, on view) and the lived experience, desires, and demands in everyday political making, from the minutia to the rallies to the campaign. The failure of the theatrical fourth wall, in other words, pushes open a new frame (this time of critique) to expose the entire event as politics.

Perhaps politics, as Brecht said, becomes most apparent in a performance that openly exhibits its own life of production. Production back-ends even a conventional staged performance: it indicates what goes on behind the scenes as a performance is politically managed, devised, or produced. Performance carries its own politics within the regulation of its production, where production—how it is produced and by whom—exposes the apparatus of support. If we accept that each arm of production has its own gravity of power, the question of production opens up a myriad of other acts of possible illusion and truth-making, all of which seem to radiate in a thousand directions, too plentiful to ever grasp without context, richly and deeply examined.

From at least the seventeenth century in the coastal region of Venezuela, as discussed in chapter 1, fiestas were organized directly next to and as a part of social services, such as care for the elderly, health care, and funeral services. Fiestas were an important part of organizing collective labor. These were events produced by primarily indigenous and Afro-descendant communities and often in *cumbes*, maroon communities where generations of people developed cultural, artistic, and political practices outside of colonial society. Where political representation was absent, other forms of governance were practiced through these performances. Not unlike the use of *capoeira* as a practice to rehearse fighting skills, performances of the devil dances are about faith and devotion and, at the same time, are forums to rehearse the politics of collective society.

Concisely, performance of this kind exposes the very logics and practice of populism. A popular cultural performance, such as the devil dances, is not a substitute for political work, nor does it mirror that which we call politics: it is in itself a political act. It is a processual event in which decision-making, arbitration of difference, and signification take place with a heightened degree of attention. Indeed, cultural performances are not merely "cultural"; they are an integral part of the making of politics in the everyday.

The interdependent relationship between populism and performance continuously points back to the question of how they are legitimated. A ritual of people wearing white wigs and felt robes is of the highest order in one performance; electing Fermín to lead the procession of the devil dances is one as well. The devil dances play a crucial role in setting new terms of inclusion and exclusion, of who is "we," and in determining what behaviors are considered acceptable inside or outside a durational social order. Linking social services, public welfare, and civic order to the devil dances shows how performance, in this case, was always a site of politic-making and is much more than a practice of symbolic or cultural value. Too often, populism is the word that stands in for and obscures political formations practiced outside of dominant institutions of power. This drives a powerful mandate not to define "populism" but to ask the question: what has been masked by this word?

Too often performance is relegated to a cultural domain outside of the law. The very conventional notion of performance as an art of illusion, staged fiction, or frivolous entertainment in a sense negates the event as practice of a political nature, as a means of enacting and enforcing laws. What goes on in the theater is, in a sense, protected from law. In some cases, ritual performances have been interpreted as elevated "above" the law, antistructural, or ontologically against the power structure or systems of law and order. While serving to critique (or avoid) the abuse of law and authority (i.e., police, etc.) in some cases, these interpretations also lead to a categorical dismissal of fiesta's political impact beyond a temporary lapse of norms.

Performance as populism thus allows us to think further about the ontological differences *within* the political, and about the erasure (i.e., depoliticization) of certain kinds of political action that for many centuries were explicitly understood as both politics and performance. At this conflux are the very questions of what constitutes ritual performance, and the ways in which festival performance in particular has erroneously been interpreted as outside of governance, against law, or outside of time and space. The suggestion, therefore, is to recognize large-scale public manifestations, like the devil dances, and other forms of festival and fiesta politics as assembly, as forum, and as a means of cultivating the public decision-making practice. This leads us to another main point.

The second argument that I make in this book is that, rather than being ancillary to political effects, performance was a constitutive, mediating factor in the emergence of populism in Venezuela. Performance can entertain, transform, and also shape the world in which it is present (see Schechner 2013). Performance also transmits rules and political logics. As I describe in the first two chapters, cultural assertions made through fiesta and carnival factored in the very organizational makeup of political life. Fiesta is more than just jovial and eruptive behavior. Fiesta politics is also an enduring method, one that joins social relations with materiality, from the fiesta life in the barrio public as discussed in chapter 2 to the construction of houses, alleyways, and public infrastructure by contingent design.

Here, performance and populism are a part of the built environment, literally made out of the social and material conditions of the barrio space as they are transformed from peripheral settlements on the outskirts of Caracas into their own centers of power. The play *Caín adolescente* staged the materiality of the barrio space, depicting the making of the *barrio adentro*, a geospatial perspective on the city and modernity—all of which broadens the possibilities of the urban popular class to organize its own public space of the barrio. As a depiction of the barrio public, the play is also very much about people—in this case, people like Juana, Juan, and Encarnación, each with their complexity of both good and bad, as they contend with the conditions of the barrio and its marginality to the city center of power.

Each character seeks freedom, redemption, and spiritual transformation in the space of the barrio. The glimmering lights of the city below, the broken steps, and the laundry hanging over the makeshift walls on the set of the play recall the barrio as a real-to-life place without embellishments. Yet the questions posed by these characters concern something beyond whether each would attain fulfillment; the play presents the contradictions and competing ideas that articulate what Chantal Mouffe calls the agonistic frontier, within the barrio space.

Evidence or traces of populism were carried over from fiesta councils when people migrated to the city. As residents moved from rural to urban environments and adapted to their circumstances, these physical sites of the barrio took shape through the customary building practices and forms of organization brought by new residents in what theorist Randy Martin calls a "mobilization" of politics taking form in space-time environments (1998, 208). These mobilizations contributed to the formation of the popular class and the revolution. Again, as George Ciccariello-Maher (2013) argues, while Chávez was—and still is—hugely important to the movement, he was also a part of a much longer lineage of the Bolivarian Revolution. I argue that this position of "inside" the barrio was constructed not only by activists in clandestine work against the state but also, importantly, through the work of artists such as Román Chalbaud, who helped to popularize and, in a sense, mainstream the barrio as a cultural-political space from the 1950s up to its transformation in the 1990s.

My aim, however, is not to find the origins of some "authentic populism" as much as it is to acknowledge a continuity of performance-based political cultures that get picked up and amplified—albeit in sometimes distorted ways—as melodrama, as realism and parody. What remains is evidence of what Thomas Nail (2015) calls a "kinopolitics" of migrant social flow. The act of circulation was not restricted to only states and institutions; theater and film—whether advertently or not—became vehicles to project a kinopolitical mobilization into the space of the barrio. Chalbaud's works reflect that continuity in the politics of barrio life, and even more so as they are depicted and creatively embellished from the theatrical set of the barrio onstage to the remaking of those barrio spaces as part of the populist state in a discourse of "inside the barrio" as initiated by endogenous organizations.

The failure of redemption seen in *Caín adolescente*, alongside the failure of the fourth republic (1958–99), is revived at a crescendo in the film *Pandemonium*, where the barrio is reimagined as an insurgent political space. The performance of "Florentino and the Devil" activates these spaces of the barrio so that they become the organizational base from which to assert political autonomy and demand new terms of governance.

This brings me to the last bridge argument of this book—namely, that the analysis of populism is incomplete without a performance lens because, methodologically, performance is indexically unique from other forms of expression. The gestural, behavioral, spatial, and interrelational dimensions of performed acts far exceed, or are at least different from, those of speech transcripts. It is the difference between a play text and the staged enactment. This is not to say that text-based media, such as the novel, are not fabulously rich forms of knowledge transfer that also challenge fixed assumptions about culture and politics and so forth. Nor do these modalities work only discretely from one another. As a mode of expression, however, performance tells us how people act politically through a radically expanded sensorium.

If performance requires a different methodological lens, one that attributes its meaning to an expanded register of affect—the gestural, the restored behaviors, the relationship between actors and audiences, and cultural perceptions of staged performance as illusion-making or as ritual truth-telling—what then does this say about populism? First is a theoretical intervention where populism, like performance, is by its nature antithetical to a singular idea, contrary to what the ideation scholars of populism contend. Populism cannot exist as an entity or singular concept since it is, in itself, the very process to negotiate those concepts. Populism is precisely the performed expression of this wrestling among contending voices in ongoing debate.

To view populism through performance forces us to reconsider the neat containers attributed to Manichaean dualisms of good versus evil. Good-versus-evil dualisms exist across the political spectrum, sometimes haunting institutional histories as much as popular appeals. Historically, and I believe also presently, people can generate and also work out and heal from the false dualisms of so-called Manichaean discourse through performance; it is one of the principal means by which oppressed communities have fought back from the imposition of monotheistic ideologies. Performances like the devil dances are purported to be about a battle of good versus evil, and yet the performance operates more as an antidote to Manichaeism precisely because its mode of production (the dance, its organizational networks, and its transmission) splinters apart good-versus-bad logics. In this case, popular performance loosens the knot instead of tightening it further. There are simply too many points for subversion, too many points of exchange in these popular networks for meanings to enclose and consolidate.

That said, the increasing popularity of the devil dances and their recent designation as cultural patrimony by UNESCO are raising new questions and debates about the effects of "support" and their potential to erode the networks of popular power. Just before his death in 2016, Cecilio Silva was concerned that the designation was changing the practice. "There are lots of little devils," his daughter Elvia Silva said, "but the infusion of financial support means that the old folks don't go out and collect from everyone, which formed part of the culture" (E. Silva 2017). Resources end up in the hands of some and are not always distributed. At the same time, the church continues to impose its own logic that goes against the traditions of *el pueblo*. The debates go on.

Like the devil dances, "Florentino and the Devil" is not just about good versus evil. Handily, Florentino is a force of good, but his role is also about common knowledge, peaceful resistance, and the patient and reasoned debunking of an anti-humanist agenda. The story recalls methods of political determination through verse, rhyming, and collective performance. The Devil, modeled after Wile E. Coyote, in Chávez's campaign videos is most definitely not the "good guy," but this *diablo*, who also appears in the posters and the advertisements of the "No" campaign, is also redeemable, even comically likeable, and exists within a familiar repertoire of highly symbolic, performed contestation. Audiences are no doubt swayed to identify with Florentino, but the Devil in this story oscillates between two points: one is the understanding of the inevitability of contestation and its rightful place in democracy, and the other is a vanishing point of exclusion located outside the nation and the limits of democracy altogether.

Moreover, there is an important epistemic dimension to these performances that must be considered. In these performances heavily influenced by indigenous and Afro-descendant belief systems, one figure is not required to replace the other; instead, there is an invitation, as Clemis García said in chapter 1, for *all* the saints to come to the party. As Diana Taylor (2003) argued, these acts of transfer are not necessarily about surrogation. Like the religious site where the Virgin of Tepeyac builds its power from the temple of Tonantzín buried underneath, politics functions within this layered episteme such that multiple possibilities surface in the performance space (ibid.). One edifice may be planted directly on top of another, and yet both remain in the present.

The populism of the Bolivarian Revolution follows many of these logics to include rather than replace. Bolívar is one such example, as a symbol that recalls the tradition of a triumphant, singular leader as status quo. He is the ultimate statesman, revered by Gómez and Pérez Jiménez and practically every president of the twentieth century. However, Bolívar is also constantly being "collectively remade" and in ways that appeal to creative and radical alternative youth groups, artists, and organizations that align themselves on the left. Each embraces Bolívar with different meanings. But this too is changing, where Bolívar now shares the performance space with other figures that were once obscured.

The multiplicity of Bolívar can be a catalyst for a radical reimagining of the state. Each Bolívar is grafted onto the previous version. Each manifestation carries with it another set of meanings, associations, and understandings. Rather than rejecting the iconic or symbolic value of Bolívar as an accessory or knockoff of state power, the performing icon of Bolívar is evidence of the popular exchange in remaking the state. As ordinary people, artists, and residents across multiple sectors of society continue to re-create Bolívar, they are also engaging politically as an expression of populism. The Bolivarianism projected through this icon, therefore, is not a mere branding of the messianic state. Rather, it is shaped by multitudes of people to become an act of deliberation and debate within Bolivarian democracy.

What is interesting is how this dynamic figure of Bolívar is constantly turning, constantly being re-signified; in many ways, it is a symbol that keeps performing, just as in the perennial recurrence of fiesta, an icon or a saint like San Juan revolves each year. Groups such as the Ruta Histórica of the Afro-descendant activists in Ocumare claimed Bolívar as a means to revisit pivotal questions about the inequities in national historical narratives, so his figure also plays a key position in the critical activism within the revolution. Revealing the underlying power dynamics of the independence revolution 200 years ago allows a national dialogue of bringing forth the histories that were silenced; the history of Venezuela's alliance with Haiti and figures like José Leonardo Chirinos, Juana the Advancer, and Matea Bolívar are now being recognized in the national pantheon as black leadership and as a significant movement of black revolutionary independence that gained power in and through the state. Currently, activists press for an even stronger commitment to enforce laws against racial discrimination and to continue a South-to-South dialogue with African nations to end systemic racism.

The questions of this book thus stretch beyond populism, because within them is a much more hard-hitting demand to recognize the Afro-descendant and indigenous political philosophy as integral and foundational to democracy. It must be noted that the Bolivarian Revolution did not set out to tear down the previous order; rather, its work was to insert itself through familiar repertoires and historical revival in order to form a new state. Rather than inventing new heroes and avatars, the revolution has been constantly recycling figures and symbols of state, reorganizing what is already there, and reasserting the revisions and multiple possibilities of interpretation at each repeated enactment. This revolution, initially anyway, did not attempt to devise an entirely new symbolic order or topple the statues of the previous regime (an act that was so dramatically staged during the war in Iraq). Like the devil dances, the revolution itself has become less a performance of subtraction and more an act of recombining and adding to a mix, of grafting onto the symbols of the previous regime.

The implications of this argument call for an expansion of political ethnography to advance the intersectional work in performance studies, cultural studies, and political science. While not partisan by affiliation, cultural performances, feasts, and ritual processions lay down purposeful social guidelines and enforcement that shed light on populist logics both inside and outside of institutions of civil society and everyday life. These practices weren't necessarily called populist previously, nor should they necessarily be called populist now. The point is not to impose yet another term. Rather, I have attempted to show how assumptions surrounding the already existing terms of performance and populism interact, persist, and influence the transfer of power. The overlap of incongruent conversations is a place to start, where the evidence of disconnection and a gap in the current analysis can hopefully contribute another piece to a much broader project of decentering Eurocentric political thought as necessarily primary in a full account of democracy.

Building on David Guss's thesis that cultural performances are sites of contestation and negotiation (2001), I have argued that performance practice serves to establish public space and redraw boundaries of inclusion and exclusion in the social-political order. Politics indeed takes place in the production of the event, and, for various reasons, the complex political nature of these events has, historically and presently, been diminished and discredited. To restore the politics in the fiesta is to speak of how ordinary people legitimate and regenerate their own culturally specific aesthetic and practice.

In the absence of a performance analysis, these many aspects of populism that I have discussed as embodiment, in spatial-material evidence, and as relational and epistemic are also missing. To shift the focus from a text-based lens to a performance-based lens changes the rubric of how we understand, measure, and analyze political influence and behaviors. Moreover, if performance carries its own political logics, then within the analysis of populism the practice of those performances must be accounted for in its fullest sensorial expression. As I've argued in this book, supporters identify as "we" and "the people," they strategically wield interpretations of dualism (good versus evil, per saints and devils), and they enact these politics through repertoires of physical expression as much as on paper or in tabulated polls.

This book placed embodiment and performance histories next to theories on populism and found that populism is understood quite differently in performance examples than in ideational surveys. Performance is an essential indicator and medium for informing these key debates in the study of populism. Performance as populism expands both the objects of study and the approach toward what counts as political in order to begin to recognize the diverse means by which people enact their own political agency.

A year after Chávez died, I visited the Palacio de Miraflores in Caracas and saw a giant banner with thousands of signatures and messages remembering the president. It looked like an enormous yearbook page that banked an entire side of the plaza. A photo exhibit stretched across the middle of the wide-open public space: Chávez next to housing projects, smiling, playing music, and immersed within crowds of people. One woman stood up against the display to be photographed with him, adding another layer to the repeating memorial. It reminded me of the altars constructed in Ocumare that drew an outpouring of civic devotion and collective sentiment. Even following Chávez's passing and the relentless campaign against the Maduro government, the legacy of fiesta politics remains.

NOTES

Introduction

1. The Revolution also entailed the Venezuelan state initiating widespread reforms in education, health care, voting drives, and neighborhood "town halls," and assemblies that generated political participation in unprecedented ways. Structural reversals were indeed evident: for example, in just over a decade, the new government reversed the poverty-index trend by nearly twofold; by 2012, the poverty rate had decreased from 49.4 to 25.6 percent (Economic Commission for Latin America and the Caribbean [ECLAC] 2004b, 55; ECLAC 2014, 50, 53; ECLAC 2004a).

2. I borrow Diana Taylor's understanding of repertoire to include "embodied practice/knowledge" in gesture, orality, dance, sports, ritual (Taylor 2003, 19–20). I also see this term important in recalling Gisela Cánepa Koch's understanding of "choregraphic repertoires" (1998) and "cultural repertoires" (2009) that I discuss later in the introduction.

3. This observation especially pertains to global media and populism studies, whereas scholars in areas such as cultural studies and the anthropology of state formation have pinpointed this problem and attempted to remedy it. See a rich literature by scholars such as George Ciccariello-Maher, Luis Duno Gottberg, Sujatha Fernandes, Tinker Salas, Naomi Schiller, and Cristóbal Valencia-Ramirez, to mention a few.

4. CELCIT is an acronym for the Latin American Center for Theater Creation and Research, which is a transcontinental organization. In Venezuela, CELCIT was once housed in the residential neighborhood of San Bernardino and was formerly led by Orlando Rodríguez.

5. The *Oxford English Dictionary* (3rd ed., 2006) defines "populism" as "the policies or principles of any of various political parties which seek to represent the interests of ordinary people; and support for or representation of ordinary people or their views; speech, action, writing, etc."

6. Manichean is an adjective referring to the dualism of good versus evil. It is derived from a Persian dualistic cosmology developed by the Iranian prophet "Mani" in the third century AD who theorized a complex struggle between forces of good and evil, later rivaling the Christian concept of paganism.

7. Scholar and poet Ngũgĩ wa Thiong'o wrote, "a performance space is never empty, it comes with its history and the social practices that define it" (1997, 19), which I discuss further in chapter 3 and 4. Ngũgĩ is of course referring to Peter Brook's famous claim that the theatrical stage is empty, which Ngũgĩ refutes in his essay cited above entitled "Enactments of Power: The Politics of Performance Space."

8. See Sara C. Motta (2011) for a comprehensive critique of the ways populism was used to unfairly discredit the emergence of popular class subjectivity in the first decade of the Chavez era, and moreover, how critiques such as those by Hawkins, and others, such as Jorge Castañeda, were used to justify foreign intervention at an early point in the revolution's development.

9. Studies on the relationship between performance and populism are fairly recent; note Benjamin Moffitt's book *The Global Rise of Populism: Performance, Political Style, and Representation* (2016). See also Arditi 2013.

10. In *Festive Devils of the Americas*, Milla Cozart Riggio et al. (2015) discuss Manichaeanism as a highly misunderstood concept. According to the *New Advent Catholic Encyclopedia* (newadvent.org/cathen/09591a.htm), its original manifestations were said to be a synthesis of Zoroastrian dualism, Babylonian folklore, Buddhist ethics, and some elements of Christianity.

11. Quoted in Rai and Reinelt 2015, 3.

12. Chantal Mouffe (2013) most recently develops this point of how Eurocentric liberal theories of democracy disavow political difference in *Agonistics: Thinking the World Politically*.

13. Richard Schechner ([2002] 2013) explains performance using a spectrum containing the points "being," "doing," "showing doing," and "explaining showing doing." The first is arguably not performance, but rather an ontic of existence. Doing and showing doing are within the realm of performed acts, with an emphasis on showing doing, which implies awareness that one's actions are on display or witnessed. At the far end of the spectrum is explaining showing doing, which Schechner attributes to the work of performance studies.

14. My translation.

15. According to Álvarez, Dagnino, and Escobar, "The term 'social movement webs' (in contrast to the more common 'networks') conveys the intricacy and precariousness of the manifold imbrications of and ties established among movement organizations, individual participants, and other actors in civil and political society and the state. The 'web' metaphor also enables us to more vividly imagine the multilayered entanglements of movement actors with the natural-environmental, political-institutional, and cultural-discursive terrains in which they are embedded" (1998, 15–16). Clifford Geertz also uses the term "webs of signification" to describe a process of participants recirculating meanings among themselves (1975, 5).

16. David Guss, in *The Festive State: Race, Ethnicity and Nationalism as Cultural Performance*, argues that cultural performances operate as modalities that enable participants to produce "new social imaginaries," reminding us that they are experienced differently by each individual who assigns them distinct meanings and functions (2001, 8–11).

17. The enclosed theater space and the professionalization of labor within it were arguably seventeenth-century European inventions.

18. For Victor Turner, "anti-structure" refers to that which is counter to "society as a structured, differentiated, and often hierarchical system of politico-legal-economic positions with many types of evaluation, separating men in terms of 'more' or 'less' " (1969, 96).

19. See Cole 2010; and Chambers-Letson 2013.

20. One example of these endogenous organizations is the artist and cultural group Nucleo Endógeno Cultural Nuevo Circo.

21. As Naomi Schiller wrote, "Liberal formulations that oppose state constraint and individual freedom are insufficient to account for how Catia TVe producers experience and work to create greater access to media production and decision making alongside official state actors. . . . For Catia TVe producers, the meaning of co-optation and of autonomy is made additionally complex because they explicitly embrace the state as a collective project under construction" (2013, 547–48).

22. By "American-born," I mean those born in the American hemisphere.

23. The cartographer who first used the name "America" was the German clergyman Martin Waldseemüller, who apparently adopted the Latin version of Amerigo Vespucci's name and feminized it from "Americus" to "America" on his amateur map of 1507. Waldseemüller sold thousands of copies of the map. In 1538, Gerardus Mercator made the name America official to South and North America.

24. Given that, prior to the European arrival, Mayans from the Yucatán traded and migrated to the area. It is also very possible and likely that cacao was traded, consumed, or cultivated on the Aragua coast in a trans-Caribbean economy well before this date.

25. See Mörner 1993, which draws on data found in the 1880–1882 Archivo de Registros de Protocolos de Maracay.

Chapter 1

1. For more on the history of the dancing devils in Venezuela, see Ramos Guédez 2009; Salazar 1984; and Strauss 2004.

2. On the theatricality of liturgical fiestas in the early sixteenth century, see Díez Borque 1987.

3. In *Inka Bodies and the Body of Christ: Corpus Christi in Colonial Cuzco, Perú*, Carolyn Dean (1999) describes the framework of Corpus Christi as the triumph of Christianity over indigenous peoples of the Andes and so-called paganism, while showing that Andeans celebrating these fiestas enacted many double and reversed meanings at the same time.

4. It is important to consider that the Inquisition was primarily a regulatory system for the propertied class to resolve disputes of debt and labor through corporal punishment. Labor disputes were among the most common reasons for being anonymously reported to the Inquisition authorities, followed by bigamy and homosexuality, or what church officials deemed as sexual transgressions.

5. Originally authored by Nicholas Eymerich circa 1320, the *Directorium Inquisitorum* included instructions for rooting out demonic beliefs. Evidence of demonic belief included people praying or lighting candles or incense to devils, or mentioning them in litany alongside the names of saints or angels. The text specifically refers to the beliefs of Muslims—those believing in Muhammad—as heretical, condemning them as demonic witchcraft.

6. See the excellent work by Carolyn Dean (1999) on this topic in the colonial context of Cuzco.

7. On the term "cultural performance," see Guss 2001.

8. In Chuao, the devils dance inside the church as well as outside, but in Cata and Ocumare (and possibly Cuyagua) the devils remain at the door.

9. For more on the idea of fiesta performance as continuously playing out a cosmic battle, one with no narrative finality, see Diana Taylor's introduction to the 1537 Corpus Christi play *Final Judgment* in Taylor and Townsend 2008, 51.

10. For more on collective ownership of these cultural performances, see Guerrero Veloz, 2001.

11. The term *suelto* is featured in "El Diablo Suelto," a song published in 1888. The songwriter, Heraclio Fernández, was from the Venezuelan state of Zulia.

12. This is not unlike a form of stoop or front-porch culture, where people sit on the steps of their houses and talk to neighbors and others passing by. In this case, people were gathered one step out of the modest one-level cinder block house. A few people sat on chairs pulled from the house, another person sat on the step, and another stood.

13. See also Carmen Alemán's (1997) account of how women and other neighborhood organizers contribute to the dances on the Aragua coast of Venezuela.

14. José Cheché Echenagucia, the *capataz* of the *cofradía* in Ocumare, said that the women's role in this performance also has an official title: *hermanas del Santísimo* (sisters of the Holy Sacrament), or *capitanas* (captains).

15. See also Ackerman 1993.

16. For scholarship on Radio Bemba, see Sujatha Fernandes's chapter "Radio Bemba in an Age of Electronic Media: The Dynamics of Popular Communication in Chávez's Venezuela," in Smilde and Hellinger 2011.

17. I visited the Aragua coast for five different stays of varying lengths (ranging from one to five weeks each) in 1999, 2007, 2008, 2010, and 2017.

18. For moral prestige in the fiestas of the Aragua coast, see Alemán 1997.

19. While this book focuses on the decade before the UNESCO designation, it is important to point out that many cultural producers are concerned about the changes since the designation. I return to this issue in the conclusion of this book.

20. These *cofradías*, which were recognized as Intangible Heritage by the United Nations in 2012, led their own process of deliberation throughout all of the communities associated with the devil dances in meetings that brought together artists, dancers, costume makers, and guardians. Thousands of participants in these performances gathered throughout the central and coastal regions of the country for this process.

21. *Cofradías* were obligated to ask *limosna* every Sunday of the year to provide services such as funerals and caring for the sick or elderly.

22. See also Foster 1953.

23. Again referring to the fiesta of Tepoztlán in central Mexico, Taylor writes, "The same organizational structures that allow for the massive performance-of-communal-self year after year have simultaneously sustained the sturdy, community-wide infrastructure and networks that date back to the pre-Conquest period" (2006, 68). These organizational systems make territorial and material claims around resources and the flows of exchange that mobilize these networks; see also Cabranes-Grant 2011, 516.

24. See Pollak-Eltz 1972, 1984.

25. See Velásquez 1979; Núñez and Pérez 1994.

26. For more on the ongoing tensions and struggles in achieving this recognition, there are several sources, including García 2004, 2007; Fernandes 2010; García and Guerrero Veloz 2003.

27. The *Cayapa Visual Revolucionaria* blogsite is an important online space for activists of the revolution: cayapavisualrevolucionaria.blogspot.com. It is important to point out that vitriolic internet trolling has for a long time targeted Chavista online communications.

28. The popular use of the word *cayapa* to mean "ganging up on one person" is widespread and found across party lines. See Britto García 2008.

29. In *Identities, Boundaries, and Social Ties*, Charles Tilly (2005) introduces the concept of "episodes" as a "continuous stream of social life," as, for example, the period in which a campaign takes place.

30. Quoted in Guss's 1993 article "The Selling of San Juan: The Performance of History in an Afro-Venezuelan Community."

31. In her essay entitled "The Potosí Principle: Another View of Totality," sociologist and Aymara activist Silvia Rivera Cusicanqui adds that a "complex and motley heterogenous ritual frame" including churches and the patron saints, libations, dance, and chants "connects distant spaces . . . rearticulating that which is deranged, joining forces to repair the 'pierced fishing net' that the cosmos became for the peoples of the Andes" (2014, n.p.).

32. For more on Manichaeanism and its relationship to festive devils, see Milla Cozart Riggio's (2015) conclusion essay in *Festive Devils of the Americas*.

33. In her (2004) essay "Scenes of Cognition: Performance and Conquest," Diana Taylor writes, "the term performance, then, suggests both a praxis and an episteme" (364).

34. As an anecdotal aside, in 2007, I wore a green T-shirt with a small black-print tiger on it to the San Juan fiestas in Ocumare, which featured the colors of a political party opposing Chávez (Chavistas, and San Juaneros, typically wear the color red). I was curious whether it would be noticed, but I did not feel in any way scrutinized. Finally, I made a comment about it, drawing attention to the color, and one organizer pointed out other multicolored shirts around me, smiling while she said, "All colors come to the fiesta."

Chapter 2

1. The Teatro de la Casa Sindical de Caracas is the Spanish name of the theater in which *Caín adolescente* debuted. It was reproduced at the Ateneo de Caracas in 1956.

2. "Popular class" refers to the majority of low-income and informal workers, loosely defined in some cases to include the middle class. The popular class could also be considered in relationship to the culture of the majority poor. The barrio, also known colloquially as *ranchos*, refers to mostly poor neighborhoods in the peripheral margins of Caracas, with some pockets in the city center and south. Consisting of dwellings mainly made of cinder block, corrugated metal, and found materials, these neighborhoods are also sometimes squatter settlements.

3. Although in the play the precise location of Juana and Juan's hometown is slightly ambiguous, in the last scene Juan suggests it was near Barlovento, about 150 miles west of Ocumare de la Costa, in the same general near-coastal region west of Caracas.

4. See Ligia Álvarez 2014. Álvarez describes the conflict of *Caín adolescente* as a loss of innocence, as those unable to work the land were lured to the capital by "an illusion of progress" (25).

5. Alejandro Velasco documents what amounted to an anti-barrio campaign from the Jiménez dictatorship, including what was dubbed a "Battle Against the Rancho!" (2015, 33). Velasco shows how the dictatorship's plan was to eradicate the barrios by literally bulldozing them down.

6. I found this referenced in Ledwith and Springett 2010, and although it is a quite a simple concept, participatory practice supports political public spaces as sites of active public debate.

7. Warner derives this idea from Nancy Fraser 1990, 62.

8. The play *Caín adolescente* also in some ways confirms a belief in the hidden dangers of these spaces, where the barrio was not necessarily laid bare for others. What is behind the sheet is still unrevealed. While one alleyway is onstage, the rest of the barrio is only intimated. The barrio in *Caín*, and later in *Pandemonium*, is thus the opposite of Jeremy Bentham's late-eighteenth-century panopticon; it is a labyrinth of hidden spaces that are seen only by those who live there.

9. The stampede at the end of *Caín adolescente* is based on the real-life tragedy that occurred on April 9, 1952, at the Santa Teresa church in Caracas during the annual Easter celebrations of San Pablo. In this tragic incident, thousands of people waited to offer their devotional prayers to the altars inside. At the entrances several uniformed men in blue directed devotees through the doorways, attempting to manage the crowd. The five o'clock mass was about to start, and even more people lined up to enter, pushing in nervously as the previous congregation tried to get out. The story, as narrated on several blog sites, suggests that someone from the left nave of the church screamed "Fire!" The resulting chaos left 50 people dead and 113 wounded, most of them older women and children who were crushed in the stampede. The police and the fire department arrived and found there was no fire, only a candle that had likely, for an instant, caught fire on a veil that hung from a woman's hat. As the corpses were piled at the church doors, the newspapers in the morning announced that the tragedy was a terrorist plot with international connections. The "connections," however dubious they may be, are interesting for our purposes, since they point out a degree of suspicion by the state that the tragedy at the Santa Teresa church was related to the Colombian Bogotazo, in which massive street riots had protested the assassination of the popularly elected leader Jorge Eliécer Gaitán on the same day four years earlier, April 9, 1948. Gaitán was extremely popular and known for demanding an end to government violence and persecution of the poor. Himself of humble origins and mixed race, he was said to be a "spellbinding orator," with one of his keynote speeches entitled "I am not a man, I am a people." He was poised to win the 1950 presidential elections, and his assassination catapulted the country into what is known as La Violencia, a period in which over 100,000 people were killed in the countryside of Colombia, mainly by government and paramilitary forces who sought to repress supporters of Gaitán.

10. See Cory Fischer-Hoffman (2014, n.p.) for a description of the conditions of police repression by Pérez Jiménez at the time when *Caín adolescente* debuted in Caracas. Fischer-Hoffman writes, "Under the dictatorship of Perez-Jimenez (1948–1958) members of the Communist Party and the political party

Democratic Action (AD) were rounded up by the secret police, and taken to concentration camps on Guasina island on the Orinoco river and the Isla del Burro on Valencia Lake. Because many of the political dissidents came from the literate working and middle classes, their testimonies of torture were recorded and some have been published and circulated in Venezuela. This vast collection of 20th-century political prisoner testimony actually constitutes its own genre of literature within Venezuela. Reported methods of torture included cigarette burns, being forced to sit on blocks of ice, the force-feeding of laxatives and being cut with razors."

11. Roughly 40 percent of the major movies in the decades after the Pérez Jiménez dictatorship (1952–58) followed theatrical productions. From the national playhouses to the screen, a cadre of intellectuals in Venezuela known as the "trilogy" of playwrights and producers—Ignacio Cabrujas, Isaac Chocrón, and Román Chalbaud—blazed the trail from the municipal stages to studios and the national screen as an embrace of "new" democracy. See Benítez 2008, interview.

12. To illustrate Chalbaud's rejection of the conditions of the country's majority poor in the political context, it is interesting to note the foreword to his later 1974 production *Los siete pecados*, in which he writes: "Considering that from the first exploitations of our natural riches, the population has tripled and the national budget is one hundred times stronger, yet the majority of the population that makes it possible for the lavish excesses of a minority, continues to be as poor as when the country depended on coffee and chocolate. Considering that the city has converted itself into a nightmare of air conditioning, loud and obnoxious, chewing on Chiclets and fawning over synthetic and canned goods. Considering that throughout the hills of staircases and tin shacks, more than half a million contemplate their lives from houses surrounded by garbage, far away from the excesses of wealth and abundance" (Chalbaud 1991, 128).

13. Between 1958 and 1960, nearly half a million people moved to Caracas from smaller towns throughout the country, marking a shift of urban migration in the middle of the century.

14. See George Ciccariello-Maher 2013 for a deeper political history of movement building in the barrios of Caracas in the decades before Chávez came to power.

15. The fact that newspaper articles featured the Holy Week fiestas is not surprising, of course, because the sample months I researched in my three years of study were the months in which the annual Semana Santa fiestas were celebrated throughout the country.

16. Again, *rancho* is another word for barrio, referring to the contingent constructions of cinder block, zinc, and paneling in which the majority of the poor reside.

17. UNEARTE is an acronym for Universidad Nacional Experimental de las Artes, which is a public university that now occupies a prominent position in the fine arts district of Caracas. See unearte.edu.ve.

18. Theater critic José Antonio Barrios Valle (2014, 57) argues that Chalbaud was the first to assume an urban marginality on stage and to give it meaning in a realist discourse in which situations and characters were relevant to a new spectator.

19. My reading of the playscript admittedly may not be the intent of the film, or the author for that matter, in regard to the potential complexity of the character

of Encarnación. In the film, as Ligia Álvarez (2014) rightly points out, Encarnación divides the house with only a motive to enrich himself and his business. The sheets across the living room are thus divisive to Juana and Juan's relationship. Transformation in the character of Encarnación arguably takes place at the end of the film after Juana visits Encarnación in prison and he realizes that her love for him was unconditional. However, it is important to point out that the film presents a definitively negative portrayal of Encarnación, as the "devil incarnate."

20. Carlos de la Torre (2016) writes of populism and the "politics of the extraordinary" as ways in which leaders benefit from extraordinary numbers of ballots in their elections, which implies an excess of promise and extraordinary virtuosity to solve the problems of society. I see the participation of voters showing up to the polls as significantly different than the staged images of Carlos Andrés Pérez in this 1973 campaign.

Chapter 3

1. For news reports on this act, see Pilkington 2006; Stout 2006; and "Chávez Calls Bush 'The Devil' " 2006. The latter article includes a transcript of the speech.

2. Quoted in "Chávez: Bush 'Devil'; U.S. 'On the Way Down' " 2006.

3. Sujatha Fernandes describes the links between protagonists in the contemporary period of revolution and cultural identity as expressed in mural art, rap, hip-hop, and popular fiestas and other popular traditions as an "idiom for expressing collective identities and developing a critical consciousness about one's place in the world" (2010, 262).

4. The first published version of *Florentino and the Devil* appeared as *El reto* (1940) and was composed of 224 verses. It appeared in *Glosas a cancionero (poemas)* (Torrealba 1940). For an example of the poem in performance, see "Florentino y el Diablo Parte 2," uploaded September 19, 2007, YouTube.com, https://youtu.be/IKNR82N2PCE. The English translation is at http://bookmaniac.org/writing/florentino-english-booklet.pdf.

5. Parallels can be drawn between the story of Florentino and the Devil and the fiddler who challenges the devil in the song "The Devil Went Down to Georgia," made popular by the Charlie Daniels Band. However, an important distinction is that Florentino's goal is not just to prove he is "best" in the land, but also to defend his right to live on the land in the face of adversity.

6. The second edition of *Glosas al cancionero* was published in 1950. In that volume, the epic poem was given a new title, *Florentino el que cantó con el Diablo*, and was composed of 477 verses. The definitive version is titled *Florentino y el Diablo,* published in 1958 with 1,219 verses. See also Araujo 1974, 55, 83.

7. See Coronil 1997. Coronil concludes that the 1958 revolution was the result of a "crystallization of collective discontent" generated from a combination of classes and social sectors (204–12).

8. Pérez called this "El gran viraje" or "The Great Turnaround" in economic policy. Carlos Andres Pérez was indicted on corruption and embezzlement charges in 1994, five years after suppressing the Caracazo.

9. For more details on the election period based on interviews with Chávez in 2000, see Gott 2005.

10. For more on the constitution and the assembly process, see Wilpert 2003.

11. To review, the first elections for Chávez took place on December 6, 1998. The MVR party received 3,673,685 votes and the nearest contender, Henrique Salas Römer, who represented a coalition against Chávez known as Project Venezuela, received 2,613,161 votes. The election results were endorsed by the Carter Center. Directly following the presidential elections, Chávez held another election to ratify constituent powers and won that election by 59.8 percent in 2000.

12. Notably, in 2002 Chávez declared that the media was his number one adversary. In Venezuela, 80 percent of current TV channels and radio stations are privately owned. Since the coup, two state channels have become a significant factor in contesting the media monopoly of those who oppose the government. The role of RCTV in the 2002 coup led directly to the government agency's refusal to renew RCTV's public broadcast license in 2006. See Lamrani 2007.

13. See Roberto Lovato's article in Foreign Policy, July 25, 2015.

14. See Fleischer 2002. Events of the April 2, 2002, coup are recounted in detail in a report by the fiscal general elected by the General Assembly. The documentary film *The Revolution Will Not Be Televised* (2002) by the Irish film company Radio Telefís Éireann cites the contradictions between media reports and the actual events filmed during the 2002 coup attempt. See also Cannon 2004.

15. My account of these events is informed by the documentary film *The Revolution Will Not Be Televised*. For more on the film's relationship to documentary production and circulation, see Schiller 2009.

16. In all, estimates to repair the cost to the oil industry were reported as up to US$13.3 billion as reported by Jones 2007, 386.

17. There was a further issue with negotiating the date of the elections, where four days later, on August 19, the vice president would complete the term. For more on this, see Hellinger 2005.

18. For the full text of the 1999 constitution in English, see "Constitution of the Bolivarian Republic of Venezuela," Human Rights Library, University of Minnesota, http://www1.umn.edu/humanrts/research/venezuela-constitution.html.

19. On June 8, 2004, CNE officials announced that the official count of signatures was 2,541,636, a figure that narrowly fulfilled the requirements to initiate the national recall referendum ballot. Issues over the validity of the signatures were eventually resolved. See Gott 2005; and Hellinger 2005.

20. Venezuela has a three-part voting procedure that requires voters to privately register their vote, verify a paper printout by fingerprint signature, and then place the paper vote in a separate box. Venezuelan elections have been reported as "an exemplary model" by the Carter Center, the Organization of American States, and the European Union. For further negotiations made regarding the date of the election, see Hellinger 2005.

21. Chacón adds that, despite these preparations, everything had changed by the end of the broadcast.

22. Antonio José de Sucre was a leader of the Venezuelan struggle for independence and a close associate of Símon Bolívar. He was known as the Gran Mariscal de Ayacucho (Grand Marshal of Ayacucho). His troops were victorious in the Battle of Ayacucho, the last battle before the Spanish military capitulated to the Independentist Venezuelan forces.

23. See also Hellinger 2005 for details of the election process. His article includes tables of the vote counts and analysis of the campaign and political

analysis. He argues that Comando Ayacucho and the organized groups on the ground did not necessarily play a significant role in mobilizing the vote. Instead, he suggests they were mired in conflict, and where there was street action they failed in getting the numbers in their districts to the polls. Nevertheless, as Hellinger reports, the numbers far favored Chávez and were verified by the OAS and Carter Center observers, among others. The opposition still claimed fraud and refused to recognize Chávez as the winner.

24. For more on media bias against the revolutionary state, see Lovler 2004, a former correspondent for CNN in Latin America.

25. For video and other examples of popular responses, see the film *Venezuela Bolívariana* (2006) by Calle y Media Colectivo. For more recent *coplas* and popular response with ethnographic accounts, see Valencia Ramírez 2008.

26. For a hip-hop version of Florentino and the Diablo, see "Florentino y el Diablo (Mc Arena / Mc Robex)," uploaded November 26, 2007, YouTube.com, https://youtu.be/5MdbznVxyJI.

27. In terms of street art, the historian Dale Graden writes in a 2013 article in *NACLA* that "street art plays an increasingly vital role in revolutionary Venezuela: it is a mode of political expression, a form of popular education and helps build a collective historical memory."

28. For more on minority interests in participatory democracies, see Cronin 1989.

29. On the limits of civil society, see Fernandes 2010. Fernandes discusses "civil society" as a term that has been adopted by anti-Chávez activists to distance institutional forms of social organization established in pre-Chávez regimes from the emerging forms of organization in the Bolivarian Revolution (1999–present). For Fernandes, tensions continue to exist between technocrats employed by the state and grassroots organizations in what she calls the "hybrid state."

30. Incidentally, Lander told Bart Jones (2004), a journalist for the *National Catholic Reporter*, that "the problem is that the poor are organizing and mobilizing. And that signifies a threat of the 'dangerous classes.' The dangerous classes are dangerous if they mobilize, if they act, if they demand." In his interview with Jones, Lander repeated his metaphor of a high-society party where "the white people, the refined people, the people who know how to speak well, who know how to hold the crystal cups to drink wine. Suddenly, into the party barge some people who don't have manners, who are poorly dressed, who haven't taken a bath and smell bad. They grab the food with their hands. They create the sensation they are taking over the country."

31. Irene Sáez was Miss Universe in 1981 and later mayor of Chacao, a wealthy municipality within Caracas.

32. See the Sam L. Slick Collection of Latin American and Iberian Posters, Center for Southwest Research and Special Collections, University of New Mexico, Albuquerque.

33. See the video clips of the Florentino y el Diablo campaign. "El Diablo pasa trabajo," uploaded May 3, 2006, YouTube.com, https://youtu.be/OvywIrI1zX8.

34. In December 2007, during the constitutional assembly referendum, which Chávez narrowly lost, the opposition coalition circulated precisely the same design in order to vote "No" *against* the Chávez initiative.

35. See the short cartoon "El Diablo pasa trabajo (humanismo)," uploaded August 15, 2014, Youtube.com, https://youtu.be/1GSg6iRat6g.

36. In July 2004, the poster circulated around the Internet as evidence of the violence implicit in Chavismo. According to one blog, the "Z" mimicked gay male speech, and the pairing of the masculine overtones of the embodiment of Chávez with the flouncy depiction of the devil in the poster feminized the opposition and thus exhibited an intolerant, even dangerous, political culture that persecuted gay men. See Duquenal 2004.

37. On his weekly television broadcast *Aló Presidente*, Chávez frequently referred to his mixed-race ethnicity, exclaiming on one occasion, "Look at my hair, look at my lips! It's obvious I come from African and Indigenous roots." See Scruggs and Rentner 2007.

38. See also Silverblatt 1988 for a discussion of Illapa-Santiago in Peru.

39. See Oliver Stone's film *South of the Border* (2010) for these news clips and, in addition, an interview in which Chávez states, "It pained me to see the lies and the disrespect towards the people. But then I realized it's all part of a game, and no matter what I do—I could dress like a priest with a nice red hat on my head and they would still call me a tyrant. The people know the truth."

Chapter 4

1. While Bolívar is commonly referred to by biographers as the liberator of each of these six nations, it is important to note that not all countries necessarily recognize Bolívar as the central figure of their country's liberation from Spanish colonial rule.

2. The statue of Simon Bolívar in New York City's Central Park was commissioned in 1921 as a gift to the United States from Venezuela during the dictatorship of Juan Vicente Gómez.

3. In "Bolívar y Ponte," Marx (1858) describes Bolívar as a coward, a dictator, "impassioned," and "wild." He also quotes Ducoudray-Holstein's description of Bolívar as passionate and indulgent, "a dark and wild aspect" and one who "becomes in a moment a madman, throws himself into his hammock, and utters curses and imprecations upon all around him." See Ducoudray-Holstein and Viollet 1831.

4. Also at issue was that the flag added an eighth star to the conventional seven stars, with respect to Bolívar's decree in 1817 that Guyana be considered an independent territory from Spanish rule. See Morsbach 2006.

5. See the article entitled "Chávez Flies the Flag for Change" (NBC News, March 13, 2006) in which a Venezuelan opposition activist, Lilian Luces, claims that the flag change was "a whim of the president." For additional coverage, see *USA Today* and the BBC News.

6. For more on the controversial flag appearance, see Marcia Ochoa's book *Queen for a Day* (2014).

7. On Bolívar and the Betancourt years, see Bercovich 2014, 23–53.

8. Various portraits of Bolívar as *moreno*, with an afro, or with a full curly beard emphasize his embodiment of Afro-descendant rights and emancipation. See Salas de Lecuna 1987.

9. See the discussion in Mills 2004.

10. For politicization among Afro-descendant communities in the Caribbean in the nineteenth century, see Dubois 2006; and Blackburn 2011.

11. The declarations of emancipation in 1816 happened first in Carúpano on June 2, and then in Ocumare on July 16. It is said that Bolívar abolished slavery on his own property during this time. See Ramos Guédez 2004.

12. According to Miguel Acosta Saignes (1967), by 1800 there were no less than 30,000 self-liberated Africans and their descendants in the northwest coastal range of Venezuela. The explorer and botanist von Humboldt claims there were 60,000 enslaved people in the haciendas in roughly the same region by the end of the eighteenth century. Africans, indigenous peoples, and their descendants constituted more than 50 percent of the population between Coro and La Guaira. The tensions between the *criollo* elite and the propertyless and mostly black, indigenous, or mestizo majority were evident leading up to the events of 1816. In 1811, Coro, Maracaibo, and Guayana preferred to be governed directly by Joseph Bonaparte rather than by the Caracas Cabildo and never accepted independence from Spain, even when it was offered.

13. A 2006 essay by the Curaçaoan researcher Eugene Edward Godfreid Presilia begins with the following introduction: "We notice a significant increase in discussions among peoples of Curaçao, Venezuela, Caribbean and other parts of the world regarding the liberation and integrationist struggles of the formerly Spanish colonized territories on the American continent. President Hugo Chávez's government and the Bolívarian revolution of Venezuela are calling world attention to historical personalities like Simón José Antonio de la Santísima Trinidad Bolívar y Palacios. In Curaçao and Dutch colonized territories, at last, the process is taking better shape, stimulating thoughts and debates on Admiral Pedro Luis Brión and Carlos Manuel Piar, two Curaçaoans proven to be exemplary figures" (1). See also Damas 2007.

14. It is important to point out that soldiers who enlisted with Bolívar had a long and difficult journey from Curaçao, nearly starving as they waited for reinforcements.

15. In several situations along the Aragua coast, I witnessed the conversations of retirees, shopowners, and fisherpeople, each with different ideas and perspectives and research that they had conducted around the topic of Bolívar's expeditions. I saw this as more than mere coincidence and an indication that the historical issues were very active as public discourse and debate among the social networks in the Ocumare area.

16. The full title in Spanish is "Ruta Bicentenaria Afrodescendientes: 'Bolívar y los Afros en la Historia de Emancipación desde los Pueblos Eje Costero de Aragua.' "

17. This form of liberational education surges from the new Ley Orgánica of Article 3.

18. Cumbuoto is known to have been a *cumbe*, or maroon (*palenque*) community.

19. This statement made by Eubel López was posted on Abrebrecha.com ("Red Afrodescendiente de Aragua," April 18, 2013). See also García 2014.

20. More recently, Guerrero Veloz became Venezuelan ambassador in the Caribbean island of Granada.

21. See François-Dominique Toussaint Louverture as quoted by Guerrero Veloz 2001, n.p.

BIBLIOGRAPHY

Interviews

Benítez, Luisa. 2008, June 10. Interview with the author. Ocumare.

———. 2010, June 10. Interview with the author. Ocumare.

Echenagucia, José "Cheché." 2007, June 15. Interview with the author. Ocumare.

———. 2008, June 12. Interview with the author. Ocumare.

García, Clemis. 2008, June 10. Interview with the author. Ocumare.

———. 2010, June 8. Interview with the author. Ocumare.

García, Luisa. 2007, June 18. Interview with the author. Ocumare.

Silva, Elvia. 2017, March. Interview with the author. Cata.

Valera, Jorman. 2008, June 8. Interview with the author. Ocumare.

———. 2010, June 3. Interview with the author. Ocumare.

Films and Theater

Arvelo, Alberto. 2014. *The Liberator*. 35mm. Film. Directed by Alberto Arvelo. Toronto: Cohen Media Group.

Buñuel, Luis. 1950. *Los olvidados*. Film. Directed by Luis Buñuel. Mexico DF: Óscar Dancigers.

Chalbaud, Román. 1974. *Los siete pecados*. Film. Directed by Román Chalbaud. Caracas: Chalbaud Productions.

———. 1997. *Pandemonium, la capital del infierno*. 35mm. Film. Directed by Román Chalbaud. San Sebastián: Chalbaud Productions.

Power, David, Kim Bartley, Donnacha O'Brien, et al. 2003. *The Revolution Will Not Be Televised*. Film. Directed by David Power, Kim Bartley, Donnacha O'Brien, et al. Dublin: Power Pictures.

Triana, Jorge Alí. 2001. *Bolívar Soy Yo*. Film. Directed by Jorge Alí Triana. Bogotá: Venevision International.

Yuyachkani, Grupo Cultural, Miguel Rubio Zapata, and Peter Elmore. 2001. *Santiago*. Lima: New York University, Hemispheric Institute Digital Video Library.

Published Sources

Ackerman, Bruce. 1993. *We, the People*. Vol. 1. Cambridge, Mass.: Belknap Press of Harvard University Press.

Acosta Saignes, Miguel. 1962. *Estudios de folklore venezolano*. Caracas: Instituto de Antropología e Historia, Facultad de Humanidades y Educación, Universidad Central de Venezuela.

———. 1967. *Vida de los esclavos negros en Venezuela*. Caracas: Hespérides.

Aguilera Vásquez, Pedro Eduardo. 2014. "Chalbaud and Williams: Un espacio para sus encuentros y desencuentros desde una poética marginal." Universidad

Nacional Experimental de las Artes (UNEARTE). *Revista Theatron* no. 24–25 (April): 62–71.

Alemán, Carmen Elena. 1997. *Corpus Christi y San Juan Bautista: Dos manifestaciones rituales en la comunidad afrovenezolana de Chuao*. Caracas: Fundacíon Bigott.

Alfonso, Pedro Antonio. 1854. *Memorias de un matancero: Apuntes para la historia de la isla de Cuba, con relación á la ciudad de San Cárlos y San Severino de Matanzas*. Matanzas: Marsal.

Álvarez, Ligia. 2014. "*Caín adolescente*: Retrato del tránsito de la inocencia del campo a la corrupción citadina." Universidad Nacional Experimental de las Artes (UNEARTE). *Revista Theatron* no. 24–25 (April): 25–36.

Álvarez, Sonia E., Evalina Dagnino, and Arturo Escobar, eds. 1998. *Cultures of Politics, Politics of Cultures: Re-Visioning Latin American Social Movements*. Boulder, Colo.: Westview.

Appadurai, Arjun. 1986. *The Social Life of Things: Commodities in Cultural Perspective*. New York: Cambridge University Press.

Araujo, Orlando. 1974. *Contrapunteo de la vida y de la muerte*. Caracas: Ed. en la Raya.

Arditi, Benjamin. 2003. "Populism, or Politics at the Edges of Democracy." *Contemporary Politics* 9, no. 1: 17–31.

———. 2007. *Politics on the Edges of Liberalism: Difference, Populism, Revolution, Agitation*. Edinburgh: Edinburgh University Press.

———. 2013. "Las insurgencies no tienen un plan—Ellas son el plan: Performativos políticos y mediadores evanescentes." *Revista Sul-Americana de ciencia política* 1, no. 2: 1–18.

Arriaga, Pablo Joseph de. (1621) 1999. *La extirpación de la idolatría en el Perú*. Cuzco, Peru: CBC, Centro de Estudios Regionales Andinos "Bartolomé de Las Casas."

Arrighi, Giovanni. 1994. *The Long Twentieth Century: Money, Power, and the Origins of Our Times*. London: Verso.

Austin, J. L. 1975. *How to Do Things with Words*. Cambridge, Mass.: Harvard University Press.

Bakhtin, Mikhail M. (1968) 1984. *Rabelais and His World*. Translated by Helene Iswolsky. Bloomington: Indiana University Press.

Barreto, Daisy. 1995. "El mito y culto de María Lionza: Identidad y resistencia popular." In *Historias de identidad urbana*, edited by Emanuele Amodio, Teresa Ontiveros, and Iris Rosas, 61–72. Caracas: Fondo Editorial Tropykos.

———. 1995. "Identidad, etnicidad, antropología." *Boletín americanista* 45: 7–21.

Barrios Valles, José Antonio. 2014. "El realism en la dramaturgia de Román Chalbaud." Universidad Nacional Experimental de las Artes (UNEARTE). *Revista Theatron* no. 24–25 (April): 54–61.

Bell, Catherine. 1992. *Ritual Theory, Ritual Practice*. Oxford: Oxford University Press.

Bercovich, Alexander Philip. 2014. *The Bolívar Archive*. Cambridge, Mass.: Harvard University Press.

Betancourt, Rómulo. 1979. *Venezuela: Oil and Politics*. Translated by Everett Bauman. Boston: Houghton Mifflin.

Blackburn, Robin. 2011. *The American Crucible: Slavery, Emancipation and Human Rights*. London: Verso.

Blough, Les. 2006. "Campaigning for the December 3rd Election: Chávez Connects with the Venezuelan People." Translated by Ramón Santiago. AxisofLogic.com. October 5. http://www.axisoflogic.com/artman/publish/Article_23164.shtml.

Boal, Augusto. 1979. *Theater of the Oppressed*. Translated by Charles A. McBride and Maria Odilia Leal McBride. New York: Urizen Books.

Bolívar, Simón. 1948. *Cartas del Libertador: 1802–1829*. Edited by Vicente Lecuna. Caracas: Banco de Venezuela, Fundación Vicente Lecuña.

Bourriaud, Nicolas. (1998) 2002. *Relational Aesthetics*. Paris: Les Presse du Reel.

Brading, Ryan. 2012. *Populism in Venezuela*. New York: Routledge.

Brandes, Stanley. 1988. *Power and Persuasion: Fiestas and Social Control in Rural Mexico*. Philadelphia: University of Pennsylvania Press.

Branford, Becky. 2004. "Analysis: Chávez at Eye of Storm." *BBC News*. August 13. http://news.bbc.co.uk/2/hi/americas/3559668.stm.

Brathwaite, Kamau. 1974. *Contradictory Omens: Cultural Diversity and Integration in the Caribbean*. Jamaica: Savacou.

Briggs, Charles, and Clara Mantini-Briggs. 2007. "'Misión barrio adentro': Medicina social, movimientos sociales de los pobres y nuevas coaliciones en Venezuela." *Salud colectiva* 3, no. 2 (May-August): 159–76.

Britto García, Luis. 2008. *Dictadura mediática en Venezuela: Investigación de unos medios por encima de toda sospecha*. Caracas: Ministerio del Poder Popular para la Comunicación y la Información.

Brown, David H. 2003. *Santeria Enthroned: Art, Ritual, and Innovation in an Afro-Cuban Religion*. Chicago: University of Chicago Press.

Bruce, Douglas. 2001. "Notes toward a Rhetoric of Animation: The Road Runner as Cultural Critique." *Critical Studies in Media Communication* 18, no. 2: 229–45.

Buck-Morss, Susan. 2009. *Hegel, Haiti and Universal History*. Pittsburgh, Pa.: University of Pittsburgh Press.

Bull, Michael, Paul Gilroy, David Howes, and Doug Kahn. 2006. "Introducing Sensory Studies." *The Senses and Society* 1, no. 1: 4–7.

Burke, Kenneth. (1945) 1969. *A Grammar of Motives*. Berkeley: University of California Press.

Bushnell, David. 2004. *Simón Bolívar: Liberation and Disappointment*. New York: Pearson Longman.

Butler, Judith. 2015. *Notes Toward a Performative Theory of Assembly*. Harvard University Press.

Buxton, Julia. 2005. "Venezuela's Contemporary Political Crisis in Historical Context." *Bulletin of Latin American Research* 24, no. 3: 328–47.

Cabranes-Grant, Leo. 2011. "From Scenarios to Networks: Performing the Intercultural in Colonial Mexico." *Theatre Journal* 63, no. 4 (December): 499–520.

Cabrujas, Ignacio. "Introduction." In *Teatro venezolano*. Caracas: Monte Avila Editores.

Cahill, David. 1996. "Popular Religion and Appropriation: The Example of Corpus Christi in Eighteenth-Century Cuzco." *Latin American Research Review* 31, no. 2: 67–110.

Cánepa, Gisela. 2009. "Esfera pública y derechos culturales: La cultura como acción," *Memoria: Revista sobre cultura, democracia y derechos humanos*, no. 5: 27–38.

Cánepa-Koch, Gisela. 1998. *Máscara, transformación e identidad en los Andes*. Lima: Fondo Editorial de la Pontificia Universidad Católica del Perú.

Cañizares-Esguerra, Jorge. 2006. *Puritan Conquistadors: Iberianizing the Atlantic 1550–1700*. Palo Alto, Calif.: Stanford University Press.

Cannon, Barry. 2004. "Venezuela, April 2002: Coup or Popular Rebellion? The Myth of a United Venezuela." *Bulletin of Latin American Research* 23, no. 3: 285–302.

Canovan, Margaret. 1999. "Trust the People! Populism and the Two Faces of Democracy." *Political Studies* 47, no. 1: 2–16.

Carlson, Chris. 2007. "Venezuelan President Clashes with the King of Spain at Latin American Summit." Venezuelanalysis.com. November 12. http://www.venezuelaanalysis.com/news/2827.

Carter Center. 2005. "Observing the Venezuela Presidential Recall Referendum Comprehensive Report." Delegation led by Jennifer McCoy. Atlanta: Carter Center, The Americas Program.

Castañeda, Jorge. 2006. "Latin America's Left Turn." *Foreign Affairs*. May/June. Available at http://www.foreignaffairs.com.

Castillo, Susana D. 1980. *El desarraigo en el teatro venezolano: Marco histórico y manifestaciones modernas*. Caracas: Editorial Ateneo de Caracas.

Chacón, Alfredo. 1979. *Curiepe: Ensayo sobre la realización del sentido en la actividad magicoreligiosa de un pueblo venezolano*. Caracas: Universidad Central de Venezuela.

———. 1983. *Poblaciones y culturas negras de Venezuela*. Caracas: Instituto Autónomo Biblioteca Nacional y de Servicios de Bibliotecas.

Chalbaud, Román. 1981. *Teatro venezolano*. Caracas: Monte Avila Editores.

———. (1955) 1991. *Caín adolescente*. In *Colección teatro 1*. Caracas: Monte Avila Editores.

Chambers-Letson, Joshua. 2013. *A Race So Different: Performance and Law in Asian America*. New York: New York University Press.

Chatterjee, Partha. 2004. *The Politics of the Governed: Reflections on Popular Politics in Most of the World*. New York: Columbia University Press.

"Chávez: Bush 'Devil'; U.S. 'On the Way Down.' " 2006. CNN.com. September 21. http://edition.cnn.com/2006/WORLD/americas/09/20/chavez.un/index.html.

"Chávez Calls Bush 'The Devil' in UN Address, Predicts Fall of 'U.S. Empire' and Calls for Major UN Reforms." 2006. *Democracy Now!* September 21. http://www.democracynow.org/2006/9/21/chavez_calls_bush_the_devil_in.

"Chávez Flies the Flag for Change." 2006. Aljazeera.com. March 13. http://www.aljazeera.com/archive/2006/03/200849142148794963.html.

Chesney, Lawrence. 2005. "El teatro a fines del siglo XX (1970–2000)." *Associació d'investigació i experimentació teatral*.

———. 2007. "Uslar pietri en el teatro venezolano." *Revista* 61, no. 2: 77–83.

Ciccariello-Maher, George. 2013. *We Created Chávez: A People's History of the Venezuelan Revolution*. Durham, N.C.: Duke University Press.

Cohen-Cruz, Jan. 2005. *Local Acts: Community-Based Performance in the United States*. New Brunswick, N.J.: Rutgers University Press.

Cole, Catherine. 2010. *Performing South Africa's Truth Commission*. Bloomington: Indiana University Press.
"Colectivo venezolano rinde homenaje a Hugo Chávez a través de teatro y ballet." 2014. MSN.com. November 29.
Comaroff, Jean, and John L. Comaroff, eds. 1993. *Modernity and Its Malcontents: Ritual and Power in Postcolonial Africa*. Chicago: University of Chicago Press.
Coronil, Fernando. 1997. *The Magical State: Nature, Money, and Modernity in Venezuela*. Chicago: University of Chicago Press.
———. 2008. "Magical History: What's Left of Chávez?" LANIC e-Text Collection. Latin American Network Information Centre. http://lanic.utexas.edu/project/etext/llilas/vrp/.
Cronin, Thomas E. 1989. *Direct Democracy: The Politics of Initiative, Referendum, and Recall*. Cambridge, Mass.: Harvard University Press.
Dagnino, Evalina. 1998. "Culture, Citizenship, and Democracy: Changing Discourses and Practices of the Latin American Left." In *Cultures of Politics, Politics of Cultures: Re-Visioning Latin American Social Movements*, edited by Sonia E. Álvarez, Evalina Dagnino, and Arturo Escobar, 33–45. Boulder, Colo.: Westview.
Damas, Eligio. 2007. "El General Manuel Piar opina sobre su fusilamiento." Aporrea.org. September 29. http://www.aporrea.org/actualidad/a41810.html.
DaMatta, Roberto. 1991. *Carnivals, Rogues, and Heroes: An Interpretation of the Brazilian Dilemma*. Notre Dame, Ind.: University of Notre Dame Press, 1991.
Das, Veena, and Deborah Poole. 2004. "Introduction." In *Anthropology in the Margins of the State*, edited by Veena Das and Deborah Poole, 3–34. Oxford: School of American Research Press.
Dauster, Frank. 1981. "Review of Susan Castillo's *El desarraigo en el teatro venezolano*." *Latin American Theater Review* 15, no. 1: 95–96.
De Certeau, Michel. 1984. *The Practice of Everyday Life*. Berkeley: University of California Press.
De la Torre, Carlos. 2010. *Populist Seduction in Latin America*. Athens: Ohio University Press.
———. 2016. "Populism and the Politics of the Extraordinary in Latin America." *Journal of Political Ideologies* 21, no. 2: 121–39.
Dean, Carolyn. 1999. *Inka Bodies and the Body of Christ: Corpus Christi in Colonial Cuzco, Perú*. Durham, N.C.: Duke University Press.
Debord, Guy. 1994. *The Society of the Spectacle*. Translated by Donald Nicholson-Smith. New York: Zone Books.
Delacour, Justin. 2004. "Spinning Lies, Damned Lies, and Statistics in Venezuela." *Narco News Bulletin*. Narconews.com. July 30. http://www.narconews.com/Issue33/article1007.html.
Di Benedetto, María Eugenia. 2000. *Pedro Pérez Delgado, Maisanta, el último hombre a caballo: Versión de una historia no "oficial."* Caracas: El Centauro Ediciones.
Diamond, Elin. 1996. *Performance and Cultural Politics*. New York: Routledge.
Díez Borque, José María. 1987. "Liturgia-fiesta-teatro: Orbítras concéntricas de teatralidad en el siglo XVI." *Cuadernos de filologia hispánica*, no. 6: 485–99. Madrid: Editorial Universitario de Complutense.

Duarte, Carlos F. 1987. *Las fiestas del Corpus Christi en la Caracas hispánica: Tarasca, gigantes y diablitos*. Caracas: Academia Nacional de la Historia.

Dubois, Laurent. 2006. "An Enslaved Enlightenment: Rethinking the Intellectual History of the French Atlantic." *Social History* 31, no. 1 (February): 1–14.

Ducoudray-Holstein, Henri Louis La Fayette Villaume, and Alphonse Viollet. 1831. *Histoire de Bolívar, par la Gen. Ducoudray-Holstein: Continue jusqu'a sa mort par Alphonse Viollet*. Paris: A. Levasseur.

Duno-Gottberg, Luis. 2004. "Mob Outrages: Reflections of the Media Construction of the Masses in Venezuela (April 2000–January 2003)." *Journal of Latin American Cultural Studies* 13, no. 1: 115–35.

———. 2009. *Social Images of Anti-Apocalypse: Bikers and the Representation of Popular Politics in Venezuela*. Raleigh: North Carolina State University, Department of Foreign Languages and Literatures.

———. 2011. "The Color of Mobs: Racial Politics, Ethnopopulism and Representation in the Chávez Era." In *Participation and the Public Sphere in Venezuela's Bolivarian Democracy*, edited by David Smilde and Daniel Hellinger. 271–97. Durham, N.C.: Duke University Press.

Duquenal, Daniel. 2004. "Homophobia and Chavismo." *Venezuela News and Views*. July 21. http://daniel-venezuela.blogspot.com/2004/07/homophobia-and-chavismo-check-one-more.html.

Economic Commission for Latin America and the Caribbean (ECLAC). 2004. *A Decade of Social Development in Latin America, 1990–1999*. Santiago: ECLAC.

———. 2004. *Social Panorama of Latin America, 2002–2003*. Santiago: ECLAC.

———. 2014. *Social Panorama of Latin America, 2013*. Santiago: ECLAC.

Elizalde, Rosa Miriam, and Luis Báez. 2004. *Chávez nuestro*. Havana, Cuba: Casa Editora Abril.

Ellner, Steve. 2005. "Revolutionary and Non-Revolutionary Paths of Radical Populism: Directions of the *Chavista* Movement in Venezuela." *Science & Society* 69, no. 2: 160–90.

———. 2008. *Rethinking Venezuelan Politics: Class, Conflict, and the Chávez Phenomenon*. Boulder, Colo.: Lynne Rienner.

———. 2015. "Chavismo on the Horns of a Dilemma: Populism and Pragmatism in Venezuela." *New Left Project*. Venezuelanalysis.com. May 22. http://venezuelanalysis.com/analysis/11391.

Ellner, Steve, and Tinker Salas, eds. 2007. *Venezuela: Hugo Chávez and the Decline of an "Exceptional Democracy."* London: Rowman and Littlefield.

Espar, Teresa. 1998. *La semiótica y el discurso literario latinoamericano*. Caracas: Monte Avila Editores.

Eymerich, Nicholas. (ca. 1376) 1578. *Directorium Inquisitorum*. Witchcraft Collection, Department of Rare and Manuscript Collections, Cornell University. http://ebooks.library.cornell.edu/cgi/t/text/text-idx?c=witch;idno=wit045.

Falcón, Fernando. 2006. *El cadete de los valles de Aragua: El pensamiento político y military de la illustración los conceptos de guerra política en Simón Bolívar, 1797–1814*. Venezuela: Universidad Central de Venezuela, Facultad de Ciencias Jurídicas y Politicas.

Fanon, Frantz. 1967. *Black Skin, White Masks*. Translated by Charles Lam Markmann. New York: Grove.

Fernandes, Sujatha. 2006. "Saints of Venezuela: Reclaiming the Religious Fiestas of Slaves." *Colorlines* 9, no. 1: 51–52.

———. 2007a. "Barrio Women and Popular Politics in Chávez's Venezuela." *Latin American Politics and Society* 49, no. 3: 97–127.

———. 2007b. "A View from the Barrios: Hugo Chávez as an Expression of Urban Popular Movements." *LASA Forum Focus* 28, no. 1: 17–19.

———. 2010. *Who Can Stop the Drums? Urban Social Movements in Chávez's Venezuela*. Durham, N.C.: Duke University Press.

Ferry, Robert J. 1981. "Encomienda, African Slavery, and Agriculture in Seventeenth Century Caracas." *Hispanic American Historical Review* 61, no. 4 (November): 609–35.

Finch, Aisha K. 2015. *Rethinking Slave Rebellion in Cuba: La Escalera and the Insurgencies of 1841–1844*. Chapel Hill: University of North Carolina Press.

Fischer-Hoffman, Cory. 2014. "Venezuela's 'Political Prisoner' Allegory." *Global Research*. October 11. Available at http://www.globalresearch.ca.

Fischer-Lichte, Erika. 2014. *The Routledge Introduction to Theatre and Performance Studies*. Edited by Minou Arjomand and Ramona Mosse. London: Routledge.

Fleischer, Ari. 2002. "Press Briefing by Ari Fleischer." Office of the Press Secretary, White House. April 12. http://georgewbush-whitehouse.archives.gov/news/releases/2002/04/20020412–1.html.

Flores, Juan. 2005. "'Pueblo Pueblo': Popular Culture in Time." In *Popular Culture: A Reader*, edited by Raiford A. Guins and Omayra Zaragoza Cruz, 72–82. London: Sage.

Flynn, Maureen. 1991. "Mimesis of the Last Judgement: The Spanish Auto de Fe." *New Century Journal* 22, no. 2: 281–97.

Forns Broggi, Roberto. 1999. "Review of *Pandemonium* by Román Chalbaud." *Chasqui* 28, no. 2 (November): 167–69.

Foster, George M. 1953. "Cofradia and Compradazgo in Spain and Spanish America." *Southwestern Journal of Anthropology* 9, no. 1 (spring): 1–28.

Foucault, Michel. 1995. *Discipline and Punish: The Birth of the Prison*. New York: Vintage Books.

Frajman, Eduardo. 2014. "Broadcasting Populist Leadership: Hugo Chávez and Aló Presidente." *Journal of Latin American Studies* 46: 501–26.

Francia, Néstor. 2005. *Campaña de Santa Inés: Revolución en la publicidad*. Caracas: Ministerio de Comunicación e Información.

Frank, Jason. 2010. *Constituent Moments: Enacting the People in Postrevolutionary America*. Durham, N.C.: Duke University Press.

Fraser, Nancy. 1990. "Rethinking the Public Sphere: A Contribution to the Critique of Actually Existing Democracy." *Social Text* 25/26: 56–80.

Freire, Paolo. 1970. *Pedagogy of the Oppressed*. New York: Herder and Herder.

Gallegos, Rómulo. 1929. *Doña Bárbara*. Barcelona: Araluce.

García, Jesús Chucho. 1989. *Contra el cepo: Barlovento, tiempo de cimarrones*. Las Colonias: Editorial Lucas y Trina.

———. 2004. "Demystifying Africa's Absence in Venezuelan History and Culture." Venezuelanalysis.com. January 15. http://venezuelanalysis.com/analysis/316.

———. 2007. "La deuda del estado venezolano y los Afrodescendientes." *Journal of Latin American and Caribbean Anthropology* 12, no. 1: 223–32.

———. 2014. "Why Are There No Barricades in Afrodescendant Communities?" *La Voz*. Venezuelanalysis.com. April 23. http://venezuelanalysis.com/analysis/10637.

García, Jesús Chucho, and Bartolome Duysens. 1999. *AfroVenezuelan Reflections: The Drums of Liberation*. Caracas: Fundación Afroamerica and CONAC.

García, Jesús Chucho, and Jorge Guerrero Veloz. 2003. *Afrovenezolanidad, racismo e interculturalidad*. Caracas: Red de Organizaciones Afrovenezolanas.

García Canclini, Néstor. (1989) 2005. *Hybrid Cultures: Strategies for Entering and Leaving Modernity*. Translated by Christopher L. Chiappari, Silvia L. López, and Renato Rosaldo. Minneapolis: University of Minnesota Press.

———. 1992. *Transforming Modernity: Popular Culture in Mexico*. Translated by Lidia Lozano. Austin: University of Texas Press.

García-Guadilla, María. 2003. "Civil Society: Institutionalization, Fragmentation, Autonomy." In *Venezuelan Politics in the Chávez Era: Class, Polarization, and Conflict*, edited by Steve Ellner and Daniel Hellinger, 179–96. Boulder, Colo.: Lynne Rienner.

Geertz, Clifford. 1975. *The Interpretation of Cultures: Selected Essays*. London: Hutchinson.

Gellner, Ernest. 2006. *Nations and Nationalism*. Malden, Mass.: Blackwell. Gonzalbo Aizpuru, Pilar. 1993. "Las fiestas novohispanas: Espectáculo y ejemplo." *Mexican Studies/Estudios Mexicanos* 9, no. 1: 19–45.

Goodwyn, Lawrence. 1978. *The Populist Moment: A Short History of the Agrarian Revolt in America*. Oxford: Oxford University Press.

Gott, Richard. 2000. *In the Shadow of the Liberator: Hugo Chávez and the Transformation of Venezuela*. New York: Verso.

———. 2005. *Hugo Chávez and the Bolivarian Revolution*. New York: Verso.

Graden, Dale T. 2013. "A Force for Transformation: The Memory of Ali Primera in the Street Art of Caracas." *NACLA: Report on the Americas* 46, no. 3 (fall): 64–71.

Graham-Jones, Jean. 2014. *Evita, Inevitably: Performing Argentina's Female Icons before and after Eva Perón*. Ann Arbor: University of Michigan Press.

Griffiths, Mo. 2003. *Action for Social Justice in Education: Fairly Different*. Maidenhead, Eng.: Open University Press.

Guerra Cedeño, Franklin. 1984. *Esclavos negros, cimarroneras y cumbes de Barlovento*. Caracas: Lagoven.

Guerrero Veloz, Jorge. 2001. *Comunidades afroaragüeñas*. Caracas: Ministerio de Educación, Cultura y Deportes; Viceministerio de Cultura; CONAC: Dirección General de Desarrollo Regional, Plan de Sobremarcha, Proyecto de Redes Socioculturales.

Guss, David M. 1993. "The Selling of San Juan: The Performance of History in an Afro-Venezuelan Community." *American Ethnologist* 20, no. 3 (August): 451–73.

———. 2001. *The Festive State: Race, Ethnicity, and Nationalism as Cultural Performance*. Berkeley: University of California Press.

Hall, Stuart. 1981. "Notes on Deconstructing the Popular." In *People's History and Socialist Theory*, edited by Raphael Samuel, 227-40. London: Routledge and Kegan Paul.

———. 1982. "The Rediscovery of 'Ideology': Return of the Repressed in Media Studies." In *Culture, Society, and the Media*, edited by Tony Bennett, James Curran, Michael Gurevitch, and Janet Woollacott, 56–90. London: Methuen.

Hamera, Judith, ed. 2006. *Opening Acts: Performance in/as Communication and Cultural Studies*. Thousand Oaks, Calif.: Sage, 2006.

Hatemi, Peter K., and McDermott, Rose. 2016. "Give Me Attitudes." *Annual Review of Political Science*, 19: 331–50.

Hawkins, Kirk. 2003. "Populism in Venezuela: The Rise of Chavismo." *Third World Quarterly* 24, no. 6: 1137–60.

———. 2010. *Venezuela's Chavismo and Populism in Comparative Perspective*. Cambridge: Cambridge University Press.

Hawkins, Kirk A., and Bojana Kocijan. 2013. "Codebook for Measuring Populist Discourse: Populist Discourse Project at Central European University."

Hellinger, Daniel. 2005. "When 'No' Means 'Yes to Revolution': Electoral Politics in Bolivarian Venezuela." *Latin American Perspectives* 32, no. 3: 8–32.

Hernandez, Juan Antonio. 2004. "Against the Comedy of Civil Society: Posthegemony, Media and the 2002 Coup d'Etat in Venezuela." *Journal of Latin American Cultural Studies* 13, no. 1: 137–45.

Hernández, Paola. 2015. "Teatro de lo Real." Paper presented at the Latin American Studies Association (LASA) Thirty-third International Congress, San Juan, Puerto Rico, May 27–30.

Herrera Salas, Jesús Maria. 2004. "Racismo y discurso politico en Venezuela." *Revista venezolana de economia y ciencias sociales* 10, no. 2: 111–28.

Hobsbawm, Eric. 1983. "Introduction: Inventing Traditions." In *The Invention of Tradition*, edited by Eric Hobsbawm and Terence Ranger. 1–14. Cambridge: Cambridge University Press.

Howes, David. 2015. "Sensation and Transmission." In *Ritual, Performance and the Senses*, edited by John P. Mitchell and Michael Bull. 153–64. New York: Bloomsbury.

Human Rights Watch. 2008. "A Decade under Chávez." Hrw.org. September 18. http://www.hrw.org/reports/2008/09/22/decade-under-ch-vez.

Irady, Benito. 2015. "Cofradias of Venezuelan Dancing Devils." In *Festive Devils of the Americas*, edited by Milla Cozart Riggio, Angela Marino, and Paolo Vignolo, 243–52. London: Seagull; Chicago: University of Chicago Press.

Jackson, Shannon. 2011. *Social Works: Performing Art, Supporting Publics*. London: Routledge.

———. 2011. "Working Publics." *Performance Research* 16, no. 2: 8–13.

Jenkins, Keith. 1991. *Re-Thinking History*. New York: Routledge.

Jones, Bart. 2004. "Venezuela: Divisions Harden after Chávez Victory." *National Catholic Reporter*. NCRonline.org. September 4. http://natcath.org/NCR_Online/archives2/2004c/090304/090304a.php.

———. 2007. *¡Hugo!: The Hugo Chávez Story from Mud Hut to Perpetual Revolution*. Hanover, N.H.: Steerforth.

Joseph, Gilbert, and David Nugent. 1994. "Popular Culture and State Formation in Revolutionary Mexico." In *Everyday Forms of State Formation: Revolution and the Negotiation of Rule in Modern Mexico*, edited by Gilbert M. Joseph and Daniel Nugent, 3–23. Durham, N.C.: Duke University Press.

Karst, Kenneth L., Murray L. Schwartz, and Audrey J. Schwartz. 1973. *The Evolution of Law in the Barrios of Caracas*. Los Angeles: University of California, Latin American Center.

Kazin, Michael. 1998. *The Populist Persuasion: An American History*. Ithaca, N.Y.: Cornell University Press.

Kester, Grant. 2011. *The One and the Many: Contemporary Collaborative Art in a Global Context*. Durham, N.C.: Duke University Press.

King, Marita. 1987. *Román Chalbaud: Poesía, magia y revolución*. Caracas: Monte Avila Editores.

Klooster, Wim. 2014. "Slave Revolts, Royal Justice, and a Ubiquitous Rumor in the Age of Revolutions." *William and Mary Quarterly* 71, no. 3 (July): 401–24.

Laclau, Ernesto. 1977. *Politics and Ideology in Marxist Theory: Capitalism, Fascism, Populism*. London: NLB.

———. 1995. "Universalism, Particularism, and the Question of Identity." In *The Identity in Question*, edited by J. Ranchman, 93–108. New York: Routledge.

———. 1999. *New Reflections on Revolutions of Our Time*. New York: Routledge.

———. 2005. *On Populist Reason*. London: Verso, 2005.

Laclau, Ernesto, and Chantal Mouffe. (1985) 2001. *Hegemony and Socialist Strategy: Towards a Radical Democratic Politics*. London: Verso.

Lamadrid, Enrique. 2003. *Hermanitos comanchitos: Indo-Hispanic Rituals of Captivity and Redemption*. Albuquerque: University of New Mexico Press.

Lamrani, Salim. 2007. "Reporters without Borders and RCTV: Disinformation and Lies." *Global Research*. September 21. Available at http://www.globalresearch.ca.

Lander, Edgardo. 2005. "Venezuelan Social Conflict in a Global Context." *Latin American Perspectives* 32, no. 2: 20–38.

Laviña, Javier, and Michael Zeuske. 2008. "Failures of Atlantization: First Slaveries in Venezuela and Nueva Granada." *Review (Fernand Braudel Center)* 31, no. 3: 297–342.

Lawrence, Louis Chesney. 2007. "Uslar pietri en el teatro venezolano." *Revista* 61, no. 2: 77–83.

Lebowitz, Michael. 2007. "Venezuela: A Good Example of the Bad Left of Latin America." *Monthly Review* 59, no. 3. https://monthlyreview.org/2007/07/01/venezuela-a-good-example-of-the-bad-left-of-latin-america/.

Ledwith, Margaret, and Jane Springett. 2010. *Participatory Practice: Community-Based Action for Transformative Change*. Bristol, Eng.: Polity.

Leech, Garry. 2013. "The Bias of Human Rights Watch." *Counterpunch*. March 14. http://www.counterpunch.org/2013/03/14/the-bias-of-human-rights-watch/.

"Ley Orgánica de los Consejos Comunales." 2012. minci.gob.ve. December 9. http://www.minci.gob.ve/2012/09/ley-organica-de-los-consejos-comunales/.

Lezra, Jacques. 2003. "The Ethic of Terror in Radical Democracy." *Arizona Journal of Hispanic Cultural Studies* 7: 173–94.

Liscano, Juan. 1950. *Folklore y cultura: Ensayos*. Caracas: Editorial Ávila Gráfica.

López, Oscar. 2014. "Peru: Sterilizing the Poor as an Economic Measure." *Cornell International Law Journal Online* 36.

López-Cano, María del Pilar, Gisela von Wobeser, and Juan Guillermo Muñoz Correa. 1998. *Cofradías, capellanías y obras pías en la América colonial*. México, D.F.: Universidad Nacional Autónoma de México.

López Maya, Margarita. 2003. "The Venezuelan 'Caracazo' of 1989: Popular Protest and Institutional Weakness." *Journal of Latin American Studies* 35, no. 1: 117–37.

———. 2004. "Venezuela 2001–2004: Actores y estrategias." *CDC* 21, no. 56: 109–32.

Lovler, Ronnie. 2004. "Fair, Responsible Media Debatable in Venezuela." University of Florida News. August 23. http://news.ufl.edu/archive/2004/08/fair-responsible-media-debatable-in-venezuela.html.

Lummis, C. Douglas. 1996. *Radical Democracy*. Ithaca, N.Y.: Cornell University Press.

Lupu, Noam. 2010. "Who Votes for Chavismo? Class Voting in Hugo Chávez's Venezuela." *Latin American Research Review* 45, no. 1: 7–32.

Maddock Dillon, Elizabeth. 2014. *New World Drama: The Performative Commons in the Atlantic World 1649–1859*. Durham, N.C.: Duke University Press.

Márquez Montes, Carmen. 1998. "El rito y la fiesta en la dramaturgia de Román Chalbaud." *Teatro* 13-14: 267–75.

Márquez Rodríguez, Alex. 2004. "Florentino y el Diablo en Santa Inés." Analitica.com. June 23. http://analitica.com/opinion/opinion-nacional/florentino-y-el-diablo-en-santa-ines/.

Marsland, William David, and Amy Louis Marsland. 1954. *Venezuela through Its History*. New York: Crowell.

Martin, Randy. 1994. *Socialist Ensembles: Theater and State in Cuba and Nicaragua*. Minneapolis: University of Minnesota Press.

———. 1998. *Critical Moves: Dance Studies in Theory and Politics*. Durham, N.C.: Duke University Press.

Martín-Barbero, Jesús. 2008. "Prácticas de comunicación en la cultura popular: Mercados, plazas, cementerios y espacios de ocio." Paper presented at the Universidad Nacional de Colombia (UNAL), Bogotá, Colombia, October.

Martz, John D. 1964. "Venezuela's 'Generation of '28': The Genesis of Political Democracy." *Journal of Inter-American Studies* 6, no. 1: 17–32.

Marx, Karl. (1858) 2009. "Bolivar y Ponte." Marxists.org. https://www.marxists.org/archive/marx/works/1858/01/bolivar.htm.

Mauss, Marcel. (1925) 1954. *The Gift: Forms and Functions of Exchange in Archaic Societies*. London: Cohen and West.

Mazoch, Leslie. 2006. "Chávez Raises New Flag with Nod to Bolívar." *USAToday.com*. March 13. http://usatoday30.usatoday.com/news/world/2006–03–12-venezuela_x.htm.

McCoy, Jennifer, and David J. Myers, eds. 2004. *The Unraveling of Representative Democracy in Venezuela*. Baltimore, Md.: Johns Hopkins University Press.

McEnaney, Tom. 2017. *Acoustic Properties: Radio, Narrative, and the New Neighborhood of the Americas*. Evanston, Ill.: Northwestern University Press.

Mendoza, Zoila. Producer/director. 2015. *The Pilgrimage to the Sanctuary of the Lord of Qoyllur Rit'i: The Walk Experience*. 44 min. Color.

Mills, Catherine. 2004. "Agamben's Messianic Politics: Biopolitics, Abandonment and a Happy Life." *Contretemps* 5 (December): 42–62.

Mitchell, Jon P., and Michael Bull, eds. 2015. *Ritual, Performance and the Senses*. London: Bloomsbury.

Modesto Bolívar, Pedro. 2006. *Ocumare, el municipio de la Costa de Oro*. Maracay, Venezuela: Pinfer.

Moffitt, Benjamin. 2016. *The Global Rise of Populism: Performance, Political Style, and Representation*. Redwood City, Calif.: Stanford University Press.

Monasterios, Rubén. 1990. *Un enfoque crítico del teatro venezolano*. Caracas: Monte Avila Editores.

Moraga, Cherríe, and Gloria Anzaldúa. 1983. *This Bridge Called My Back: Writings by Radical Women of Color*. New York: Kitchen Table.

Moreiras, Alberto. 2001. *The Exhaustion of Difference: The Politics of Latin American Cultural Studies*. Durham, N.C.: Duke University Press.

Mörner, Magnus. 1993. *Region and State in Latin America's Past*. Baltimore, Md.: Johns Hopkins University Press.

———. 2004. *Historia de Ocumare de la costa entre 1870 y 1960*. Stockholm: Instituto de Estudios Latinoamericanos de la Universidad de Estocolmo.

Morón, Guillermo. 1996. *Libro de amigos: Homenaje a Guillermo Morón*. Caracas: Academia Nacional de la Historia.

Morris, Pam, ed. 1994. *The Bakhtin Reader: Selected Writings of Bakhtin, Medvedev, and Voloshinov*. London: E. Arnold.

Morsbach, Greg. 2006. "New Venezuela Flag Divides Nation." *BBCNews.com*. March 13. http://news.bbc.co.uk/2/hi/americas/4800202.stm.

Motta, Sara C. 2011. "Populism's Achilles' Heel: Popular Democracy beyond the Liberal State and the Market Economy in Venezuela." *Latin American Perspectives* 38 no. 1 (176): 28–46.

Motta, Sara C., and Mike Cole, eds. 2013. *Education and Social Change in Latin America*. New York: Palgrave Macmillan.

Mouffe, Chantal. 2007. "Artistic Activism and Agonistic Spaces." *Art & Research* 1, no. 2. http://www.artandresearch.org.uk/v1n2/mouffe.html.

———. 2013. *Agonistics: Thinking the World Politically*. London: Verso.

Mudde, Cas, and Cristóbal Rovira Kaltswasser. 2012. *Populism in Europe and the Americas: Threat or Corrective for Democracy?* Cambridge: Cambridge University Press.

Mueller, Jan-Werner. 2014. "'The People Must Be Extracted from within the People': Reflections on Populism." Constellations Lecture, Princeton University, Princeton, N.J., March

Myers, David J. 2004. "The Normalization of Punto Fijo Democracy." In *The Unraveling of Representative Democracy in Venezuela*, edited by Jennifer McCoy and David J. Myers, 11–32. Baltimore, Md.: Johns Hopkins University Press.

Nail, Thomas. 2015. *The Figure of the Migrant*. Palo Alto, Calif.: Stanford University Press.

Negri, Antonio. 1999. *Insurgencies: Constituent Power and the Modern State*. Minneapolis: University of Minnesota Press.

Newcomb, Steven T. 2008. *Pagans in the Promised Land*. Golden, Colo.: Fulcrum.

Ngũgĩ wa Thiong'o. 1983. *Barrel of a Pen: Resistance to Repression in Neo-Colonial Kenya*. London: New Beacon Books.

———. 1997. "Enactment of Power: The Politics of Performance Space." *TDR: The Drama Review* 41, no. 3: 11–30.

———. 1998. *Penpoints, Gunpoints, and Dreams: Toward a Critical Theory of the Arts and the State in Africa*. New York: Oxford University Press.

Norris, Andrew. 2006. "Ernesto Laclau and the Logic of the Political." *Philosophy & Social Criticism* 32, no. 1: 111–34.

Núñez, Rocío, and Francisco Javier Pérez. 1994. *Diccionario del habla actual de Venezuela: Venezolanismos, voce indígena, nuevas acepciones*. Caracas: Universidad Católica Andrés Bello, Centro de Investigaciones Lingüticas y Literarias.

Ochoa, Marcia. 2014. *Queen for a Day: Transformistas, Beauty Queens, and the Performance of Femininity in Venezuela*. Durham, N.C.: Duke University Press.

Ochoa Espejo, Paulina. 2011. *The Time of Popular Sovereignty*. University Park, Pa.: Penn State University Press.

Ortiz, Fernando. 1921. "Los cabildos y fiesta afrocubanos." *Revista bimestre cubana* 16 (January/February): 5–39.

———. (1920) 1960. *La antigua fiesta afrocubana del "Dia de Reyes."* Havana: Ministerio de Cultura.

Ortíz, Manuel Antonio, et al. 1982. *Diablos danzantes de Venezuela*. Caracas: Fundación la Salle de Ciencias Naturales.

Ostiguy, Pierre. 2009. "The High and the Low in Politics: A Two-Dimensional Political Space for Comparative Analysis and Electoral Studies." Helen Kellogg Institute for International Studies Working Paper #360. July. http://kellogg.nd.edu/publications/workingpapers/WPS/360.pdf

Oviedo y Baños, Joseph de. 1723. *Historia de la conquista y poblacion de la Provincia de Venezuela*. Madrid: D. Gregorio Hermosilla.

Panizza, Francisco, ed. 2005. *Populism and the Mirror of Democracy*. London: Verso.

Pastor, Roberto Viciano, and Rubén Martinez Dalmau. 2001. *Cambio proceso constituyente en Venezuela (1998–2000)*. Caracas: Editorial Tirant lo Blanch.

Pearson, Mike, and Michael Shanks. 2001. *Theatre/Archaeology*. London: Routledge.

Pilkington, Ed. 2006. "Chávez Attacks 'Devil' Bush in U.N. Speech." *Guardian*. September 21. Available at http://www.theguardian.com.

Podur, Justin. 2004. "Venezuela: Florentino the Devil and the Opposition." Killingtrain.com. August 14. Archived copy available at https://podur.org.

Pollak-Eltz, Angelina. 1968. "The Devil Dances in Venezuela." *Caribbean Studies* 8, no. 2: 65–73.

———. 1972. "Magic, Sorcery and Witchcraft in Venezuela—Some Considerations." *Review of Ethnology* 3, no. 21: 161–68.

———. 1974. *Vestigios africanos en la cultura del pueblo venezolano*. Caracas: Universidad Católica Andrés Bello, Instituto de Investigaciones Históricas.

Poole, Deborah, and Veena Das. 2004. *Anthropology in the Margins of the State*. Santa Fe, N.M.: School of American Research Press.

Postel, Charles. 2007. *The Populist Vision*. New York: Oxford University Press.

Presilia, Eugene Edward Godfreid. 2006. "Carlos Manuel Piar and Pedro Luis Brion: Curaçaoans Struggling Together with Simón Antonio Bolívar y Palacios for Liberation from Colonialism and Racism." Afrocubaweb.com. June 17. http://www.afrocubaweb.com/eugenegodfried/piar-brion.htm.

Prieto, Miguel Angel. 1995. "Funcionamiento del calendario compuesto." Ponencia "La Tradición Indígena Mariche." Ateneo de Caracas.

———. 2000. "El origen de la rueda del sol (calendario solar compuesto), en petroglifos de Venezuela." *Diario Chacao*, March 10.

———. 2010. *Cayapa-Asaque: Modo de producción communal, economia communal y modo de vida entre los Mariche-Cumanogoto, los arcaicos navegantes de suramérica*. Caracas: Fundación Educacional Simón Rodríguez.

Rai, Shirin M., and Janelle Reinelt, eds. 2015. *The Grammar of Politics and Performance*. New York: Routledge.

Rama, Ángel. 1976. "A la búsqueda de la nacionalidad por el teatro." *Escena* 11 (CONAC, Caracas): 33–37.

Ramos Guédez, José Marcial. 2004. "150 años de la abolición de la esclavitud en Venezuela: De José Leonardo Chirino a José Gregorio Monagas." *Tierra firme* 22, no. 85: 17–32.

———. 2009. "Orígenes de la festividad de los diablos danzantes en Venezuela." *Boletín de la Academia Nacional de la Historia*, no. 366 (June): 165–73.

Ramos-Smith, Maya. 1998. *Censura y teatro novohispano, 1539–1822: Ensayos y antología de documentos*. Vol. 1. México, D.F.: Consejo Nacional para la Cultura y las Artes, Instituto Nacional de Bellas Artes, Centro Nacional de Investigación e Información Teatral Rodolfo Usigli: Escenología, A.C.

Raphael, Timothy. *The President Electric: Ronald Reagan and the Politics of Performance*. Ann Arbor: University of Michigan Press.

"Red Afrodescendiente de Aragua reafirmó resaldo contundente al Presidente Nicolás Maduro." 2013. Abrebrecha.com. April 18. http://www.abrebrecha.com/275214_Red-Afrodescendiente-de-Aragua-reafirm%C3%B3-respaldo-contundente-al-Presidente-Nicol%C3%A1s-Maduro.html.

Riggio, Milla Cozart, ed. 2004. *Carnival: Culture in Action—The Trinidad Experience*. New York: Routledge.

Riggio, Milla Cozart, Angela Marino, and Paolo Vignolo. 2015. *Festive Devils of the Americas*. Chicago: Seagull/University of Chicago Press.

Rivera Cusicanqui, Silvia. 2014. "The Potosí Principle: Another View of Totality." *Emisférica* 11, no. 1. http://hemisphericinstitute.org/hemi/en/emisferica-111-decolonial-gesture/e111-essay-the-potosi-principle-another-view-of-totality.

Roach, Joseph. 1996. *Cities of the Dead: Circum-Atlantic Performance*. New York: Columbia University Press.

———. *It*. 2007. Ann Arbor: University of Michigan Press.

Rodríguez, Omar. 2007. *El cine de Román Chalbaud*. Ph.D. diss., University of British Columbia, Vancouver.

Rodríguez-Bobb, Arturo. 2004. *At the Other Side of the Atlantic: Ensayo sobre la esclavitud del negro: Razón, violencia estructural y racismo institucional en el discurso de los intelectuales colombianos del siglo XVI al siglo XIX*. Berlin: Wissenschaftlicher Verlag Berlin.

Rovira Kaltswasser, Cristóbal. 2014. "Latin American Populism." *Constellations* 21, no. 4: 494–504.

Ruhl, Sarah. 2006. "Re-Runs, Repetition, Theatre." In *Popular Forms for a Radical Theatre*, edited by Caridad Svitch and Sarah Ruhl, 28–42. South Gate, Calif.: NoPassport.

"Ruta Bicentenaria Afrodescendiente." 2010. Redesculturalesafroaragua.blogspot.com.es. http://redesculturalesafroaragua.blogspot.com.es/p/ruta-bicentenaria-afrodescendiente.html.

Salas de Lecuna, Yolanda. 1987. *Bolívar y la historia en la conciencia popular*. Colombia: Ediciones de la Universidad Simon Bolívar.

———. 2004. "'La revolucion bolivariana' y 'la sociedad civil': La construccion de subjectividades nacionales en situacion de conflict." *Revista venezolana de economia y ciencias sociales* 10, no. 2: 91–110.

———. 2005. "Los imaginarios colectivos y su relación con el modelo cultural." In *Cultura, política y sociedad: Perspectivas latinoamericanas*, edited by Daniel Mato, 241. Buenos Aires: CLACSO.

Salazar, Rafael. 1984. *Diablos danzantes de Venezuela: Orígenes y celebraciones en Caracas, Naiguatá, Cata y Turiamo*. Caracas: Miguel Ángel García e Hijo.

Sandoval, Chela, and Latorre, Guisela. 2008. *Chicana/o Artivism: Judy Baca's Digital Work with Youth of Color*. Cambridge, Mass.: MIT Press.

Schechner, Richard. 1985. *Between Theatre and Anthropology*. Philadelphia: University of Pennsylvania Press.

———. (2002) 2013. *Performance Studies: An Introduction*. 3rd ed. New York: Routledge.

Schiller, Naomi. 2009. "Framing the Revolution: Circulation and Meaning of *The Revolution Will Not Be Televised*." *Mass Communication and Society* 12, no. 4: 478–502.

———. 2011. "Catia Sees You: Community Television, Clientelism, and Participatory Statemaking in the Chávez Era." In *Venezuela's Bolivarian Democracy: Participation, Politics, and Culture under Chávez*, edited by David Smilde and Daniel Hellinger, 104–30. Durham, N.C.: Duke University Press.

———. 2013. "Reckoning with Press Freedom: Community Media, Liberalism, and the Processual State in Caracas, Venezuela." *American Ethnologist* 40, no. 3 (August): 540–54.

Scolieri, Paul A. 2010. *Dancing the New World: Aztecs, Spaniards, and the Choreography of Conquest*. Austin: University Press of Texas.

Scruggs, T. M., and Simon Rentner. 2007. "Venezuela: The Rise of Afro-Venezuelan Music to the Present Day Hugo Chávez Era." *Afropop Worldwide*. September 29. http://www.afropop.org/wp/6059/t-m-scruggs-afro-venezuela/.

Selbin, Eric. 2010. *Revolution, Rebellion, Resistance: The Power of Story*. New York: Zed Books.

Shifter, Michael. 2006. "In Search of Hugo Chávez." *Foreign Affairs* (May/June). https://www.foreignaffairs.com/articles/venezuela/2006–05–01/search-hugo-ch-vez.

Silverblatt, Irene. 1988. *Moon, Sun, and Witches: Gender Idologies and Class in Inca and Colonial Peru*. Princeton, N.J.: Princeton University Press.

Smilde, David, and Daniel Hellinger. 2011. *Venezuela's Bolivarian Democracy: Participation, Politics, and Culture under Chávez*. Durham, N.C.: Duke University Press.

Sommer, Doris. 1991. *Foundational Fictions: The National Romances of Latin America*. Berkeley: University of California Press.

Sontag, Susan. 1970. "Introduction: Posters: Advertisement, Art, Political Artifact, Commodity." In *The Art of Revolution: Castro's Cuba, 1959–1970*, edited by Dugald Stermer, vii–xxiii. London: Pall Mall.

Stout, David. 2006. "Chávez Calls Bush 'the Devil' in U.N. Speech." *New York Times*. September 20. http://www.nytimes.com/2006/09/20/world/americas/20cnd-chavez.html.

Strauss, David Levi, and Michael Taussig. 2005. "The Magic of the State: An Interview with Michael Taussig." *Cabinet* 18 (summer). http://cabinetmagazine.org/issues/18/strauss.php.

Strauss, Rafael K. 2004. *El diablo en Venezuela: Certezas, comentarios, preguntas*. Caracas: Fundación Bigott.

Street, John. 1997. *Politics and Popular Culture*. Philadelphia: Temple University Press.

Sulai Capponi, Anna. 2006. "El culto de Santiago entre las comunidades indígenas de Hispanoamérica: Símbolo de comprensión, reinterpretación y compenetración de una nueva realidad spiritual." *Imaginario* 12, no. 13: 249–77.

Svitch, Caridad. 2006. "Popular Forms for a Radical Theatre." In *Popular Forms for a Radical Theatre*, edited by Caridad Svitch and Sarah Ruhl, 8–27. South Gate, Calif.: No Passport.

Taggart, Paul. 2000. *Populism*. Buckingham, Eng.: Open University Press.

Tapia, José León. 1974. *Maisanta: El último hombre a caballo*. Caracas: Centro Editor.

Taussig, Michael. 1980. *The Devil and Commodity Fetishism in South America*. Chapel Hill: University of North Carolina Press.

———. 1997. *The Magic of the State*. New York: Routledge.

Taylor, Diana. 2003. *The Archive and the Repertoire: Performing Cultural Memory in the Americas*. Durham, N.C.: Duke University Press.

———. 2006. "Performance and/as History." *TDR: The Drama Review* 50, no. 1 (spring): 67–86.

———. 2007. "Remapping Genre through Performance: From 'American' to 'Hemispheric' Studies." *PMLA* 122, no. 5 (October): 1416–30.

———. 2016. *Performance*. Durham, N.C.: Duke University Press.

Taylor, Diana, and Sarah J. Townsend, eds. 2008. *Stages of Conflict: A Critical Anthology of Latin American Theatre and Performance*. Ann Arbor: University of Michigan Press.

Tilly, Charles. 2005. *Identities, Boundaries, and Social Ties*. Boulder, Colo.: Paradigm.

Tinker-Salas, Miguel, Gregory Wilpert, and Greg Grandin. 2009. "Academics Respond to Human Rights Watch Director's Defense of Venezuela Report." Venezuelanalysis.com. January 12. http://venezuelanalysis.com/analysis/4106.

Torrealba, Alberto Arvelo. 1940. *Glosas a cancionero (poemas)*. Caracas: Editorial Elite.

———. 1940. "Leyendas de la llanura." *Revista nacional de cultura*. Caracas: CONAC.

Touraine, Alain. 1997. *What Is Democracy?* Boulder, Colo.: Westview.

Trinkunas, Harold A. 2004. "The Military: From Marginalization to Center Stage." In *The Unraveling of Representative Democracy in Venezuela*, edited by Jennifer McCoy and David J. Myers, 50–70. Baltimore, Md.: Johns Hopkins University Press.

———. 2010. "The Transformation of Venezuela." *Latin American Research Review* 45, no. 3: 239–47.

Trouillot, Michel-Rolph. 1995. *Silencing the Past: Power and the Production of History*. Boston: Beacon.

Turner, Victor. 1969. *The Ritual Process: Structure and Anti-Structure*. Chicago: Aldine.

———. 1974. *Dramas, Fields, and Metaphors: Symbolic Action in Human Society*. Ithaca, N.Y.: Cornell University Press.

Urbinati, Nadia. 2014. *Democracy Disfigured: Opinion, Truth and the People*. Cambridge, Mass.: Harvard University Press.

Valencia Ramírez, Cristóbal. 2008. "Hemos Derrotado el Diablo! Chávez Supporters, Anti-Neoliberalism, and Twenty-First-Century Socialism." *Identities: Global Studies in Culture and Power* 15, no. 2: 147–70.

———. 2009. "Active Marooning: Confronting Mi Negra and the Bolivarian Revolution." *Radical History Review* 103: 117–30.

———. 2015. *We Are the State! Barrio Activism in Venezuela's Bolivarian Revolution*. Tucson: University of Arizona Press.

Velasco, Alejandro. 2015a. *Barrio Rising: Urban Popular Politics and the Making of Modern Venezuela*. Oakland: University of California Press.

———. 2015b. "The Commune in One Place: Promise and Contradiction in the 23 de Enero." Paper presented at "The Communal State and the Quest of Inclusion in Venezuela: Theoretical Debates and Empirical Challenges." Latin American Studies Association, San Juan, Puerto Rico, May 27.

Velásquez, Nelly. 1979. *Llano del Hato: Cuatro relaciones solidarias de producción*. Universidad de los Andes, Facultad de Humanidades y Educación.

———. 1981. "Algunos criterios para el estudio de las particularidades socioculturales en las sociedades campesinas: El caso de Llano del Hato." In *Anuario 1981*. Mérida: Facultad de Humanidades y Educación, Universidad de los Andes.

Vivas, Fabricio. 1993. "La economía colonial." In *Los tres primeros siglos de Venezuela: 1498–1810*, edited by Pedro Grases, Pedro Cunill Grau, et al., 378–460. Caracas: Grijalbo.

Walker, Julia A. 2003. "Why Performance? Why Now? Textuality and the Rearticulation of Human Presence." *Yale Journal of Criticism* 16, no. 1 (spring): 149–75.

Warner, Michael. 2005. *Publics and Counterpublics*. New York: Zone Books.

Weyland, Kurt. 2013. "The Threat from the Populist Left." *Journal of Democracy* 24, no. 3: 18–32.

White, Heather Rachelle. 2005. "Between the Devil and the Inquisition: African Slaves and the Witchcraft Trials in Cartagena de Indies. *The North Star: A Journal of African American Religious History* 8, no. 2 (spring).

Williams, Gareth. 2002. *The Other Side of the Popular: Neoliberalism and Subalternity in Latin America*. Durham, N.C.: Duke University Press.

Wilpert, Gregory. 2003. "Venezuela's New Constitution." Venezuelanalysis.com. August 27, 2003. http://venezuelanalysis.com/analysis/70.

———. 2012. "The 47-Hour Coup That Changed Everything." Venezuelanalysis .com. April 4. http://venezuelanalysis.com/analysis/6922.

Worsley, Peter. 1969. "The Concept of Populism." In *Populism: Its Meanings and National Charateristics*, edited by Ghita Ionescu and Ernest Gellner, 29–61. London: Weidenfeld and Nicolson.

INDEX

Page references in *italics* refer to illustrations.